T0157480

Liszt Recomposed

Liszt Recomposed

∽

Exploring Intertextual Fluidity in Song

Nicolás J.F. Puyané

THE BOYDELL PRESS

First published 2024
The Boydell Press, Woodbridge

ISBN 978 1 83765 047 7

The Boydell Press is an imprint of Boydell & Brewer Ltd
PO Box 9, Woodbridge, Suffolk IP12 3DF, UK
and of Boydell & Brewer Inc.
668 Mt Hope Avenue, Rochester, NY 14620–2731, USA
website: www.boydellandbrewer.com

A catalogue record for this book is available
from the British Library

The publisher has no responsibility for the continued existence or accuracy of URLs for
external or third-party internet websites referred to in this book, and does not guarantee
that any content on such websites is, or will remain, accurate or appropriate

Contents

List of Illustrations

Figures

The author and publisher are grateful to all the institutions and individuals listed for permission to reproduce the materials in which they hold copyright. Every effort has been made to trace the copyright holders; apologies are offered for any omission, and the publisher will be pleased to add any necessary acknowledgement in subsequent editions.

Tables

List of Musical Examples

Acknowledgements

The extraordinarily supportive musicological community in Ireland, and in particular the SMI (Society for Musicology in Ireland), deserve my sincerest thanks. It has supported my research monetarily, but more importantly it provided a welcoming, encouraging, and invaluable proving ground for my research. Discussions during numerous conferences and symposiums over the past decade with colleagues and international scholars have enriched my work deeply. While there are too many names to mention in this regard, I will nevertheless make some exceptions: Lorraine Byrne Bodley, Harry White, Christopher Morris, Patrick Devine, Antonio Cascelli, Cathal Twomey, Anja Bunzel, Majella Boland, Zbigniew Granat, Natasha Loges, Bláithín Duggan, and Bryan Whitlelaw.

I am grateful to the staff at Klassik Stiftung Weimar, Musée Marmottan Monet, Kunsthaus Zürich, and the Morgan Library and Museum New York who were able to deal with all of my requests in such a helpful manner. The many anonymous individuals involved in the digitisation and public dissemination of rare and out-of-print works whose continued efforts have made many research endeavours, especially my own, much more convenient and economically viable also deserve my gratitude. I would also like to thank the staff at Boydell and Brewer, for their professionalism, enthusiasm, and attention to detail, and in particular Michael Middeke for his unwavering belief, support, and guidance. Lastly, I wish to thank my wife Alison for her love and support.

Introduction

No comparable portion of Liszt's output has received less attention from scholars than his songs and recitations for solo voice. The studies described below include virtually everything ever published about these pieces, many of them among the masterpieces of nineteenth-century European music.[1]

As recently as 2009, this paragraph still greeted the reader leafing through Michael Saffle's *Franz Liszt: A Research and Information Guide* at the opening of the section marked 'Works for Solo Voice'. This issue of acknowledging the quality of Liszt's significant contribution to the art of song, while simultaneously recognising that they (the songs) are not widely known, has a long history going back at least as far as 1879, to the first edition of the *Grove Dictionary of Music and Musicians*. Francis Hueffer's entry on Liszt in that 1879 edition noted that the composer's contribution to the Lied had 'not hitherto been sufficiently appreciated by his critics', and that in reference to his setting of Goethe's 'Über allen Gipfeln ist Ruh', '[Liszt] has rendered the heavenly calm of the poem by his wonderful harmonies in a manner which alone would secure him a place amongst the great masters of German song.'[2]

Liszt's Lieder contain some of his most experimental writing, incorporating many ideas that would later be explored in other genres, such as the highly chromatic introduction to 'Die Loreley', the tone-painting piano figurations in '(A/I)m Rhein, im schönen Strome', and the daring harmonic ambiguity of the second setting of 'Wer nie sein Brot mit Tränen aß'. In 2005, Alan Walker identified this repertoire as a 'missing link' between the works of Robert Schumann and both Hugo Wolf and Gustav Mahler.[3] Moreover, Walker claimed that the history of the Lied is incomplete without taking Liszt's contribution into account, a view endorsed by Ben Arnold, Rena Charnin Mueller, and Susan Youens.[4] And yet, despite such high praise and a growing recognition of their quality – as evidenced by an increasing

[1] Michael Saffle, *Franz Liszt: A Research and Information Guide*, 3rd edn (New York: Routledge, 2009), p. 444.

[2] Francis Hueffer, 'Liszt, Franz', *Grove Dictionary of Music and Musicians (A.D. 1450–1879)*, ed. George Grove, 4 vols (London: MacMillan & Co., 1879), vol. 2, p. 148.

[3] Alan Walker, *Reflections of Liszt* (Ithaca: Cornell University Press, 2005), p. 150.

[4] Ben Arnold, 'Songs and Melodramas', in Ben Arnold (ed.), *The Liszt Companion* (London and Westport, CT: Greenwood Press), p. 403; Rena Charnin Mueller, 'The Lieder of Liszt', in James Parsons (ed.), *The Cambridge Companion to the Lied* (Cambridge: Cambridge University Press, 2004), p. 168; Susan Youens, 'Heine, Liszt, and the Song of the Future', in Christopher Gibbs and Dana Gooley (eds), *Franz Liszt and His World* (Princeton: Princeton University Press, 2006), p. 39.

number of recordings as well as some excellent recent articles and chapters – there has been no monograph in English on the Lieder.

Any study wishing to tackle Liszt's Lieder is immediately confronted with a 'Liszt problem' that perhaps has its most obvious comparison with the well-documented 'Bruckner problem': that is, one of numerous extant versions, sometimes radically altered, many of which have equal claims to 'authenticity'[5] – what Rena Charnin Mueller calls the *Fassungsproblem* (the versions problem). That this issue has up to now not been adequately addressed is easily borne out by the difficulty in answering a simple question: how many songs did Liszt compose? The answer varies greatly depending on whether one considers different versions of songs as separate works. But if we take all versions, including unpublished and incomplete variants, the number stands at close to 160 separate items. Liszt set at least eighty-seven texts to music for solo voice. Sixty-four of those are German texts, of which twenty-five exist in at least two versions and these works span a period of over forty years, from 1842 to 1885. It is these multi-version Lieder that are the focus of this book.

It was necessary to limit the number of chosen compositions so that the works selected would be examined in reasonable detail. I chose to look at only the Lieder, as they by themselves form the largest grouping – greater than the sum of all of Liszt's songs in other languages. Moreover, the Lied has more concrete and developed genre associations that help inform part of the discussion on the contemporaneous reception of his Lieder in Chapter 3. I also chose to limit the versions examined in close readings to those that were published within Liszt's lifetime. There were several reasons for adopting this approach. Firstly, limiting my study to the versions published within his lifetime afforded me a balance whereby I would be able to look, in detail, at the differences between versions while still having sufficient space to examine a sizeable proportion of his multi-version songs. By focusing on published versions, I could also make more confident assertions about Liszt's motivations as these versions can be viewed as arrival points of intentionality. In other words, although he might later change his mind, each published version represented Liszt's final wish on the matter, at least at that stage. By avoiding intermediate versions, prevarications are avoided, and what is instead presented are a series of 'final thoughts'. However, it is worth emphasising that this was done purely for reasons of space and is in no way meant to suggest that studies incorporating intermediate versions are not of great value.

In this book I explore Liszt's evolving relationship to the Lied as a genre through an intertextual examination of a selection of his multi-version Lieder. I conceptualise multiformity as being an inherent quality of the compositional process and as an opportunity to shed light on Liszt's evolving ideas on composition in general and his changing view of the Lied in particular. Part I (Chapters 1 and 2) addresses

---

[5]   It should also be noted that the phrase the 'Liszt problem' was used for a period to describe two unrelated, but similar, claims in Liszt studies: firstly, that the majority of Liszt's prose works were in the main written by either Marie d'Agoult or Princess Caroline zu Sayn-Wittgenstein; and secondly, that Liszt's early orchestral works were orchestrated by a number of his copyists, most notably Joachim Raff. It is now widely accepted that neither of these 'Liszt problems' held any water.

two questions: firstly, why study Liszt's songs from an intertextual perspective? And secondly, why focus on multi-version Lieder? Moreover, Part I also examines Liszt's compositional practice, teaching, performance style, and views on composition and editing. Through this examination I suggest that the establishment of an *Urtext* for many of Liszt's works would deny them one of their most inherent qualities: multiplicity or fluidity.

Part II (Chapters 3 and 4) focuses on investigating the role that external forces played in shaping Liszt's revisions. Firstly, in Chapter 3, the unfavourable reception of his early Lieder and the role that genre expectations played in forming this reception are discussed. Secondly, in Chapter 4, his roles as an accompanist during his virtuoso years and as Kapellmeister during his Weimar years are shown to have been materially different performing and composing environments, and each of these environments would have informed his continually evolving Lied aesthetic.

Part III is split across three chapters. It is a series of intertextual close readings of twelve of Liszt's Lieder. However, these intertextual readings are concerned not so much with connections of those Lieder to other works, but with those between different texts of the same Lieder. Leaning heavily on the work of textual scholar John Bryant, these readings are described as fluid-text readings. No one particular version or text of a Lied is privileged as being definitive; rather, each is seen as an expression of Liszt's thoughts or compositional intentions at a particular time.

Finally, in the Epilogue – after showing how multi-version works can be fruitfully reconceptualised as fluid texts by creating close readings that reflect those works' multiformity – I propose that fluid-text editions, which make multi-version works more navigable, would better equip scholars and performers to pursue this mode of critical inquiry. After a brief survey of existing music-based digitisation projects such as the Online Chopin Variorum Edition (OCVE) and Schubert Online, various modes of implementation are investigated. A distinction is drawn between digitisation projects that function more as digital repositories of original documents and those that would seek to be seen as a 'true' edition of those works. The need to create fluid-text editions in digitally native formats is put forward. I assert that fluid-text editions would be more useful if they were to avoid merely recreating the original documents in a digital format, and instead present the variability of those works in a graphic manner that is more easily navigable and comprehensible to users unfamiliar with comparing many versions of the same work.

PART I

CHAPTER 1

(Inter)Textual Preferences: The Elusive Quest for *Urtexts* in the Lieder of Franz Liszt

❧

> The frontiers of music are never clear-cut: beyond its framing silence, beyond its inner form, it is caught up in a web of references to other music: its unity is variable and relative. Musical texts speak among themselves.
>
> —Michael Klein, *Intertextuality in Western Art Music*[1]

After just three virtuosic pages in *Intertextuality in Western Art Music* – that link Eco, Bloom, Grass, Foucault, Barthes, Kristeva, and Bakhtin – Michael Klein feels suitably justified in using the above provocative statement to move the discussion from literature to music. Though it could be seen as a red flag by those who prefer a formalist approach to reading music, I believe it would be an error to see it this way. Klein does not dispute that there is meaning and an inner logic to be found within the limits of a piece of music; rather, he points us in the direction of the myriad of references, meanings, and interpretations that lie beyond the somewhat arbitrary 'within/without' distinction. To state that Franz Liszt is a highly intertextual composer would be more than an understatement. He is a composer whose works wholeheartedly encourage us to view them from an intertextual perspective. Approximately half of his compositions are directly based on the musical works of other composers – these include the numerous transcriptions, arrangements, paraphrases, and fantasies – while the vast majority of his original works also draw their inspiration overtly from other works of art. Sources of inspiration could include paintings, sculptures, folktales, literature, and especially poetry. When one considers how strongly Liszt perceived the interrelationships between the arts, as explained in his open letter to Hector Berlioz, it is not difficult to understand how the range of sources that Liszt drew upon was so wide and diverse in both medium and character.

> The beautiful in this special land became evident to me in its purest and most sublime form. Art in all its splendor disclosed itself to my eyes. It revealed its universality and unity to me. Day by day my feelings and thoughts gave me a better insight into the hidden relationship that unites all works of genius. Raphael and

---

[1] Michael Klein, *Intertextuality in Western Art Music* (Bloomington and Indianapolis: Indiana University Press, 2005), p. 4.

Michelangelo increased my understanding of Mozart and Beethoven; Giovanni Pisano, Fra Beato, and Il Francia explained Allegri, Marcello, and Palestrina to me. Titian and Rossini appeared to me like twin stars shining with the same light. The Colosseum and the Campo Santo are not as foreign as one thinks to the Eroica Symphony and the Requiem. Dante has found his pictorial expression in Orcagna and Michelangelo, and someday perhaps he will find his musical expression in the Beethoven of the future.[2]

Even when one considers Liszt's works that have generic titles, such as the two Ballades, the two Polonaises, the Berceuse, or the Sonata in B minor, it must be recognised that they are all highly and self-consciously architextual. That is, they play on the preconceived notions associated with those genres and directly evoke the music of other composers that are closely associated with those genres: Chopin in the first three of the examples above, and Beethoven – especially the late piano sonatas – in the B minor sonata. Moreover, Liszt could draw upon multiple sources or intertexts to compose music that acts as a sort of critical commentary.[3] It is also worth noting that Liszt's transcriptions, whether more literal or in the mode of a fantasy, would also have this quality of commentary upon the work that is being transcribed. According to Charles Rosen:

> It is not simply the melodies of *Don Giovanni* that Liszt transcribed but the dramatic situations and the sense of the whole opera. The title, *Réminiscences de Don Juan*, must not be taken as a series of isolated memories but as a synoptic view of the opera, in which the different moments of the drama exist simultaneously: what Liszt reveals is the way they are interrelated.[4]

Similarly, the textual transcendence – or transtextuality as Gérard Genette would term it – of the Sonata in B minor has given rise to a huge amount of scholarly literature, even though the concept of intertextuality is rarely mentioned, transtextuality even less so. Indeed, the perceivable connection of Liszt's sonata to other works of art has inspired a small library's worth of articles, chapters, and dissertations. To recount all these here is not necessary and far beyond the scope of this book.

[2] Franz Liszt, *An Artist's Journey: Lettres d'un bachelier ès musique, 1835–1841*, ed. and trans. Charles Suttoni (Chicago: Chicago University Press, 1989), p. 186. The letter is dated 2 October 1839 and was published in the *Gazette Musicale de Paris* on 24 October 1839.

[3] Joanne Cormac, 'Intertextuality, Subjectivity, and Meaning in Liszt's *Deux Polonaises*', *The Musical Quarterly*, 102:1 (Spring 2019), 111–52, https://doi.org/10.1093/musqtl/gdz005. Cormac makes a convincing case that Liszt's Polonaises reference not only Chopin's Polonaises, but also Liszt's biography on Chopin, and the genre of the funeral march and his own piece, *Funérailles*. See also Jonathan Kregor, *Program Music* (Cambridge: Cambridge University Press, 2015) pp. 120–25. Liszt's symphonic poem *Tasso: Lamento e Trionfo* references the works of both Goethe and Byron. Liszt's music here can be seen as a syncretic commentary on the idea of the Tasso figure. It includes allusions to the historical figure and literary versions in the same way as comparative literature on the notion of Frankenstein's monster may just as easily reference Mel Brooks or Boris Karloff as Mary Shelley.

[4] Charles Rosen, *The Romantic Generation* (Cambridge, MA: Harvard University Press, 1995), p. 530.

Conveniently, though, Alan Walker assembled a taxonomy of five types of theories that attempt to explain the 'extra-musical' meaning of the sonata:

i. The sonata is a musical portrait of the Faust legend, with 'Faust,' 'Gretchen,' and Mephistopheles' themes symbolizing the main characters.

ii. The sonata is autobiographical; its musical contrasts spring from the conflicts within Liszt's own personality.

iii. The sonata is about the divine and the diabolical; it is based on the Bible and on Milton's *Paradise Lost*.

iv. The sonata is an allegory set in the Garden of Eden; it deals with the Fall of Man and contains 'God,' 'Lucifer,' 'serpent,' 'Adam,' and 'Eve' themes.

v. The sonata has no programmatic allusions; it is a piece of 'expressive form' with no meaning beyond itself – a meaning that probably runs all the deeper because of that fact.[5]

Liszt would have surely enjoyed that his 'riddle of the sphinx' has engaged performers and musicologists for over a century. The above interpretations are indeed compelling, any one of which may well have formed part of Liszt's inspiration; however, the fact that Liszt chose the simple designation 'sonata' seems rather to highlight the work's architextual aspects with respect to genre, and the mastery and manipulation of form. That analysts still debate whether the work is in one, three, four, or any number of movements is surely the point. It is a sonata, at least on one level, concerned with sonata form. The ambiguity or rather the multiplicity of possible interpretations is very consciously built into its structure, and thus forms a sort of commentary on the notion of sonata form. This does not preclude the possibility of Liszt's having composed the sonata with a programme in mind; instead, I am suggesting that by choosing to keep any programme private Liszt's intention was to highlight the work's connection to the genre as a whole, and thus he seems to be addressing both his contemporaries and predecessors. The sonata is far from being Liszt's only work in two-dimensional sonata form, or arguably even his most sophisticated use of it, not to mention the myriad of other works that are in a modified sonata form. Therefore, I would suggest that Liszt placed immense importance on the work's designation.

The progressive and forward-looking nature of much of Liszt's music is also apt to provoke a type of ahistorical intertextual reading described by Klein as 'allowing us the pleasure of reading Brahms as if he were the father of Beethoven, or Chopin as if he inspired Bach'.[6] There is also a tendency to view his works, especially those in his experimental idiom, as being validated by later developments rather than directly influencing them. In other words, we are often reminded of later composers when listening to his music. The later composers most often linked with Liszt in this way are Debussy, Ravel, Bartók, Scriabin, and Schoenberg. It is hoped with this necessarily brief discussion that the reader is convinced that Liszt's works are ripe for intertextual study such as seen in Paul Roberts's recent book, *Reading Franz*

---

[5]   Alan Walker, *Franz Liszt*, 3 vols, rev. edn (Ithaca, NY: Cornell University Press, 1989), vol. 2, p. 150.

[6]   Klein, *Intertextuality in Western Art Music*, p. 11.

Liszt (2022), which situates Liszt's piano works in a rich cultural milieu and examines their connections to poetry and literature.[7] However, in this chapter I do not re-tread Klein's arguments as to how or why we should study musical works from an intertextual perspective. Instead, I argue that although the works of Liszt are particularly well-suited to intertextual readings in the broadest sense, studying his multi-version Lieder allows us to engage in a form of intertextual analysis, one that helps us to better understand the development of his relationship with the genre.

In this book I focus mostly on one type of intertextual relationship: revision.[8] As multi-version works have intertextual connections with themselves due to their multiple texts, by looking to the compositional environment that created them we can account for the impulses that drove their creation. While this may seem like a headlong charge into intentional fallacy territory, it is meant, rather, as a recognition that each version's creation would have required a concerted effort on Liszt's part and that by investigating the composer's compositional and performance environments, we are seeking to uncover the forces that would have been pushing him towards rewriting and/or republishing his vocal works. Studying Liszt's revisions allows us to chart his development on several levels. Firstly, we explore the changes in effect that Liszt's revisions make to the affective quality of each song. Secondly, we examine how these changes reflect a change in relationship with the songs' intertexts, in many cases not only the poetic text, but also the larger work from which that text was drawn, for example, Goethe's *Faust*. And finally, we question how these changes reflect the architextual evolution of the song – that is, how these revisions are indicative of a development in aesthetic with regards to genre.

In *The Musical Work: Reality or Invention?* Jim Samson proposed that the rise of the *Werktreue* ideal (being true to the work) in the mid-nineteenth century led to the devaluation of works of a more fluid nature. Samson posits that this led to, in part at least, the diminution of the importance of improvisation and consequently the reputations of composers whose works invite performer modification/input, such as Rossini.[9] Accepting this, it is clear how works existing in multiple published versions would also have been devalued. That each version was at one time sanctioned by the composer would in fact make matters worse. Their existence would be interpreted as a lack of confidence on the part of the composer or evidence of a composition's inherent weakness. Inevitability is often cited as an enviable quality in a composition; compositions that exist in multiple versions, by definition, fail to meet this condition

---

7   Paul Roberts, *Reading Franz Liszt*, (London: Rowman & Littlefield / Amadeus Press, 2022).

8   Revision, according to Robert S. Miola, is the closest form of intertextual relationship. Miola, 'Seven Types of Intertextuality', in M. Marrapodi (ed.), *Shakespeare, Italy, and Intertextuality* (Manchester: Manchester University Press, 2004), p. 13.

9   Jim Samson, 'The Practice of Early-Nineteenth-Century Pianism', in Michael Talbot (ed.), *The Musical Work: Reality or Invention?* (Liverpool: Liverpool University Press, 2000), p. 112.

and must therefore be inferior. The existence of multiple versions calls into question their worth, simply by virtue of the existence of the other versions. The relative value or merit in each version is not considered; their existence is enough to damn them.

This view, however, was not all-pervasive in the nineteenth century. Robert Schumann noted the value of studying various versions of a work when reviewing Liszt's *Grandes Études*. When comparing the first and second versions of the etudes that would eventually become the *Études d'exécution transcendante*, Schumann wrote:

> On making this comparison we immediately perceive the difference between the pianist of then and now, and find how the latter has gained in richness of means, brilliancy, and fullness; while we cannot fail to observe that the original simplicity, which is natural to the first flow of youthful talent, is almost entirely suppressed in its present form. In addition, the new version provides a criterion for the artist's present more intense way of thinking and feeling. Indeed, it affords us a glimpse into his secret intellectual life with the result that we often remain undecided whether not to envy the boy more than the man, who appears unable to find peace.[10]

Without a doubt, it is the glimpsing of this 'secret intellectual life' that is one of the many benefits that can be garnered from looking at multiple versions of the same work. The same rationale has also been used to appreciate early sketches and drafts of visual works. Johann Georg Sulzer wrote:

> Sketches, when they are by the great masters, are often more highly prized than works more completely realized, for all the fire of imagination, often dissipated in the execution of the work, is to be met in them. The *Entwurf* is the product of genius. The working out is primarily the doing of Art and of Taste.[11]

Both Karen Karbeniener and Gay Allen Wilson make similar observations regarding the many published versions of Walt Whitman's *Leaves of Grass*.[12] And in his

---

[10] Robert Schumann, *On Music and Musicians*, ed. Konrad Wolff, trans. Paul Rosenfeld (New York: Pantheon Books Inc., 1946), pp. 146–7.

[11] Richard Kramer, *Unfinished Music* (Oxford: Oxford University Press, 2008), p. 13. Originally from Johann Georg Sulzer, 'Entwurf', in *Allgemeine Theorie der schönen Künste*, 2 vols (Leipzig: Weidmann, Reich, 1771–4), vol. 2, p. 80. A similar thought, but now related to music by Sulzer, is found on p. 208: 'the fantasies of great masters, and especially those that are performed out of a certain abundance of feeling and in the fire of inspiration, are often works of an exceptional power and beauty that could not have been composed in a reflective state of mind.'

[12] 'The interest in reading through the first edition of *Leaves of Grass*, then, derives not only from looking at it as a point of departure for later editions, but also from marvelling at this remarkable, as-yet mysterious first effort.' Karen Karbeniener, introduction to Whitman, *Leaves of Grass: First and 'Death-bed' Editions* (New York: Barnes & Noble Books, 2004), p. 6; 'Whitman spent nearly four decades trying to produce a book that would satisfy him and he finally died content with his effort ... Nevertheless, the reader will understand the "authorized" Leaves of Grass better by knowing something of its growth or transmutation. In some ways the last is superior to all previous editions, but it did not grow naturally like the rings of a tree as Whitman and his first biographers liked

chapter on Liszt's song revisions, Ben Arnold draws upon the writing of poet Barry Wallenstein to illustrate this same point:

> We often take it for granted that the poet who is master of his craft will produce in his final version his best poem. We assume that though the poet may sacrifice many lovely touches and lines, he will finally make his poem better in the final analysis. If the reader follows this assumption too religiously, he will miss the point that the two versions often present not merely a poem getting better, but two separate experiences, each valuable and interesting in its own right. Too, it is possible for the poet, with his eye and sensibility controlled by many concerns, to make his final poem best in relation to his developing vision, but inferior to the earlier version.[13]

Wallenstein's writing is highly applicable to Liszt's revisions, as they were not all produced concurrently, in contrast to Schubert, who on occasion would produce a number of highly contrasting settings within a short space of time.[14] Rather, Liszt returned to some of his early Lieder after a span of over fifteen years. Thus, Wallenstein's notion of the developing vision of the poet is especially relevant, as is his notion of appreciating each version on its own terms. In reference to the operatic transcriptions and fantasies, Kenneth Hamilton succinctly lays out the benefits to the scholar of viewing the many extant stages of Liszt's compositions, while also highlighting some obstacles to doing just that:

> The problem is not simply that some of Liszt's more important fantasias are either totally unknown, or studied only in distorted versions, but that the fascinating information yielded by manuscripts of both published and unpublished works on Liszt's compositional technique has been ignored too. The conclusions drawn from a study of manuscript revisions vitally reinforce the evidence of the various versions of the published pieces in any study of his musical development. Unfortunately, comparison of published editions is not as straightforward a task

---

to think. It did not, in other words, grow by accretion, by accumulating layer on layer of new tissue. This final version might better be compared to a house built from the wreck of former houses, with new materials used for the annexes. Each edition of Leaves of Grass reveals, if studied with sufficient care, a great deal of the poet's life, his moods, emotional crises, ambitions, and ripening philosophy … If Whitman had preserved in each poem more or less as he first published it, and had arranged his poems in the chronology of their composition, we would have in the final collection a record on his inner life—not strictly autobiography, but a record of his spiritual and poetic development.' Gay Wilson Allen, introduction to Whitman, *Leaves of Grass* (New York: Penguin, 1980), pp. xviii–xix.

[13] Ben Arnold, 'Visions and Revisions, Looking in Liszt's Lieder', in Michael Saffle and Rossana Dalmonte (eds), *Liszt and the Birth of Modern Europe: Music as a Mirror of Religious, Political, Cultural, and Aesthetic Transformations*, Proceedings of the International Conference Held at the Villa Serbelloni, Bellagio (Como), 14–18 December 1998 (Hillsdale, NY: Pendragon Press, 2003), pp. 253–80 (p. 253). Quoting Barry Wallenstein, *Visions and Revision: An Approach to Poetry* (New York: Thomas Y. Crowell, 1971), pp. 10–11.

[14] Lorraine Byrne Bodley, *Schubert: A Musical Wayfarer* (London and New Haven: Yale University Press, 2023), p. 80.

as it might seem. Several pieces have never been republished and some editions have remained unidentified in the catalogues.[15]

Hamilton not only advocates the use of manuscripts and intermediate versions to study Liszt's compositional technique and its development; he also highlights the lack of any edition that adequately reflects the multiplicity of these works.

Paradoxically, it could be argued that works that have been continually revised throughout a composer's life tell us more about a composer's aesthetic development than a series of single-version works. An early work that is then revised by a composer at a later stage in their career affords us the opportunity to see how that composer handles the same material at various times. A comparative study of a revised version with its earlier incarnation(s) will not only make the contrast between earlier and later aesthetics more easily perceived, but also help in charting the composer's technical development or other relevant expertise that may have been acquired in the intervening years. In contrast, a single-version work may be the result of the composer being either completely satisfied with their essay, or conversely so dissatisfied that the work in question was simply abandoned. Moreover, in song composition the composer's choices in a single-version work can be difficult to separate from the poetic text. That is, the artistic choices can be argued to stem from the poem rather than from changes in the composer's aesthetic. Therefore, unlike a comparative study of multiple-version works, a comparative study of single-version works will not be in the position to compare like with like. Any pronouncements regarding a composer's development will naturally come couched in caveats. Therefore, I would posit that, on this point, there is more to be gleaned from comparing the early and later versions of 'Am Rhein, im schönen Strome' (1841 and 1855) than comparing 'Il m'aimait tant' (1840) with 'Wie singt die Lerche schön' (1855). When comparing the two versions of 'Am Rhein', the differences can be more easily discerned as the products of a more mature composer working in a different environment and reacting to the reception of their earlier works and performing a sort of self-criticism, as Liszt is working with the same material both times. With the two unrelated songs, separating these issues from the differences that naturally arise from setting two different poems is more difficult.

This may seem polemical, but it can be helpful to consider Brahms, a composer who famously destroyed preliminary sketches and drafts of his compositions, thus leaving a catalogue mostly devoid of multi-version works. One major notable exception in Brahms's catalogue is his youthful piano trio, op. 8 in B major. It was originally published in 1854, but Brahms returned to the work after his publisher, Simrock, acquired the rights to it, along with several other early works in 1888. The revision was completed in 1889 and published in 1891, and although the first 62 bars of the piece are almost identical in both versions, thereafter they diverge greatly. Interestingly, and out of character for Brahms, he suggested to Simrock that the first version should not be retracted and that both versions be published together. This work affords the scholar the unique opportunity in Brahms's catalogue to study his

---

[15] Kenneth Hamilton, 'The Opera Fantasias and Transcriptions of Franz Liszt: A Critical Study' (PhD diss., University of Oxford, 1989), p. iv.

early and late styles within the scope of a single work. In doing so, it also highlights the danger of considering a work's organicism as actually being an inherent quality of the composition, as opposed to being merely a stylistic trait. A work that progresses in a seemingly organic and inevitable way only appears to do so. *Ars est celare artem.*[16] Multi-version works remind us that compositions are never really inevitable, and that at every turn a myriad of possibilities is open to the composer.

The case having been made for the importance of examining earlier versions of Liszt's works, it is nevertheless instructive to consider Liszt's own view of his revisions. With few exceptions, he was generally not enthusiastic about keeping his earlier versions in his catalogue of works. Indeed, Liszt was clear in not wishing his revisions of the *Études d'exécution transcendante* and the *Harmonies poétiques et religieuses* to be seen as alternative versions to their earlier incarnations. They were to supersede the original versions and Liszt even went to the trouble of attaching a brief preface to the *Harmonies* disavowing the earlier version of the stand-alone piece *Harmonies poétiques et religieuses* that was later recomposed into *Pensée des morts.*[17] With the transcendentals Liszt was adamant that the publisher Härtel add 'Seule Édition Authentique, revue par l'Auteur' to their edition. In a letter to Alfred Dorffel, dated 17 January 1855, Liszt declared:

> I recognise only the Härtel edition of the 12 Studies as the *sole legitimate one,* which I also clearly express by a note in the catalogue, and I therefore wish that the catalogue should make no mention of the earlier ones. ... I consider it very profitable to correct one's mistakes as far as possible, and to make use of the experiences one gains by the editions of the works themselves. I, for my part, have striven to do this; and, if I have not succeeded, it at least testifies to my earnest endeavour.[18]

That Liszt sought to replace his older works is enlightening, as it does indeed speak to his having found fault with some of his earlier essays. But more than that, it helps clarify part of his motivation for undertaking such large-scale revision projects. Nevertheless, even though it is clear that Liszt preferred the later versions of his works, it seems that the wiser course would be to follow Barry Wallenstein's exam-

---

[16] Latin maxim of unknown origin, often translated as 'True art conceals the means by which it is achieved' or 'True art is to conceal art'.

[17] The *Études d'exécution transcendante,* S. 139/LW A172 (Leipzig: Breitkopf & Härtel, 1852), are extensively revised versions of the *Grandes études,* S. 137/LW A39 (Vienna: Haslinger, 1839). The stand-alone piece *Harmonies poétiques et religieuses,* S. 154/LW A18 (Leipzig: Hofmeister, 1835), was revised between 1840 and 1847 and then fully recomposed as the fourth piece from *Harmonies poétiques et religieuses,* S. 173/LW A158 no. 4, *Pensée des morts* (Leipzig: Kistner, 1851).

[18] The note in the catalogue reads: 'Der Autor erklärt hiermit für ungültig die frühen bei anderen Verlegern erschienenen Ausgaben der Werke, welche in diesem Catalog mit einem bezeichnet sind. – N.B. für den Stecher – das unter beigefügte Nota-bene daf nicht weggelassen bleiben' ('The author hereby declares invalid the early editions of the works published by other publishers, which are marked with this symbol in this catalogue. — N.B. For the engraver — the attached Nota-bene must not be left out'). Rena Charnin Mueller, 'Liszt's Tasso Sketchbook: Studies in Sources and Revisions' (PhD diss., New York University, 1986), p. 73.

ple via Ben Arnold and not only look for the 'lovely touches' that can be discarded in later versions, but also use them to chart the 'developing vision' of the composer. Our ability to study the various iterations of these works should be clear. It gives us an opportunity to witness the compositional development of a major composer by getting an instructive glimpse into their workshop.

Liszt's Lieder make numerous intertextual references and allusions similar to the ones mentioned above. However, due to his predilection for regularly revising his works, even published ones, the nature of these intertextual links develops greatly in complexity over time. And it is this development that is the focus of this book. In order to capture multi-version works successfully, I believe it is necessary to understand the works from the process that produced them – that is, the circumstances that produced the multiple texts. In contrast to a viewpoint that focuses solely on the end point of the process, if we view composition as an activity where reworking and revision are inherent and normal aspects of that activity, we can then view the multiple texts and versions of a work as records of this process. By then examining the many versions of a work, we can chart the numerous varying designs that formed each version. This is even the case for versions that are not directly related from a musical perspective, such as re-settings or versions that were compositional exercises. In these cases, the later versions can often be interpreted as reactions against previous explorations rather than as stemming directly from them.[19] Regardless, knowing what a composer discarded can be as valuable as knowing what was retained. One such paradigm that views 'the work' in this way is the 'fluid text'.[20]

Its strength as a concept is that it views each version from the point of view of the composer, or at least of whichever actor initiated its creation. It reflects the realities of the compositional process rather than an unrealisable ideal. Multiple versions – whether they are published revisions, sketches, or intermediate drafts or variants – are seen as naturally stemming from the writing process. The major implication of this is that no one version of the work – or more accurately, no one text – represents the work in its entirety, but rather a version of the work at a particular time. John Bryant uses the differences in the Folio and Quarto texts of Shakespeare's *King Lear* to describe the notion of textual fluidity and our natural resistance to it:

> we expect *Lear* to be *Lear*. And yet there are variant *Lears*, not simply because that play has been interpreted differently in essays and books or even in multiple performances, but because the text of *Lear* in the folio is radically different from that of the Quarto. Still, we expect one *Lear*, indeed we want one *Lear*, and hundreds of years of editing have worked toward trying to insist upon one *Lear*.[21]

[19] Further to this point, the idea of composing against previous works in a genre could be seen as a composer not wanting to repeat themselves.

[20] Coined by the textual scholar John Bryant, the term 'fluid text' refers to a work that exists in multiple versions. The fluid text sees the work as residing not in any one text, but rather as evolving over a span of time with each surviving version or text representing an iteration of that work along its compositional journey. Each text is reflective of a certain amount of energy that has gone into creating it, whether it is a composer's revision, an editor's excision, or emendation, or indeed the result of action by any other actor.

[21] John Bryant, *The Fluid Text* (Ann Arbor: University of Michigan Press, 2002), p. 3.

Bryant argues that the fluid text is a natural result of the writing/composing process since 'writing is fundamentally an arbitrary hence unstable hence variable approximation of thought'.[22] Nearly ninety years earlier than Bryant, in 1910, Busoni famously made a similar assessment: 'notation is itself the transcription of an abstract idea. The moment that the pen takes possession of it the thought loses its original form.'[23] Liszt expressed himself similarly in 1880: 'What interested me most is Flaubert's lengthy method of work in eager search of the *mot juste*, suitable, expressive, simple, and unique. I know similar torments in music.'[24] The common idea being articulated is that because the writing or composing process is, in essence, always inadequately struggling to capture thought, it naturally invites the composer not only to revise (in the narrow sense of the word, as in to fine-tune a work), but also to engage in wide-ranging revisions or recompositions. If we consider thought to be an inherently fluid phenomenon, we can then agree with Busoni that writing/composing rather than capturing thought instead captures an approximation of thought. And so, works that exist in many versions simply reflect the reality of the compositional process. Bryant highlights the many forces that may impact the creation of a variety of texts:

> The very nature of writing, the creative process, and shifting intentionality, as well as the powerful social forces that occasion translation, adaptation, and censorship among readers – in short, the facts of revision, publication, and reception – urge us to recognize that the only 'definitive text' is a multiplicity of texts or rather the fluid text.[25]

Regarding Liszt's songs, the possible reasons for his revising his compositions are manifold, including but not limited to initial poor reception and disappointing sales, along with a changing compositional aesthetic, and the concomitant change in the nature of the intended performer and venue. It is thus helpful to consider the revisions with these forces in mind to see if the changes made to earlier works reflect these concerns. I propose that the concept of textual fluidity can be successfully adopted from textual scholarship as an alternative framework with which to understand multi-version musical works.[26]

Even though Bryant, like Busoni, describes writing as an iterative process, where with each successive version the composer/writer attempts to refine or revise their

[22] Ibid., p. 1.

[23] Ferrucio Busoni, *The Essence of Music and Other Papers*, trans. Rosamond Ley (London: Rockliff Publishing Corporation, 1957; repr. New York: Dover Publications, 1987), pp. 87–8.

[24] Ben Arnold, 'Liszt as Reader, Intellectual, and Musician', in Michael Saffle (ed.), *Liszt and His World* (Stuyvesant, NY: Pendragon Press, 1998), p. 42.

[25] Bryant, *The Fluid Text*, p. 2.

[26] Bryant purposefully eschews using the term 'textual instability' to avoid the natural tendency to view the succession of versions as aesthetic improvements. This dampens the urge to introduce 'stability' by attempting to establish the primacy of one version. Bryant warns against making the 'teleological assumption' that the final version represents the 'fulfilment of an author's previously inchoate, but now realised intentions'. Ibid., p.5.

vision to a closer approximation of the compositional impulse/thought, each version may not necessarily be a more successful approximation of those thoughts.[27] It is imperative, therefore, not to discard early or intermediate versions of works, especially if they were published within the composer's lifetime. The main assertion here is that there is a wealth of understanding to be gleaned from the examination of multiple versions, which would otherwise be lost if we remained focused solely on the final version of a work.[28]

On this point it may be worth considering the following thought experiment. Consider Franz Liszt in the final stages of preparing his Sonata in B minor for publication in 1853. As the piece nears completion Liszt crosses out the work's finale, composes a new one, and pastes this new finale onto his manuscript. The sonata is then printed in 1854 with the new finale, and the work becomes familiar and widely disseminated in this form. In 1924 the original finale is first published in the critical notes of the 'old Liszt complete edition' edited by Liszt's pupil José Vianna da Motta for Breitkopf & Härtel. The critical opinion is almost universal that in discarding the original finale Liszt is held to have made the correct decision. The original finale is commonly considered overly bombastic in tone and lacking the aura of mystery, harmonic invention, thematic/motivic integration, and sense of closure of the second finale.

Now imagine the same scenario except that the finales have been reversed, with the widely acclaimed ending crossed out (Liszt perhaps believing that his non-traditional ending would hinder the work's acceptance) and instead the more conventional genre-compliant ending inserted at the last minute. In this situation what is the modern editor to do? Or indeed performer, scholar, or teacher. Should we consider the first or the second ending the 'real' one, or perhaps both? What factors should we consider when arriving at our decision? Should we consider the rationale behind Liszt's last-minute revision? Were there any external factors – such as the reception of previous works or an intervention by a publisher, editor, or even intended performer – that may have come to bear on his decision? Or more controversially, should we choose the ending that we consider the most artistically satisfying, regardless of the composer's wishes? The purpose of this thought experiment is to highlight the fact that many decisions regarding the editing of multi-version works are far from clear-cut, and to propose that we should avoid ideologically rigid positions.

---

[27] For example, Harold Bloom regards the 1855 edition of Walt Whitman's *Leaves of Grass* as superior to the later revised ones: 'As is often the case, Whitman's first thought was his best.' Bloom, *The Western Canon* (New York: Harcourt Brace, 1994), p. 266. This is especially pertinent to this discussion as Whitman believed his final 'death-bed' edition of 1892 as being definitive; it is also a clear case of a critic knowingly diverging from a poet's own assessment. Bloom is not alone in venerating the 1855 edition, and Malcolm Cowley's introduction to a 1959 reprint is clear in his preference for the first edition. Walt Whitman, *Leaves of Grass* (New York: Viking Press, 1959), pp. vii–xxxvii. And indeed, the many commemorative editions of the 1855 version are also evidence to this effect.

[28] A prosaic example of the pervasiveness of the teleological position – much to my amusement – is that when I was writing this passage the autocorrect function suggested I change the term 'final version' to 'definitive version'.

If this line of thinking seems altogether too speculative, consider that a less extreme version of this situation does exist with Robert Schumann's C Major Fantasy, op.17 – and that music publisher G. Henle Verlag's treatment of that work demonstrates the problematic nature of establishing a fixed text for a multi-version work. Moreover, it also shows that the musical work concept (the work as a fixed object) still plays an active role in modern music editing. The Henle edition of the *Fantasie* published between 1987 and 2003 included Schumann's original ending – an ending that was discovered by Alan Walker and has been favoured in performance by some eminent pianists, notably Charles Rosen and Jeffrey Siegel. However, since 2003 Henle have not included this original ending with their edition, although it is still available on their website. Explaining the decision to remove the ending from their printed editions, Wolf Dieter Seiffert wrote:

> In my view, the decision of that time was a mistake. Because of the worldwide circulation and use of our editions, we as editors and publishers have a much higher responsibility in dealing with music texts than do performing musicians. Schumann's will here is unambiguous. He did not want played the measures superseded in his view. He clearly cancelled them and notated what he wanted. He conscientiously proofread the first edition. This alone is Schumann's last word. This we must respect. Our idea of a 'work' would crumble to dust in the end were we to decide arbitrarily and from case to case at our own discretion what is 'better' or 'worse'. The floodgates would be open to capriciousness. As much as it is highly interesting for the scholar and interpreter to see how the C major Fantasy came to be what it is today, an Urtext edition has little to do with the workshop. At most in special cases, we can portray in more detail revision stages in the editorial apparatus or in an appendix. But suchlike actually belongs in the apparatus of a complete edition. We do not want to present our customers with preliminary stages, but with the correct text as legitimated by the composer.[29]

It may be argued that the Henle edition discussed above is somewhat of an aberration, and that the tendency has been, in general, to include variants in modern editions. However, as many modern critical editions continue to be marketed as *Urtext* editions, I would suggest that this speaks to the value that is still attached to the term especially to its target market, that is, performers, students, and pedagogues.[30] Indeed, the above example demonstrates an editorial perspective in direct opposition to the concept of the social text as described by Jerome J. McGann in

---

[29] Wolf-Dieter Seiffert, 'Will versus Caprice. On the Closing Measures of Robert Schumann's C Major Fantasy Op. 17', 20 August 2012, http://www.henle.de/blog/en/2012/08/20/will-versus-caprice-dealingwith-the-closing-measures-of-robert-schumann's-c-major-fantasy-op-17/> [accessed 17 January 2023].

[30] Both Christopher Hogwood and James Grier have aptly described the constraints and limitations of the *Urtext* approach especially for multi-version works; they adroitly have also highlighted the inaccuracy of the term in describing the editorial method often employed by such editions. Even though the etymology of the word would suggest favouring the oldest text, this is rarely ever the case. As the word itself is suggestive of a primal text from which other later texts derive, it seems also to invite editors to create a single text. Nevertheless, its continued cachet seems difficult to deny. Christopher Hogwood, 'Urtext, que me veux-tu?', *Early Music*, 41:1 (2013), 123–7 (p. 123); James Grier,

A Critique of Modern Textual Criticism – a concept that has multifarious ramifications for how we consider both the composition and reception of musical works, especially multi-version works. It has been hugely influential in the fields of textual scholarship and literary theory, and as James Grier has convincingly argued, should be incorporated into the critical editing of music.[31] I would suggest that the urge, evident in the above extract, to want to 'stabilise' multi-version works stems from a strict adherence to the musical work concept. This point of view is exemplified by Georg Feder's view of the musical work:

> The Western composer writes down his developed mental image or imagination in musical notation. Then the work is sung and played for the first time according to this musical text. Further performances are again conversions from notation into sound, although many musicians do them from memory after a certain amount of time. In terms of subtle nuances, no performance is like another; each presupposes the activation and actualisation of the interpreter's mental images. Thus, the work is more than the individual audible interpretation, even if it is one by the composer himself. It is more than the sum of individual performances and more than the notated text. It is neither a real nor an ideal matter, but rather an 'intentional' one: the mentally imagined creation, which the composer has written out in notated form so that it is audibly realized through the imagination of the singer and player, and it speaks to the imagination of the listener.[32]

As Feder was an influential figure in the practice of music editing his views on the musical work are worth noting. Feder is also clear in his opinion that 'one speaks of a "work" only when there is a notated composition'.[33] It is my contention that even though Feder based his description closely on the work of Polish philosopher Roman Ingarden (1893–1970), he has not, in fact, given an accurate account of Ingarden's conception of the musical work. In *The Work of Music and the Problem of Its Identity*, Ingarden did propose that the musical work was an intentional object and that the musical work has a certain amount of 'indeterminateness which can only be removed in performance'.[34] Ingarden stated that 'because of the imperfection of musical notation, the score is an incomplete, schematic prescription for performance'.[35] Ingarden's concept of concretisation to describe an instantiation or

The Critical Editing of Music: History, Method, and Practice (Cambridge: Cambridge University Press, 1996), pp. 10–12.

[31] Jerome J. McGann, *A Critique of Modern Textual Criticism* (Charlottesville, VA: The University Press of Virginia, 1992; originally Chicago: University of Chicago Press, 1983), pp. 42–44. It should be noted that James Grier cites McGann as a major influence, specifically in this regard, on his own work. Grier, *The Critical Editing of Music*, p. xiii.

[32] Georg Feder, *Music Philology: An Introduction to Musical Textual Criticism, Hermeneutics, Editorial Technique*, trans. Bruce C. MacIntyre (Hillsdale, NY: Pendragon Press, 2011), pp. 14–15.

[33] Feder is writing here from a philological perspective; nevertheless, I believe his description to be problematic. Ibid., p.14.

[34] Roman Ingarden, *The Work of Music and the Problem of Its Identity*, ed. Jean Gabbert Harrell, trans. Adam Czerniawski (London: MacMillan Press, 1986), pp. 116–17.

[35] Ibid., p. 116.

realisation of a work through performance is an important one. That is, a work can only become an aesthetic object to be appreciated through performance. In this way, the score can be viewed as a set of schematic descriptors, that if followed within acceptable limits, can create an instantiation of the work. However, although due to convention, Ingarden might agree that the score acts similarly to Feder's description, he in fact does not at all consider the score an essential part of the musical work:

> To the same extent that a sign is different from the object it designates, a score is different from the musical work that is designated by it. The ontic connection between the work and the score consists only in a correlation created conventionally. Nor is this correlation in every respect isomorphic; the same work may be 'inscribed' within different notational systems; also, the work is not univocally in every respect defined in its properties by the score. The work possesses characteristics that do not pertain to the score and vice versa. The work of music includes sounds, or strictly speaking, tonal qualitative aspects, melodic qualities, and qualitative characteristics of various kinds of harmony and disharmony (in the original, proper meaning of the word). None of this forms part of the score nor characterizes it. The work is determined by various rhythmic and dynamic properties that it would make no sense to look for in the score. In contrast to a literary work, in which language organized in its two-stratum structure forms a part, so that the work cannot even be perceived without its linguistic double strata, the relationship between a musical work and its score is much looser and more distant. Not only can a work of music in principle be heard without the aid of the score – we do not usually 'read' musical works, though this of course does happen when we learn to play a particular work – but when we hear the work and perceive it aesthetically in the fullness of its properties and complete concretion, the score remains totally outside the work's range. Even those who know the score do not include it within the work's boundaries. Thus, the score not only is different from the musical work but also does not form any part of it and does not form any of its layers (assuming that talk of strata with reference to a musical work were at all acceptable). This does not contradict the fact that a musical work is intentionally designated by the score in cases where the score exists and that the score itself is intentionally designated by the composer's creative acts, so that ultimately the musical work has its source of existence and its properties in these acts. Where the composer has not notated his work, however, has not fixed it in a score, the work is derived directly from his creative intentional acts, intentions that are sometimes immediately realized in a performance by the composer himself.[36]

Ingarden's notion that the score does not form any part of the musical work and that the relationship between a work and its score is not isomorphic is hugely significant, as it allows for a much broader conception of the musical work than is often articulated by those who cite Ingarden.[37] So, while it may appear that I am pushing at open

---

[36] Ibid., pp. 36–7.

[37] Feder is not alone in mischaracterising Ingarden's conception. Philip Tagg, for example, writes of 'the notational centricity of Ingarden's philosophising on the Ontology of music' which as we can see in the cited extract is not an accurate description. Tagg, *Kojak: 50 Seconds of TV Music* (New York: The Mass Media Music Scholar's Press, 2001), p. 59.

doors when I suggest that notions such as the work concept, *Werktreue*, and *Urtext* are not well suited to the study of multi-version works, the above example (Henle's removal of Schumann's original ending) shows how these concepts do indeed still influence musical discourse. For the purposes of this discussion, I will use the term 'musical work' to refer to any musical composition or piece of music, and the term 'work concept' to describe the historical conceptualisation of musical works that sees each work as a closed, unified, and fixed composition that is uniquely identified by its score. This is Leo Treitler's formulation of the musical work concept. It should be noted that I do not wish to imply that Treitler subscribes to this point of view (quite the opposite in fact), but rather that I am using his description of it for its conciseness and acuity.[38]

The philosophical origins and the implication of the emergence in the early nineteenth century of both the musical work concept and the *Werktreue* ideal were charted in Lydia Goehr's *The Imaginary Museum of Musical Works*. And it is Goehr's notion of the musical work as a regulative concept that is of most relevance to this book.[39] Goehr proposed that the emergence of *Werktreue*, literally translated as 'faithfulness to a work', has meant that notions of textual fidelity have dominated or at least underpinned much musical discourse since the nineteenth century. With the establishment of the *Werktreue* ideal as a regulative concept, several problems arise for the performer or scholar when confronted with a multi-version work, especially if those versions happen to be significantly contradictory and have relatively equal claims to 'authenticity'. Firstly, how does one reconcile the differences between versions, to perform or study the work in detail? Or indeed, how does one decide between versions? It is my contention that without the 'necessary' tool (a clear reading and stable text) to tackle their respective endeavours, performers and scholars shy away from works that exist in multiple versions lest they, among other reasons, engage with the 'wrong' version. Much of the difficulty in this scenario arises from the impulse to view the musical work as a fixed object. While this fixed-object viewpoint has been challenged in recent years by authors such as Jeffrey Kallberg

---

[38] Leo Treitler, *With Voice and Pen: Coming to Know Medieval Song and How It Was Made* (Oxford: Oxford University Press, 2003), p. 246.

[39] In Goehr's formulation: 'Regulative concepts are delimiting. They indirectly suggest to the participants of a practice that only certain beliefs and values are to be held and only certain kinds of actions are to be undertaken. In this sense, regulative concepts are structuring mechanisms that sanction particular thoughts, actions, and rules as being appropriate. Thus, for example, performing a work involves employing the appropriate regulative concept(s). One shows one's knowledge and understanding of these concepts when one, for example, complies with a score, plays these notes and not others, plays in such a way as to indicate respect for the genre musically and historically conceived.' Thus, viewing the musical work as a regulative concept it is possible to see how the emergence of being true to a composer's intentions (*Werktreue*) became of utmost importance in musical practice. Lydia Goehr, *Imaginary Museum of Musical Works: An Essay in the Philosophy of Music* (Oxford: Oxford University Press, 1992), p. 104.

with respect to Chopin's works, it is a concept that needs further and continued re-examination.[40]

The emergence of *Urtext* editions in the twentieth century can be seen as directly emanating from that of the *Werktreue* ideal and the work concept in the nineteenth century. An *Urtext* edition of a work is one that, according to the editor, best (re) presents the intentions of the composer. It should be noted that publishers often vary significantly in their methods of arriving at those intentions and how best to present them, or even on the fundamental question of whether first or final intentions are to be favoured.[41] This leads naturally to the conclusion that editing must be viewed as an interpretive act.

The rise in the popularity of *Urtext* editions, to the point of near fetishisation, especially in pedagogical and academic circles, has also led to a common misconception: that what we primarily deal with as performers and scholars when studying a score is the work itself, rather than a text, its medium of preservation and transmission (between composer and performer). In 1976 Alfred Brendel warned of this issue by suggesting that *Werktreue* can easily morph into *Texttreue*. That is, striving to remain faithful to the intentions of a composer may lead to pedantic and overly literal readings of a given text. Moreover, Brendel objected to the etymology of the word itself: 'the term *Werktreue* smacks of credulous parade-ground solemnity.'[42] Similarly, in 1997 prominent pianist and teacher Russell Sherman wrote, 'The score is fixed, and its instructions are an infallible inviolable canon. … Stray from its boundaries and you are branded a heretic, infidel, or genius. … The *Urtext* is the holy and primordial code.'[43] Leaving aside Sherman's ironic style, this passage nevertheless captures how the *Werktreue* ideal can exert a powerful influence over a musical discourse even if Sherman's motives are to poke fun at it. More recently in 2020, Daniel Leech-Wilkinson's *Challenging Performance* convincingly argues that performance norms based on the notions of *Urtext*, authenticity, and the composer's intentions have inhibited performers and stifled the development of creative performance practices in Western classical music.[44] And also from 2020, Julian Dodd's *Being True to Works of Music*, while not actually using the term *Werktreue*, concerns itself almost entirely with the notion of authenticity of performance in Western art music. Furthermore, it would be difficult to believe that Dodd did not choose his title as a play on the term *Werktreue*.[45] This is not to say that Dodd subscribes

---

[40] Jeffrey Kallberg, *Chopin at the Boundaries: Sex, History, Musical Genre* (Cambridge, MA: Harvard University Press, 1996), pp. 161–230.

[41] Many of these approaches are described in depth in Feder, *Music Philology*; and Grier, *The Critical Editing of Music*. Jerome McGann highlights this conflict among editorial methods in McGann, *A Critique of Modern Textual Criticism*, pp. 5–6.

[42] Alfred Brendel, 'Werktreue – An Afterthought', in *On Music: Collected Essays* (London: JR Books, 2007), pp. 30–41, p. 30.

[43] Russell Sherman, *Piano Pieces* (New York: North Point Press, 1997), p. 138.

[44] Daniel Leech-Wilkinson, *Challenging Performance: Classical Music Performance Norms and How to Escape Them*, version 2.04 (30.iv.21) <https://challengingperformance.com/the-book/> [accessed 05 May 2023].

[45] Julian Dodd, *Being True to Music* (Oxford: Oxford University Press, 2020).

to the notion that score compliance is the only barometer with which to judge a performance's authenticity. Interestingly, he argues that performances that are not completely score-compliant can be even more authentic than compliant ones if they display what he terms interpretive authenticity – that is, performances that display a profound understanding of work, although Dodd argues that this understanding is built upon knowledge of the score.

Which leads us directly to Liszt's own views on performance authenticity: 'The letter *killeth* the spirit.'[46]

The above pronouncement should not be taken to indicate that Liszt maintained a cavalier attitude towards the authority of the score, although he was ambivalent on the matter throughout his life. In the 1830s he was known, as his open letter to George Sand in the *Gazette Musicale de Paris* demonstrates, to add trills, arpeggios, and cadenzas even to the works of Beethoven:

> During that time, both at public concerts and at private salons … I often performed the works of Weber and Hummel, and let me confess to my shame that in order to wring the bravos from the public that is always slow, in its awesome simplicity, to comprehend beautiful things, I had no qualms about changing the tempos or the composers' *intentions* [my italics]. In my arrogance I even went so far as to add a host of rapid runs and cadenzas, which, by securing ignorant applause for me, sent me off in the wrong direction – one that I fortunately knew enough to abandon quickly. You cannot believe, dear friend, how much I deplore those concessions to bad taste, those sacrilegious violations of the SPIRIT and the LETTER, because the most profound respect for the masterpieces of great composers has, for me, replaced the need that a young man barely out of child-hood once felt for novelty and individuality. Now I no longer divorce a composition from the era which it was written, and any claim to embellish or modernize the works of earlier periods seems just as absurd for a musician to make as it would be for an architect, for example, to place a Corinthian capital on the columns of an Egyptian temple.[47]

This letter was meant to indicate his move away from excesses in performance, which is further evidenced by Berlioz's account of Liszt's contemporaneous performance of Beethoven's op. 106 – an account that highlights, among other things, Liszt's apparent fidelity to the score:

> In support of my opinion, I can cite the reaction of everyone who heard him play Beethoven's great sonata, that sublime poem regarded by almost all pianists till now as the riddle of the Sphinx. A modern Oedipus, Liszt interpreted in such a way that the composer must have quivered with joy and pride in his grave. Not one note was omitted; not one added (I was following the score). Not a single

---

[46] Letter to Richard Pohl in 1853. Michael Short (ed. and trans.), *Liszt Letters in the Library of Congress* (Hillsdale, NY: Pendragon Press, 2003), letter 103, p. 96. I have used an older-style translation to make the biblical allusion clearer. 2 Corinthians 3:4–6: 'for the letter killeth, but the spirit giveth life' (King James version). This passage is often rendered in French 'car la lettre tue, mais l'Esprit vivifie'. The original text of the letter reads: '<u>la lettre tue l'Espirit</u>' [Liszt's underlining].

[47] Liszt, *An Artist's Journey*, pp. 17–18.

tempo change occurred that the text did not call for; no inflection, no idea was weakened or diverted from its true intent. In the slow movement above all, in the playing of that extraordinary hymn which Beethoven's genius seems to have sung to itself while gliding alone through the immensity of space, he constantly maintained himself at the height of the author's thought. Nothing more can be said, but anything less would be wrong, because it is true. It was the ideal performance of a work reputed to be unperformable. In his playing of a work still barely understood, Liszt proved himself to be the pianist of the future. To his great honour.[48]

However, we should not take from this that Liszt had experienced a complete sea change in his outlook. Just a few years after Berlioz's review, an account – from 2 July 1840 in the *London Times* of a performance of Handel's Fugue in E minor by Liszt – indicates how far removed our own notions of textual fidelity were from that era:

His performance commenced with Handel's fugue in e minor, which was played by Liszt with an avoidance of everything approaching to meretricious ornament, and indeed scarcely any additions, except a multitude of ingeniously contrived and appropriate harmonies, casting a glow of colour over the beauties of the composition, and infusing into it a spirit which from no other hand it ever before received.[49]

Indeed, throughout the 1840s Liszt was still being censured by critics for the liberties he was wont to take, and accounts from his masterclasses from as late as the 1870s and 1880s show Liszt giving advice such as 'you need not take that so literally' versus 'for the sake of an effect the player must never do the exact contrary of what the composer wrote'.[50]

Liszt's aesthetic allowed him to give pianists licence to alter a work when it was virtuosic in character; however, if it was a work by a great master, alterations were not to be made. Indeed, there are numerous accounts from Liszt's later years of him chastising students for taking liberties with Beethoven and Chopin. In contrast, he encouraged Sophie Menter to make her own revisions to his fantasy on Meyerbeer's *Les Huguenots*.[51] Bernhard Stavenhagen's piano roll recording of Liszt's *Deux légendes: no. 2, Saint François de Paule marchant sur les flots* is likewise, another example of extensive modifications made by a performer that were, according to

---

48 Hector Berlioz, *Berlioz on Music: Selected Criticism, 1824–1837*, ed. Katherine Klob, trans. Samuel N. Rosenberg (Oxford: Oxford University Press 2015), p. 235.

49 'Liszt's Recitals', *The London Times*, 2 July 1840, p. 6, cited in Adrian Williams, *Portrait of Liszt: By Himself and His Contemporaries* (Oxford: Clarendon Press, 1990), p. 135. Regarding this same performance, Kenneth Hamilton suggests that the 'exquisite tact' described in the *Times* review may have consisted of mostly just octave doublings of the kind found in the Liszt edition of the same fugue from later in his life. Hamilton, *After the Golden Age* (Oxford: Oxford University Press, 2008), p. 23. However, while this would indeed account for the 'exquisite tact', I am not convinced that such doublings would 'cast a glow of colour [my italics] over the beauties of the composition', and therefore suggest that the later Liszt edition represents a more sober version than the 1840 review suggests.

50 Hamilton, *After the Golden Age*, pp. 228 and 219.

51 Ibid., p. 36.

Stavenhagen, sanctioned by Liszt.[52] Yet another of Liszt pupil's, Arthur Friedheim, also made piano roll of the second legend with a modified ending to the work, which Liszt had also apparently endorsed, further supporting the view that Liszt's concept of the musical work does not always sit well with the notion of an *Urtext*.

Liszt's seemingly contradictory statements on fidelity to the score can be reconciled if we take into account his view on notation. Liszt seems to have what Ian Pace terms a 'descriptive view' of notation, namely that musical notation was a representation of musical thought and that it should be viewed as descriptive rather than prescriptive. Attitudes towards notation and how it should be interpreted have obviously changed over time, with Stravinsky famously being the *ne plus ultra* of advocating a literal approach that gives the composer supreme authority over a performance relegating the performer to the role of executant. This is in sharp contrast to the view that sees the performer as an interpretive co-creator of the work. The distinction between the two approaches implies that a descriptive view of the score gives the performer a range of possibilities that primarily describes what not to do, and what not to omit, rather than an exact representation of what they should *literally* do.[53] Evidence that Liszt subscribed to this view is found in his numerous comments that express his exasperation with the notation's inability, if followed too literally, to express musical thought accurately:

> the composer is necessarily forced to have recourse to inept or indifferent interpreters who make him suffer through interpretations that are often literal, it is true, but which are quite imperfect when it comes to presenting the work's ideas or the composer's genius.[54]

Similarly, in a letter to Dr Sigmund Lebert, Liszt explains the difficulties of capturing the subtleties of tempo rubato. What is especially noteworthy is the fact that Liszt believes that certain elements in performance are left to the discretion of the player. He also seems to indicate that the more gifted the player, the more licence is forthcoming:

> My endeavour with this work is … to make the edition a practical one for teachers and players … I added a goodly amount of fingering and pedal marks … with regard to the deceptive *Tempo rubato*, I have settled the matter provisionally in a brief note (in the finale of Weber's A-flat major sonata); other occurrences of the rubato may be left to the taste and momentary feeling of gifted players. A metronomical performance is certainly tiresome and nonsensical; time and rhythm

[52] *Deux légendes*, S.175 No.2 /LW A. 219 No.2, *Saint François de Paule marchant sur les flots*. The piano roll contains numerous significant changes of texture and passage work throughout the piece. A commercial CD recording of the Hupfeld Animatic roll no. 51416 (1912/13) is Great Pianists on Piano Rolls, Phonographie 5027.

[53] Ian Pace, 'Notation, Time and the Performer's Relationship to the Score in Contemporary Music', in Darla Crispin (ed.), *Collected Writings of the Orpheus Institute: Unfolding Time: Studies in Temporality in Twentieth-Century Music* (Leuven: Leuven University Press, 2009), p. 155.

[54] Liszt, *An Artist's Journey*, p. 35.

must be adapted to and identified with the melody, the harmony, the accent, and the poetry ... But how to indicate all this? I shudder at the thought.[55]

In relation to the performance of late Beethoven from the letter to Richard Pohl previously cited, Liszt wrote:

> In many cases even the rough, literal maintenance of the time and of each continuous bar | 1, 2, 3, 4, | 1, 2, 3, 4, | clashes with the sense and expression. There, as elsewhere, the letter killeth the spirit, a thing to which I will never subscribe, however specious in their hypocritical impartiality may be the attacks to which I am exposed.[56]

Likewise, Liszt abhorred the then newer trend towards overly literal readings of works, especially those written in the Classical style. In a letter to J.W. von Wasielewski in 1857, Liszt describes this as an abdication of interpretive responsibility:

> There is in Art a pernicious offence, of which most of us are guilty through carelessness and fickleness; I might call it the Pilate offence. Classical doing, and classical playing, which have become the fashion of late years, and which may be regarded as an improvement, on the whole, in our musical state of things, hide in many a one this fault, without eradicating it: – I might say more on this point, but it would lead me too far.[57]

Liszt was adamant about the performer's need to engage actively with a work in order to create a successful performance:

> It is annoying that virtuosos, both instrumentalists and singers, behave towards the works they perform as if they were simple reciters. Virtuosity is not a passive slave. All the attractions of a work depend on it to some extent. It can resuscitate all a work's charms ... or it can destroy it.[58]

Liszt's use of the term 'resuscitate' is most telling in this regard, as it suggests that a detached and cold reading of the notation is not sufficient to 'breathe life' into a composition. Indeed, as Liszt was one of the first virtuoso composers to regularly perform other composers' works in concert, he was keenly aware of limitations of notation. Throughout the 1830s and 1840s his works are full of idiosyncratic notational innovations that belie not only a desire to capture the nuances of musical thought more accurately/minutely, but also to demonstrate the wide variety of subtle nuances that are necessary in performance. What is interesting to note, however, is that Liszt moved away from this highly detailed approach in the 1850s. From the Weimar period (1848–61) onwards, Liszt's works have in general fewer expression marks, especially articulation and dynamic markings. This should not of course be taken to signify that these works would require less attention to control of micro

---

55 Franz Liszt, *Letters of Franz Liszt*, ed. La Mara, 2 vols (New York: Greenwood Press, 1969), vol. 1, p. 194.

56 Short, *Liszt Letters in the Library of Congress*, letter 103, p. 96.

57 *The Letters of Franz Liszt*, vol. 1, p. 315.

58 Walker, *Franz Liszt*, vol. 3, p. 223. Walker cites Henri Gil-Marcheux, 'LISZT: À propos de la technique de piano de Liszt', *Revue musicale*, 9/7 (1928), 76–88, at p. 76.

dynamics, but rather that Liszt felt these issues could be left to the discretion of the individual performer.

Therefore, I would suggest that any examination that takes into account how Liszt performed, wrote, taught, and composed will determine that Liszt's attitudes towards composition and performance were such that his works are not best served by burying their inherently fluid nature in the editorial process. Indeed, the textual condition of Liszt's works forces us to cast away long-held assumptions regarding the ontology of the musical work. The pervasiveness of the *Werktreue* ideal – that authenticity of performance can only exist through a faithfulness to a composer's intentions – appears to not sit easily with the notion of there being equally valid versions of the same work that are dramatically different from one another; this is because it raises the question as to which version really represents or best represents the composer's intentions. Leaving aside the problem of whether a composer's intentions can be known solely from a score, when we are confronted with a work that exists in multiple published versions (all of which have at one time represented the composer's last word) the difficulty of attempting to bestow *Urtext* status to one text above all others becomes apparent.[59] This is especially the case when a performing tradition around that work has emerged that does not necessarily display a preference for the later versions of that work. Such is the case in Liszt's *Petrarch Sonnets*, which are normally performed in the early quasi-operatic version dating from 1842 and not the more sober version from 1882.[60]

[59] I would draw a distinction between multi-version works where the various versions have been published with the composer's imprimatur, in contrast to works where the various versions remained unpublished within the composer's lifetime. This is not necessarily to privilege published versions, but rather to consider the various forces that may have come to bear on the musical text as it went through the process of being published.

[60] Franz Liszt, *Tre sonetti del Petrarca*, S. 270a / LW N. 14/1 (Vienna: Haslinger, 1846); *Tre sonetti del Petrarca*, S. 270b / LW N. 14/2 (Mainz: Schott, 1883).

CHAPTER 2

Palimpsests: Variants, Recompositions, and Resettings

∽

Our greatest error is to attempt to make 'scientifically' rigid a phenomenon that is fluid.

—Alfred B. Lord, *The Singer of Tales*[1]

This chapter explores Liszt's compositional processes and methods of revision. After examining these I present a framework to describe the several types of revision procedures that he employed. Liszt's willingness to return even to published pieces and mine them anew speaks of a mind that could envisage multiple possibilities. In a letter to Karl Klauser in 1863, thanking Klauser for his transcription of *Les Preludes*, Liszt describes not only his predilection for revision, but also, with a certain self-awareness, interesting notions regarding textual fidelity and a keen sense of what the ontological implications of naming a work 'an arrangement' are. Importantly, Liszt links this indelible urge to wish to refine, improve, and update works continually with the true artistic temperament:

> It is with great pleasure that I have examined your work as ingenious as it is accurate and successful. It demonstrates a perfect understanding of the score and at the same time displays the application of the best means of the art of writing for the piano. – Receive, my dear Sir, my most sincere compliments, to which you are entitled, and please do not find it strange if the satisfaction you gave me led me to add some modifications to your manuscript. The fact is that the passion for variants and what seems to me improvements of the style possesses me to an uncommon degree and increases with age. I do not apologize too much, because it is the persistent search for the best possibilities that characterizes the true artist. – Thus, since you have been so kind as to do to my preludes the honour of occupying yourself with them, I have followed your example by rewriting the last six pages [!], by which I would like to give to the pianist a full and free quarry to obtain an effect more salient than a literal fidelity to the score does. I ask you to consider this licence as the most certain proof of the entire approval that I give to your work, which will be very pleasant to me to see published under the title which I

---

[1] Alfred B. Lord, *The Singer of Tales* (Cambridge, MA: Harvard University Press, 1960), p.101.

indicated on the manuscript, by subtracting the word 'arrangement' which does not seem suitable to me. So, let's just set the title thus:

> *Les Préludes*, Symphonic Poem for Orchestra of F. Liszt.
> Piano Score by K. Klauser. (With some additions by F. Liszt.)[2]

It is interesting to note that Liszt believes this solo piano version by Klauser of *Les Préludes* is not an arrangement, but that it actually represents the work, simply realised on a piano rather than with an orchestra. This distinction should not be overlooked, as it implies that Liszt viewed works as independent of the means to realise them. Liszt often used the word 'arrangement' himself, so this is not an expression of dissatisfaction with the term in general, but rather a judgement that it does not apply in this case.

Liszt's belief that a musical work may be considered a separate entity from the means used to realise it is further evidenced by his own revisions of the orchestral version of *Les Préludes* during its composition. In this case Liszt incorporated revisions in the two-piano version of the symphonic poem back into Raff's fair copy of the orchestral score that was used as the engraver's copy for the Breitkopf & Härtel edition of 1856. Thus, when switching back and forth between mediums, he would occasionally carry changes between them.[3] That Liszt sought to write idiomatically for whatever genre or instruments he was working on is clear. However, and as the example of *Les Préludes* demonstrates, this does not mean that Liszt was only concerned with a form of translation when creating a version of a work in a new genre. Indeed, Liszt's compositional urge was such that he was wont to make revisions that would on occasion cross genres and instruments before making their way back to the 'original'.

Liszt was occasionally happy to have two versions of the same piece in the same genre co-exist without the newer one supplanting the older one. Also, numerous versions were all published within his lifetime having been proof-read by the composer, and so, at one stage at least, each represented his final word. More importantly, though, the impetus to revise the works was not foisted upon him as a condition either to publish or perform them, as even though the Lieder had many contemporary detractors, there were always some distinguished individuals willing to perform these works. It should be noted too, that while Liszt did seek advice from specialists such as Joachim Raff for orchestration in the early symphonic poems, the works in question are generally considered wholly Liszt's, and so later versions should not be taken to be interventions from editors or other parties.[4] The reason for highlighting the previous point is to reinforce the fact that the impetus for his revisions stemmed

---

[2] *Franz Liszt's Briefe*, ed. La Mara, 8 vols (Leipzig, 1905), vol. 8, p. 161. Translation is my own.

[3] Rena Charnin Mueller, 'Liszt's Tasso Sketchbook: Studies in Sources and Revisions' (PhD diss., New York University, 1986), pp. 111–12.

[4] A notable exception is the transcription for violin and piano of Hungarian Rhapsody no. 12, which could be described as a collaborative work, as Joseph Joachim completed Liszt's sketched-out violin part. William Wright, 'Chamber Music,' in Ben Arnold (ed.), *The Liszt Companion* (Westport, CT: Greenwood Press, 2002), p. 220.

from his own creative impulses. Liszt often went far beyond minor changes when altering his works; thus, subsequent versions can offer insights into his compositional processes and evolving aesthetic principles. Comparing two versions of the same song and highlighting differences between them allows us to explore Liszt's evolving compositional style. By situating these works in their cultural context, we can also explore his motivations for revising them.

Rena Charnin Mueller raises many of the pertinent taxonomic issues that arise when studying Liszt's multi-version works, especially when Liszt transfers a work to another genre:

> It is necessary to create both a typology of the sources and a typology of Liszt's works, and to try and determine when a work becomes a different work, when it is a preliminary (but finished) version, and when an 'arrangement' for a different medium becomes a different piece entirely. Liszt had always been bothered by the strictures that prevented the transference of music from one medium to another, and he saw no reason why it should not be possible for the greatest vocal music by Mozart (*Don Giovanni*) or Schubert (*Winterreise, Schwanengesang*) to be performed at the keyboard by a great pianist. He was unconcerned that he was accused of bowdlerizing the music because he felt himself to be faithful to the intent of the composer he was transcribing. So too was he faithful to these dictates when he shifted an original work from song to piano or from piano to orchestra.[5]

In his 1973 review of the first four volumes of the *Neue Liszt-Ausgabe*, published by Edito Musica Budapest, Philip Friedheim is scathing at the editorial decision to publish only the final versions of Liszt's works:

> The *Neue Liszt-Ausgabe* is apparently not designed to be a general edition at all. For even though the general preface to the first volume of the series announces at its beginning that 'the New Liszt Edition (NLE) is to present all Franz Liszt's musical works in a form which will satisfy all musicological and practical requirements' p. vi, we read further on in this same preface that 'the NLE presents Liszt's works in their final form. Variant versions of complete works are only included where significant parts of the early version are not included in the final version' p. vi. Now, at least to one reader, these statements are mutually contradictory because of the simple fact that Liszt as much as, if not more than, any other composer of his stature continually revised, altered, and otherwise varied the published versions of his compositions throughout his lifetime … a case can be made to support the contention that there is no final form for these compositions and that they exist rather as a series of possibilities always in the process of change, even as Liszt himself altered his compositions when he played them in public … Neither the scholar nor the performer will be able to look to this edition for the definitive publication of Liszt's music, but will continue to rely on the earlier edition insofar as it satisfies his needs.[6]

---

5   Mueller, 'Liszt's Tasso Sketchbook', pp. 108–9.

6   Ibid., p. 18. Quoting a review by Philip Friedheim, *Journal of the American Musicological Society*, 26:1 (Spring 1973), 171–4, at p. 172.

Interestingly, Friedheim discusses Liszt's works in terms that come close to describing the fluid text as conceptualised by Bryant. Thankfully, the situation regarding the NLE has changed significantly since Friedheim's review. In 2005, Editio Musica Budapest (EMB) began issuing supplemental volumes that include earlier versions of works. However, the fact that these are separate editions from the 'main' works makes viewing any particular work in all its iterations unnecessarily difficult and costly. Moreover, the segregation carries with it the implicit value judgement that the final versions are to be considered definitive. As a result, the impression is created that these supplemental volumes contain versions which, while possibly of musical interest, are little more than a curiosity and not a vital part of the work. By segregating the alternative versions in separate volumes from the 'definitive' versions, EMB is cementing the teleological viewpoint. More recently EMB – recognising the importance of alternative versions in the music of Liszt – has begun issuing some of the more popular works of Liszt in separate editions that include earlier incarnations, such as *Après une lecture du Dante* (2016), the *Six Consolations* (2016), and the Ballade no. 2 in B minor. However, it should be noted that the final version in these editions is still always referred to as definitive. In contrast with this stance, prominent Liszt scholars Kenneth Hamilton, Rena Charnin Mueller, Ben Arnold, and the aforementioned Philip Friedheim have all supported the viewpoint that privileging the *Fassung letzter Hand* is not always advisable when studying Liszt's multi-version works.

Liszt's Compositional and Revision Processes

> Our task in the present day is to approach the Liszt compositional materials as the composer himself did. We cannot start with the preconceptions that have been overlaid on musical source scholarship by the study of Mozart, or Beethoven, or Wagner. We have to establish Liszt's train of thought; however anomalous it may be to what we are used to and allow the path to lead us where it will.[7]

The work of Rena Charnin Mueller has been pivotal in clarifying many of the issues relating to the dating of manuscripts in the Weimar archive as well as providing invaluable information regarding the location of numerous sources, and also describing Liszt's working methods. Her 1986 dissertation has been central to many subsequent studies and although she does not explicitly call for the adoption of a model such as the fluid text, it is clear that she was not satisfied that the then contemporary musicological methods were adequate for dealing with Liszt's music. Mueller describes Liszt's compositional process thus:

> Apart from the nine surviving sketchbooks, some with 'idea' sketches and others with full-fledged drafts of works, the Liszt sources are for the most part complete MSS of works in all genres that were corrected again and again by the composer,

---

[7] Rena Charnin Mueller, 'Sketches, Drafts, and Revisions: Liszt at Work,' in Detlef Altenburg and Gerhard J. Winkler (eds), *Die Projekte der Liszt-Forschung: Bericht Über Das Internationale Symposion Eisenstadt*, 19–21 October 1989 (Eisenstadt: Burgenland Landesmuseum, 1991), pp. 23–34, at p. 29.

with pages inserted over a period of years as the revision process continued. We may lack the original Liszt exemplar in some cases, but we usually have several successive stages of a work in copies prepared by his resident scribes, which are rendered legitimate by Liszt's corrections and revisions. One must, however, determine which sources have primacy over others, and to do this we must examine the nature of the sources.[8]

It is therefore reasonable to conclude that the title of this sub-section is, perhaps, misleading as Liszt's revision process was inextricably intertwined with, and forms an integral part of, his composition process, not only at the initial stages but also, occasionally, even well after publication. In short, Liszt may not have finished composing a piece before it was published. This is not to suggest that Liszt would publish unfinished compositions, but rather that he did not perceive publication as being definitive or terminal, and thus there was no ideological barrier to returning to an earlier work in order to 'update' it. Mueller has suggested that many of the criticisms levelled at Liszt stem from his compositional process, which was in marked contrast to both predecessors (Beethoven) and contemporaries (Chopin, Schumann, and Wagner). Mueller, however, does not fall into the logical fallacy of assigning a qualitative judgement to this. Instead, she recognises that Liszt's process was merely his own.

Liszt's method was not to formulate a large-scale formal plan from the start; instead, Liszt composed in small discrete sections. These sections were then manipulated (each of which might still be in a considerable state of variability) and then melded into a larger whole. This took on many forms including the re-ordering of sections and moving the individual sections to different pitch levels, along with many of the variation techniques associated with thematic transformation. Initially, in Mueller's opinion, this was done with little consideration for the overall form of the work, but rather as an experimental stage in which the musical potential of each section was explored. Mueller identified that a common thread in these sections was not that they had common harmonic or melodic elements, but that Liszt tended to compose sections that had multiple possible resolutions, thus allowing for more flexibility than might be expected in the latter stages of composition. Perceptively, Mueller highlights the importance assumed by the connecting material between sections and repetition in Liszt's music due to this process. She views this process as going hand in hand with Liszt's adventurous harmonic palette, as bold harmonic moves would be necessary to link harmonically remote passages convincingly.[9]

Mueller also links this process with Liszt's method of anthologising his works into sets after they had been composed. Numerous examples of this abound, but it is especially evident in both the first two books of the *Années de pèlerinage*, and *Harmonies poétiques et religieuses*. In essence, this could be described as the process of imposing an order on pre-existing music *ex post facto*. Liszt would work this way at both the macro and micro level, that is, not only the re-ordering of pieces within sets, but also sections within pieces, and within those sections themselves. With such

---

8   Rena Charnin Mueller, 'Reevaluating the Liszt Chronology: The Case of "Anfangs wollt ich fast verzagen"', *19th Century Music*, 12:2 (1988), 132–47 (p. 133).

9   Mueller, 'Liszt's Tasso Sketchbook', pp. 328–37.

a process, it is easy to see how Liszt could find a seemingly inexhaustible supply of variations for his compositions, especially given his restless nature and boundless energy. It is a process that is in marked contrast to the organicism that sees inevitability as an ideal quality to strive for in a composition.

Both Kenneth Hamilton and Rena Charnin Mueller are of the opinion that Liszt composed a great quantity of music mentally, before producing any manuscript copies. Of course, all composition is in the mind: this is simply to indicate the lack of manuscript workings at the preliminary stages of a composition's life. And by quantity, the emphasis here is on how far along the composition process Liszt could bring a piece mentally, not necessarily the number of pieces. This has some unfortunate consequences for those wishing to create a fluid-text edition of Liszt's works, as a great many iterations of numerous works have unfortunately been lost to posterity. Numerous works such as the fantasy of Meyerbeer's *Les Huguenots* were performed (by Liszt) before a finished manuscript was produced and, likewise, the now-lost *Fantasia on Il Pirata* was both performed and advertised before it had been written down:

> On the evidence of these surviving sources, however, we must acknowledge that an immense amount of intricate composition went on inside Liszt's head, and that pieces were fully formed, in a manner of speaking, before he put pen to paper. It is not necessary to distinguished [*sic*] between MSS of 'original' compositions and those based on the music of other composers: the process was apparently the same in both cases.[10]

Liszt's early training with Carl Czerny is often cited as being crucial to the development of his improvisational ability, and both Hamilton and Mueller link it to Liszt's predilection for revision.[11] While this is hardly in dispute, I would suggest that training under Salieri may have also been influential in developing this side of Liszt's compositional methods. Salieri was known to instruct his students, including Schubert, in the art of *partimento*.[12] Peter van Tour describes *partimento* as: 'a notational device ... applied both in playing and in writing activities and used for developing skills in the art of accompaniment, improvisation, diminution, and counterpoint.'[13] Salieri was also known to assign his students the task of setting the same text numerous times. Therefore, it is possible to see how Liszt would have developed an ability to see the compositional potential in simple musical materials and in the works of others.

Interestingly, as Rena Charnin Mueller noted, Liszt's compositional process seems to have been the same whether working on original material or on material originating with another composer.[14] That he would invest so much creative effort

---

[10] Mueller, 'Liszt's Tasso Sketchbook', p. 106.

[11] Ibid., pp. 4–8.

[12] Lorraine Byrne Bodley, 'Salieri, *Partimento* and the Beginnings of Creation', in *Schubert: A Musical Wayfarer* (London and New Haven: Yale University Press, 2023), pp. 57–86.

[13] Peter van Tour, *Counterpoint and Partimento: Methods of Teaching Composition in Late Eighteenth-Century Naples*, Studia Musicologica Upsaliensia, 25 (Uppsala: Uppsala Universitet, 2015), p. 19.

[14] Mueller, 'Reevaluating the Liszt Chronology', p. 133.

in works that were by their nature derivative seems to have been the object of both bewilderment and consternation to those within the composer's circle. Composer Joachim Raff, who briefly worked as one of Liszt's copyists, implored him in 1850 not to expend so much effort on such works. In relation to the Fantasia and Fugue on the Chorale 'Adnos, ad salutarem undam' from Meyerbeer's *Le Prophète*, Raff wrote:

> I have gone through the Prophète Fugue with great interest. You know, it is a mystery to me how you can take such pains over the arrangement of a theme such as this? With the same expenditure of invention, you could easily have produced an original composition of the highest significance and one would never again have to hear it said that you have to fasten on to Meyerbeer because of a lack of original invention. I know what you will answer: 'This is my wish.'[15]

The motivation for naming this chapter 'Palimpsests' is twofold. Firstly, to acknowledge Liszt's actual physical methods of revision, that is, the scraping off of unwanted notes on manuscripts followed by the marking up with pencil, crayon, and paste-overs to create texts which, in certain cases, quite literally have layers. And secondly, to reference the work of literary theorist Gérard Genette whose pioneering study in the field of intertextuality, *Palimpsests: Literature in the Second Degree*, has much to offer in the way of conceptualising, both the interrelationship between texts, and successive revisions of a given text.[16] Thus, Genette's concepts are readily applicable to a study of song revision.

Genette adopts Julia Kristeva's term 'intertextuality' but uses it in a more restricted sense as one of five sub-types of transtextuality.[17] Genette defines transtextuality as

---

[15]   Kenneth Hamilton, 'The Opera Fantasias and Transcriptions of Franz Liszt: A Critical Study' (PhD diss., University of Oxford, 1989), p. 10, citing Helene Raff München, 'Franz Liszt und Joachim Raff im Spiegel ihrer Briefe', Die Musik, 1:2 (Berlin, 1901), p. 866.

[16]   Gérard Genette, *Palimpsests: Literature in the Second Degree*, trans. Channa Newman and Claude Doubinsky (Lincoln, NE, and London: University of Nebraska Press, 1997).

[17]   Genette describes five sub-types 'in order of increasing abstraction, implication and comprehensiveness'. *Intertextuality* is the actual presence of one text within another, as in quotations, plagiarism, or allusion. Of *paratextuality* Genette writes that the 'para' prefix should be understood to function similarly to how it does in the words 'paramilitary' or 'parafiscal'. This is the relationship between a text and its paratext. The paratext is the text that surrounds the main body of the text such as the title, subtitle, preface, forewords, even chapter headings, and so on. Genette lists many more examples, but it is not necessary to repeat them all here. Metatextuality consists of criticism and commentary: 'It unites a given text to another, of which it speaks without necessarily citing it.' It is explicit criticism or commentary about a given text in another text, without necessarily citing the text, such as a review. *Hypertextuality*: this concerns the relationship between a given text (the hypertext) and an earlier text (the hypotext), whereby the hypertext is derived from the hypotext, through a process of transformation. The hypertext is based on the hypotext but it does not take the form of a commentary and does not necessarily explicitly mention or reference its hypotext. Genette offers the example of two hypertexts, Virgil's *Aeneid*, and Joyce's *Ulysses*, which are derived from the same hypotext, the *Odyssey*, through different processes. *Architextuality* describes the relationship of a given text as part of a genre or genres and is

'all that sets the text in a relationship, whether obvious or concealed, with other texts'.[18] It is the fourth sub-type, hypertextuality, that is the focus of Genette's study, as is the case in this book. Hypertextuality is applicable to the process of song revision in two ways: firstly, with the notion that art song in general is by its very nature a hypertextual art form. An art song is often based on a pre-existing independent text, one that was not necessarily intended to be sung, when it was written, and therefore is a prime example of hypotext moving to hypertext.[19] Secondly, during the revision processes of a song, hypertextual relationships between the various iterations of that song are created. It is this second type of hypertextual relationship that is the focus of this chapter. Genette states that a hypertext is generated from a hypotext through the process of transformation. He describes two fundamental forms of transformation:

> A text, literary or not, can undergo two antithetical types of transformation … These two operations consist in one case of abridging the text – we shall call that reduction – and in the other we shall call it augmentation. But there are many ways to reduce or extend text.[20]

The two basic types of reduction that Genette describes are excision and concision (see Table 2.1 below). Excision is simply the removal of part of the existing text, whereas concision which also removes text preserves the idea, but in a shortened form. These two varieties of transformation operate directly on the hypotext and thus both operations only produce a new version of the hypotext. The third form of reductive transformation, condensation, is related to concision, but is different in scope. Whereas concision reduces individual elements of a whole text into a series of reductions, condensation views the text as a whole and reduces it in one whole operation. Genette suggests 'summary' as the most appropriate common-usage term for this type of transformation. The first two of these transformations have direct equivalents in music. However, it is not readily possible to summarise a musical work *in music*. That said, arguably the wordless functional analyses of Hans Keller come close to this idea, as do Liszt's own operatic paraphrases or *Réminiscences*. Abridgement in music, though related, is a quite a different operation and is more akin to a series of large-scale excisions.

Augmentation is likewise divided up into three operations by Genette: firstly, extension, which describes the simple addition of new material to an existing section; and secondly, expansion, which describes the lengthening or enlarging of pre-existing material. The third operation is termed amplification, which Genette describes as 'the obverse of a condensation' and as a 'synthesis and convergence of the two others' (extension and expansion).[21]

---

related to the notion of an archetype. Genette cautions against viewing these categories as discrete without any overlapping, or indeed as an exhaustive list.

[18] Genette, *Palimpsests*, p. 1.

[19] Genette explicitly touches on music in this capacity as an art that can be understood to engage in a wide array of hypertextual procedures. Ibid., pp. 386–92.

[20] Ibid., p. 228.

[21] Ibid., p. 262.

Table 2.1. Genette's six types of hypertextual transformation.

Reduction	Augmentation
Excision	Extension
Concision	Expansion
Condensation	Amplification

It is necessary to clarify some terminology that has often been used somewhat interchangeably within the discussions of this repertoire or in general discussions of works that exist in multiple versions. Musically equivalent terms that describe as accurately as possible the transformations effected by composers when returning to their works, and similarly terms that accurately describe the resulting interrelationships between the various hypertexts produced by the revision process, would be a useful addition to the musical lexicon. To (re)use Rena Charnin Mueller's phrase regarding Liszt's sketches, drafts, and revisions, there has been 'a syntactical and taxonomic inadequacy' when discussing the issues of multi-version works, and most especially his Lieder. Indeed, many articles and chapters that introduce Liszt's songs often make little reference to the alternative versions of songs – let alone recordings or recital programmes, which often do not detail which version is being performed.

A map is not the territory it represents, but, if correct, it has a similar structure to the territory, which accounts for its usefulness.[22]

—Alfred Korzybski

Korzybski's assertion is useful to keep in mind when drawing up a framework or categorisation of Liszt's multi-version Lieder. The notion that an abstraction based upon something is not the thing itself is relevant, as it warns us against unduly weighting the significance of findings yielded by reductive methods of interpretation and analysis. A Schenkerian graph or even a harmonic reduction in this respect is similar to Korzybski's map. For example, an approach that prepared graph reductions to compare the level of change in the *Ursatz* and middle-ground levels as an indicator of how related one version of a song was to another, while commendable, would dispense with many aspects contained within the actual text of the songs. This is not to say that surface-level features would necessarily be ignored, but their significance may be underplayed. It should be noted that the intention here is not to imply that harmonic structures (both small- and large-scale) or voice leading should be ignored; on the contrary, they should be viewed as vital dimensions of the work, but not the only ones.

---

[22] Alfred Korzybski, *Science and Sanity: An Introduction to Non-Aristotelian Systems and General Semantics*, 5th edn (Brooklyn: Institute of General Semantics, 1994), p. 58.

This study, in contrast to previous ones, builds upon Genette's work on transformation between literary texts. It focuses on the changes that composers make to a document, the musical score, rather than on changes to abstractions. This approach then evaluates the transformations that Liszt performs when he revises a song and in doing so creates a new text. By giving significance to the surface layer, every change can be evaluated and considered. Thus, this study, like the concept of the fluid text, approaches the works and their revisions from the point of view of the composer and the process rather than the finished product.

In contrast to using a simple two-category system to describe each version as either related or not-related, I view the revisions as operating on a spectrum of relatedness (see Table 2.2 and Figure 2.1 below). I categorise distinct types of revisions by the operations that the composer performs on the actual musical text. I propose that all settings of a text by the composer, whether musically related or not, should be grouped together and then ordered chronologically according to the date of composition, if it can be determined, or the date of publication. This first point follows what has been established in the *Grove* catalogue prepared by Rena Charnin Mueller and Maria Eckhardt. This arrangement highlights not only the chronological production of each of the versions, but also the nature of the revisions contained in each new document and their relationship to the earlier published versions.

I will use the terms first version, variant, recomposition, partial recomposition, and resetting to describe five types of versions. As has already been stated, there were many other types of unpublished versions created during the composer's lifetime, but in this book it is important to distinguish between these unpublished versions (sketches, drafts, etc.) and published ones. Given my limiting this study to published versions as they all would have represented, at one point in time, the composer's *Fassung letzter Hand*, it is fruitful to compare these various 'final' versions because they represent arrival points of intentionality; this is in contrast to drafts and sketches which present the work at its most fluid, and hence at its most fluid from the point of view of intentionality. These unpublished documents/versions, however, should and would of course be included in the production of a fluid-text edition.

Once these terms are adopted, it becomes much easier to describe how each version of a song is related. For example, the second version of 'Freudvoll und leidvoll' is a resetting of the poetic text, whereas the third version is a recomposition of the first version. Or the second version of 'Der Fischerknabe' is a recomposition as the whole song has been transformed, while the second version of 'Es war ein König in Thule' is a partial recomposition, as some music was left unchanged but the changes in the altered sections are too extensive for it to be considered a variant.

First Version

This is the first published setting of the text by Liszt. The inclusion of this category may seem superfluous; however, it is necessary if we are to perceive each song as an entity that evolves over time, and each version as a snapshot of the work at that point in time. All subsequent versions are considered as emanating from this version, even the ones that are not directly musically related. I believe that musically unrelated versions of settings of the same text by the same composer should be grouped together, a point that will be further elaborated on in the resetting section.

Table 2.2. Proposed framework for categorising versions.

First Version	The first published setting of the text.
Variant	Describes a version where changes to a work do not drastically alter the overall effect, but rather intensify or refine it. Most features and characteristics are retained, and the changes are usually localised to just a few bars.
Recomposition	Liszt uses material from a previous version and refashions it to such a degree that it may be considered a separate composition: that is, the changes are wide-ranging and significant, but are not sufficient to obscure the genealogy of the work. Changes in a recomposition are often felt throughout the song, such as a change in metre or texture. Motivic material is changed either through rhythmic or melodic transformation but is still recognisable.
Partial Recomposition	Some material from an earlier version has been included unchanged but includes other sections that are greatly altered either through recomposition or the addition of new material. This also includes the reordering of sections, and/or the removal of older parts, thus creating a new meaning and context for older music to inhabit.
Resetting	A version that shows no direct musical link between versions apart from sharing the same source material, namely, the poetic text. It bears no musical resemblance to any previous setting of the same text.

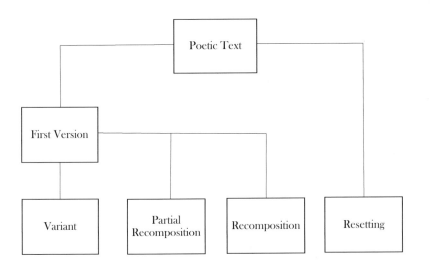

Figure 2.1. Relationship between types of versions.

Variant

'Variant' describes the type of revision that is most closely related to the first version. Here the overall nature of the work is not changed drastically, and the changes are not wide-ranging. This is where Liszt's changes to a work may be minor or cosmetic, and do not fundamentally alter the overall effect, but rather seek to intensify or refine it. Most features and characteristics are retained, but most importantly the changes in this type of revision are localised. The significance of this factor should not be underestimated. Large-scale excisions or additions are avoided, although some harmonic changes may be included. The changes are small enough that the overall form of the song is not dramatically altered. By keeping the changes local and bookending them with unaltered material, Liszt creates a relationship between variant versions where it would be possible to interchange bars between versions to create a speculative version. Any bar(s) from one variant version could be exchanged into another variant version, without changing the overall form or character of the song. Although somewhat controversial, the practice of piecing together a performer's version from several authentic variants is advocated by John Rink, one of the editors of the new Chopin Edition Peters and a director of the OCVE (Online Chopin Variorum Edition), as a way of imbuing Chopin's works with an improvisatory character.[23] Since in a variant the changes can be small, perhaps even located to just one bar, these versions can function like an *ossia* and be viewed as a set of alternatives. In reference to Chopin's works, Jim Samson describes this process:

> Chopin too was an inveterate reviser, as the complexity of the manuscript sources indicates. Yet in his case it was the quest for an unattainable perfection that motivated his endless fine-tuning of the individual work. There are few rival versions in Chopin, for his inclination was to keep tinkering with the existing version, glossing even its published score.[24]

Liszt was fond of this type of revision too, but, as will be further discussed, he was also wont to make far more radical and far-reaching revisions. As an aside, Samson points out how this practice is at odds with modern editorial practice, further making the case for the adoption of a method which more adequately deals with fluid works such as these.

> The result is often a lengthy source chain, extending to multiple impressions of the (often divergent) first editions, and beyond that to autograph glosses on scores belonging to family and pupils; all immensely perplexing to the modern editor.[25]

This practice is only perplexing, however, if the editor wishes to obscure or otherwise stabilise the work's inherent fluidity. If the editor chooses to present these

---

[23] John Rink, 'The Virtual Chopin', video introducing the Online Chopin Variorum Edition, published by Cambridge University, 21 March 2013: <https://www.youtube.com/watch?v=GJDnc_nZT-A> [accessed May 2023].

[24] Jim Samson, *Virtuosity and the Musical Work* (Cambridge: Cambridge University Press, 2003), pp. 107–8.

[25] Ibid., p. 108n.

variants as an intrinsic part of the work itself, its aesthetic make-up, and its cultural milieu, then the issue becomes a technical rather than a philosophical one: that is, not *which* version should be presented/published, but rather *how* best to present all the variants/versions.

Recomposition

This describes a version in which the composer reuses material from a previous setting and refashions it to such a degree that the overall character of the work is changed. This may result from rhythmic or melodic transformation, or the addition of new material. Changes are made that are not sufficient to obscure the genealogy of the work, but are sufficient in scope for the work to be considered a separate composition. Changes in this category are often not local, but global. That is, they have an effect throughout the song, including but not limited to changes in metre, key, accompaniment texture, and alteration of pre-existing melodic or rhythmic motifs. The key point regarding the last two features is that even though motifs can be altered significantly, they are still perceived as being related to the first version. Kenneth Hamilton describes the point in relation to the *Petrarch Sonnets* that went through radical recompositions in both their solo piano versions and song form:

> Frequently the revisions do not represent an ascending line of development but rather an indication of how Liszt reacted to the musical idea at that time. In the case of the Petrarch Sonnets, for example, the recomposition is so extensive and the stylistic divergences so massive that the final versions are best regarded as separate pieces rather than revisions of the earlier songs.[26]

A suitable test to evaluate whether a version would be best described as a variant or a recomposition would be to assess whether it is possible to substitute any bar from the later version into the equivalent position in the older version. If a version has undergone metric changes or significant changes to texture the result would be jarring, even if the harmonic structure were identical. Thus, when listening to or examining the score of a recomposition it should be instantly recognisable as a different version, whereas, with a variant, it would be necessary to reach a specific point in the work to be able to determine it as such. This may seem a somewhat circular definition, but it helps illustrate the point.

Jim Samson aptly describes this form of revision, where even the importance of the shared elements between works has been changed, in reference to the wide-ranging recomposition of the *Étude en douze exercises* into the *Grandes Études*:

> Liszt's re-workings are of a different order altogether from Chopin's. As I have already noted, he enlarged the figures of his earlier exercises into performance-orientated events in which structure and surface are forced apart, and in which the reconstituted figures tend to function as ornament, gesture or colour, subordinated to larger melodic statements that are varied and transformed in what Dahlhaus described as an 'ever-changing array of masks and guises'. The materials of the *Grandes Études* are in this sense unamenable either to figurative

---

[26] Hamilton, 'The Opera Fantasias and Transcriptions of Franz Liszt', p. 7.

recycling or to thematic working. They are excessive in several senses, including the sense in which they threaten to exceed the work. Liszt's reworking, then, changed the earlier exercises utterly, redefining their genre where Chopin's op. 25 had confirmed the genre of op. 10. Thus, any element that remains intact in the journey from exercises to etudes is in no sense an essence. It is by no means clear that we even have different configurations of an idea, for the idea (to use a loaded term, which will shortly be explored) has itself changed. Again the polarities are striking. The shared materials of the *Etudes en douze exercices* and the *Grandes Études* serve to highlight the difference in aesthetic, whereas the different materials of the two Chopin cycles emphasise their shared aesthetic.[27]

It should be noted that just because a recomposition could be considered a new work does not mean that it is independent from its hypotext. Indeed, if there is clear musical genealogy between the versions, it makes sense to highlight the link between versions, even if they are radically different, perhaps even more so.

Partial Recomposition

Partial recomposition describes a grey area where what might be considered a variant contains large sections of interpolated new or revised material, or where there are large excisions that change the character of the work considerably but some music is retained unchanged. In the latter case, as some music remains in situ, it could be argued that as the changes are large-scale they are nevertheless local, and it is thus a variant. However, with large-scale additions or excisions, the composer is not exchanging like for like and thus the proportion of the work has changed, making an exchange of sections between versions impossible. I therefore propose the adoption of the term 'partial recomposition'. 'Es war ein König in Thule' (LW N9; S278) would be a case in point; new material sits side by side with unchanged sections, and there are sections of significant length where the piano texture is modified to a large degree, such as the chromatic passages just before the song's coda. Both versions of the song begin identically, but very soon divergences appear that make the two versions unmistakably different, even though material that is identical in both versions does again return.

It could be argued that this category is superfluous as any major changes will invariably change the proportions of the whole work and thus changes of this nature could be simply labelled recompositions. However, I believe it is a useful and necessary category because it distinguishes those recompositions where significant portions of first-version material remains unchanged, such as in the aforementioned 'Es war ein König in Thule', from recompositions where not a single bar is identical to the first version, such as in 'Der Fischerknabe'. The point is not to create terms that are ontologically true in all cases, but simply more accurate.

Resetting

The final category, resetting, is the most straightforward revision to define. This describes a completely altered version that shares no musical material with a pre-

---

[27] Samson, *Virtuosity and the Musical Work*, p. 109.

vious version of the same poetic text, except perhaps some general and/or generic connections such as key signature or general mood – although, of course, these need not be the same either. For a song to be considered a recomposition it needs to be possible to show a direct musical link between versions, without reference to the poetic text. If this is not possible, it would be considered a resetting. It might be viewed as reflecting the composer's changed view of the text, or serving to highlight another aspect of the text and thus depicting a different reading of it. Liszt's resettings are occasionally written in such a way as to obscure any link between two versions of the song. In doing so, Liszt has self-consciously composed in opposition to the earlier version. In this way, paradoxically, the two songs become related, by being so self-consciously different from one another – the second version forming a type of commentary, in negation, on the first. For example, the first two versions of 'Freudvoll und leidvoll' (LW N23); Liszt seems to have used the duality present in the poem's incipit to compose two versions of the song which are polar opposites, in terms of mood, musical material, and even key signature, the first written in A flat major, the second in E major. That these two settings were first published side by side in the same edition speaks to this point.

Clandestine Recomposition

A sixth category could also be included, describing the instances where a composer reuses material in a piece without acknowledging its debt to an older composition. I have found only one possible instance of this in Liszt's Lieder, and so have not included it in my formal schema.

It should be added that, like Genette when describing his five forms of intertextuality, I make no claim to the exhaustiveness of this list. That is, it may well be possible to define other forms of revision categories. Furthermore, the preceding framework, precise works, and definitions are intended to act as signposts to aid scholars in their attempts to understand the motivations, conditions, and other external forces that may have come to bear on a composer when revising their work. This is not a rigid schema that attempts to shoehorn versions neatly into discrete categories; indeed, versions that fall into grey areas are to be expected. And indeed it depends to some degree on the criteria chosen to compare between versions. The criteria used in this study to evaluate the changes between versions included text-setting, text painting, vocal demands, piano texture, harmonic analysis, key scheme, as well as performance issues. These were deemed the most suitable to display Liszt's aesthetic and compositional development in relation to the Lied.

Table 2.3 displays how the proposed terminology regarding revisions could be incorporated into existing catalogues. To avoid having a table with over 150 entries at this point, it is limited to just Liszt's Goethe Lieder that are examined in close readings in Part Three of this study. A brief perusal of the table reveals how the existing numbering systems do not encapsulate either the quantity of authentic editions published within Liszt's lifetime or their compositional interrelationship. An aspect that may seem strange is the absence of a date of composition column; this was done intentionally to draw attention to the fact that fixing upon a single date in Liszt's works in many cases may in fact be arbitrary. As has been discussed before, Liszt often worked for extended lengths of time on compositions, occasionally shelving

Table 2.3. Versions of Liszt's Goethe Lieder published during Liszt's lifetime: arranged chronologically and showing revision type.

Catalogue Searle/ Grove	Title	Edition	Revision Type
S.275/1 LW N8	Mignons Lied ('Kennst du das Land') (first version)	Berlin: Schlesinger 1843	First version
S.275/2 LW N8	Mignons Lied ('Kennst du das Land') (second version)	Berlin: Schlesinger 1856	Variant of first version
S.275/3LW N8 S.275/3	Mignons Lied ('Kennst du das Land') (third version)	Leipzig: Kahnt 1863	Recomposition of first version
S.370 LW N8	Mignons Lied ('Kennst du das Land') (fourth version) (orchestral accompaniment)	Leipzig: Kahnt 1862	Recomposition of third version
S.278/1 LW N9	'Es war ein König in Thule' (first version)	Berlin: Schlesinger 1843	First version
S.278/2 LW N9	'Es war ein König in Thule' (second version)	Berlin: Schlesinger 1856	Partial recomposition of first version
S.279/1LW N10	'Der du von dem Himmel bist' (first version)	Berlin: Schlesinger 1843	First version
S279/2 LW N10	'Der du von dem Himmel bist' (second version)	Berlin: Schlesinger 1856	Partial recomposition of first version
S.279/3 LW N10	'Der du von dem Himmel bist' (third version)	Leipzig: Kahnt 1860	Recomposition
S.280/1 LW N23	'Freudvoll und leidvoll' (first version)	Vienna: Haslinger 1848	First version
S.280/1 LW N23	'Freudvoll und leidvoll' (second version)	Vienna: Haslinger 1848	Resetting
S.280/2 LW N23	'Freudvoll und leidvoll' (third version)	Leipzig: Kahnt 1860	Recomposition of first version
S.297/1 LW N34	'Wer nie sein Brot mit Tränen aß' (first version)	Vienna: Haslinger 1848	First version
S.297/1 LW N34	'Wer nie sein Brot mit Tränen aß' (second version)	Berlin: Schlesinger 1859	Variant of first version
S.297/2 LW N34	'Wer nie sein Brot mit Tränen aß' (third version)	Leipzig, Kahnt 1860	Resetting

them for a significant period before returning to them, and so it may be more useful to display a range of time when it is known that Liszt worked on a composition or a particular version of a composition. This information should of course be included whenever it is possible to do so.

The purpose in devising the above methods was to highlight the variety of compositional processes that Liszt carried out when returning to his works, and to use these insights to describe the nature of each version more accurately. By highlighting the composer's processes, a discussion can be constructed that captures how these revisions affect each of the triumvirate of actors involved in the creation of the aesthetic experiencing of a musical work, namely, the composer, the performer(s), and the audience. Moreover, by distinguishing distinct types of changes and their effects, it becomes possible to identify, in a less speculative way, Liszt's motivations and intentions when returning to his works.

PART II

CHAPTER 3

Crossing the Horizon of Expectations: The Contemporaneous Reception of Liszt's Early Lieder

∽

We begin by understanding that writers are social beings shaped not simply by social pressures, but by their self-conscious attempts to find a relation to those external pressures. Their 'autonomy', if it exists at all, is in their resistance to the elements that give them shape: their language, family or associates, and cultural ideologies.

—John Bryant, *The Fluid Text*[1]

Following on from Bryant's notion that writers are not isolated actors divorced from external factors when producing their works, by highlighting the writer's or composer's connection to their society and the external forces that were exerted upon them, we can better understand the artistic choices behind their revisions. That is, do they comply with the pressures and expectations, or do they exert their autonomy and resist them? Part II of this study (Chapters 3 and 4) concentrates on exploring how and why Liszt's revisions were shaped by various external forces. Chapter 3 will explore the predominantly negative response to Liszt's early Lieder. This reception is examined with Hans Robert Jauss's concept of the 'horizon of expectations' in mind. The overwhelmingly negative responses to Liszt's innovative impulses are seen as the composer's failure to stay within the bounds of what was expected of the genre. In addition, Liszt's Saint-Simonian leanings are considered as a motivating factor in his willingness to attempt to expand the boundaries of the genre.

The work of literary theorist Hans Robert Jauss has been critical to the development of reception theory and history. Jauss's concept of the 'horizon of expectations' is especially pertinent to this study. The horizon of expectations denotes the set of assumptions or preconceptions about a literary work that a reader has when they encounter that literary work. It is shaped by the reader's previous literary/artistic experiences and by societal and/or cultural forces, and it in turn shapes the way a reader interprets and assigns aesthetic value to a literary work. Jauss describes the importance of the horizon of expectations thus: 'The coherence of literature as an

---

[1] John Bryant, *The Fluid Text* (Ann Arbor: University of Michigan Press, 2002), p. 99.

event is primarily mediated in the horizon of expectations of the literary experience of contemporary and later readers, critics, and authors.'[2]

It should be noted, that as each reader creates their own horizon of expectations, formed by forces that are time-variable, a horizon of expectations is itself not fixed but instead is also time-variable. Not only will each subsequent generation of readers have their own cultural and societal preconceptions that inform how they interpret any literary work, but the interaction between the reader and the text may cause a shift in their horizon. Each reader's encounters with a literary work further informs, confirms, shifts, or even breaks the boundaries of their own horizon of expectations. In this way, the horizon of expectations should be viewed as a constantly shifting individualised set of cultural assumptions and preconceptions that informs each reader's experience with a text. Jauss posits that the 'aesthetic distance' between the reader's horizon of expectations and the text's fulfilment of those expectations or, indeed, failure to do so are central to our understanding of a work's contemporaneous reception:

> the horizon of expectations of a work allows one to determine its artistic character by the kind and the degree of its influence on a presupposed audience. If one characterizes as aesthetic distance the disparity between the given horizon of expectations and the appearance of a new work, whose reception can result in a 'change of horizons' through negation of familiar experiences or through raising newly articulated experiences to the level of consciousness, then this aesthetic distance can be objectified historically along the spectrum of the audience's reactions and criticism's judgment (spontaneous success, rejection or shock, scattered approval, gradual or belated understanding).[3]

Using the example of Cervantes's *Don Quixote*, Jauss demonstrates how an author can play on an implied or intended audience's knowledge of genre and style (part of their horizon of expectations) to great effect:

> The interpretative reception of a text always presupposes the context of experience of aesthetic perception: the question of the subjectivity of the interpretation and of the taste of different readers or levels of readers can be asked meaningfully only when one has first clarified which trans-subjective horizon of understanding conditions the influence of the text.
>
> The ideal cases of the objective capability of such literary-historical frames of reference are works that evoke the reader's horizon of expectations, formed by a convention of genre, style, or form, only in order to destroy it step by step – which by no means serves a critical purpose only, but can itself once again produce poetic effects. Thus, Cervantes allows the horizon of expectations of the favourite old tales of knighthood to arise out of the reading of Don Quixote, which the adventure of his last knight then seriously parodies.[4]

---

2   Hans Robert Jauss, *Towards an Aesthetic of Reception*, trans. Paul de Man (Minneapolis: University of Minnesota Press, 1982), p. 22.

3   Ibid., p. 25.

4   Ibid., pp. 23–4.

The important point raised is that many of the effects an author – or composer in our case – wishes to create are dependent on an audience's knowledge of genre, style, or form. That is, they are contingent on the composer correctly gauging their audience's knowledge of them. The composer can then confirm or challenge an audience's horizon of expectations to create a diverse array of effects. There are countless examples of composers very consciously engaging with this form of manipulation in order to heighten the effect of their compositions: from Haydn's unconventional harmonic interpolations and unexpected placement of rests and fermatas to create comic effects, to Liszt and Paganini devising feats of instrumental virtuosity that defied what their audiences thought possible on their respective instruments in order to create awe and disbelief.[5] Interestingly, Jauss goes on to assert that the amount of aesthetic distance allowed by the conventions of a genre or style determines an important characteristic of that style. That is, if no aesthetic distance is allowed between the conventions of the genre and the appearance of a new work, the genre or style approaches what Jauss rather pejoratively terms 'culinary or entertainment art':

> The way in which a literary work, at the historical moment of its appearance, satisfies, surpasses, disappoints, or refutes the expectations of its first audience obviously provides a criterion for the determination of its aesthetic value. The distance between the horizon of expectations and the work, between the familiarity of previous aesthetic experience and the 'horizonal change' demanded by the reception of the new work, determines the artistic character of a literary work, according to an aesthetics of reception: to the degree that this distance decreases, and no turn toward the horizon of yet-unknown experience is demanded of the receiving consciousness, the closer the work comes to the sphere of 'culinary' or entertainment art [*Unterhaltungskunst*]. This latter work can be characterized by an aesthetics of reception as not demanding any horizonal change, but rather as precisely fulfilling the expectations prescribed by a ruling standard of taste, in that it satisfies the desire for the reproduction of the familiarly beautiful; confirms familiar sentiments; sanctions wishful notions; makes unusual experiences enjoyable as 'sensations'; or even raises moral problems, but only to 'solve' them in an edifying manner as pre-decided questions.[6]

The assertion is that an art form's pliability – in terms of its audience's horizon of expectations – determines how 'artistic' it is or, perhaps more accurately, how progressive it is. The implied value judgement by Jauss is that art that is not progressive, that is, art that does not challenge the accepted norms of a style or genre, has little or no aesthetic value. This is a view that should be challenged, and there are innumerable counterexamples in literature and music, from the novels of P.G. Wodehouse or the music of Elgar,[7] or indeed Bach. None of these challenged the accepted norms

---

5   Alfred Brendel, *On Music: Collected Essays* (London: JR Books, 2007), pp. 92–8; Mai Kawabata, *Paganini: The Demonic Virtuoso* (Rochester, NY: The Boydell Press, 2013), pp. 16–17.

6   Jauss, *Towards an Aesthetic of Reception*, p. 25.

7   *Pace* J.P.E. Harper-Scott, *Edward Elgar: Modernist* (Cambridge: Cambridge University Press, 2006).

of style or genre of their respective eras; however, it is far beyond the scope of this book to enter into a discussion of this here. Nevertheless, this notion that the aesthetic distance between a work and the horizon of expectations of its audience (or, as Jauss terms it, 'horizonal change') is useful when examining both the reception of a work and its audience's cultural values. And it is through this lens of horizonal change that we will view the contemporaneous reception of Liszt's Lieder.

At this point, it is also worth recognising that there is some overlap between Genette's five levels of intertextuality as described in Chapter 2 and Jauss's horizon of expectations. Indeed, an audience's ability to perceive a work's architextuality similarly to that of its author or composer determines whether the work succeeds or fails in fulfilling that audience's horizon of expectations. Gerald Prince, in his foreword to Genette's *Palimpsests*, asserts that the object of poetics, as described by Genette, is the study of a text's textual transcendence – the study of how a particular text links with other texts. The insight reached is that all literature is among other things, made with or composed of pre-existing literature. It refers to, comments on, or contains elements, either in part or in whole, of previous literature. Thus, reasons Prince, it is important to know the canon.[8] Liszt not only knew the musical canon as well as anyone in his day, but he was also instrumental in shaping and forming it: playing, performing, editing, teaching, and adapting works from the Baroque to the then most recent contemporary compositions from across Europe. This activity of engaging with what Peter Burkholder calls 'museum pieces' could be understood as driving Liszt's compositional urge in a historicist direction. Burkholder describes the change in the mainstream towards a historicist inclination thus:

> Of course, the problem of creating musical works of lasting value was not in fact the problem that most of the master composers had sought to solve in their music. An often far more urgent problem was to create music which had current value, however ephemeral: providing music for a specific function, whether that be ceremony, worship, public entertainment, dancing, or amateur music-making. When they were revived, however, works of dead composers had lost whatever original social function they had served and were valued exclusively as autonomous works of art. Once the concert hall became a museum, the only works appropriate to be performed there were *museum pieces* – either pieces which were already old and revered or pieces which served exactly the same function, as *musical works of lasting value which proclaimed a distinctive musical personality which rewarded study, and which became loved as they became familiar* [Burkholder's Italics].[9]

However, Liszt's tendency towards this form of historicism seems to have also been influenced by the Saint-Simonian movement and their view of history. Even though he never became an official member of the movement, Liszt became closely associated with the Saint-Simonians in the early 1830s. While the composer did publicly

---

8   Gerald Prince, foreword to Gérard Genette, *Palimpsests: Literature in the Second Degree*, trans. Channa Newman and Claude Doubinsky (Lincoln, NE, and London: University of Nebraska Press, 1997), p. x.

9   J. Peter Burkholder, 'Museum Pieces: The Historicist Mainstream in Music of the Last Hundred Years,' *The Journal of Musicology*, 2:2 (Spring 1983), 115–34 (p. 119).

distance himself from the movement in the latter part of the 1830s and early 1840s, Ralph P. Locke has argued convincingly that this was merely so as not to be associated with its more controversial elements. Instead, Locke suggests that Liszt was in fact profoundly influenced by Saint-Simonian thought throughout his life.[10]

Two complementary perspectives on the Saint-Simonian view of history from French scholar Greg Kerr and historian Goran Blix help us to understand the progressive underpinnings of Liszt's compositional urge. Kerr describes how Saint-Simonians looked at history to divine the causes of previous changes in order to influence future progress:

> Particular to Saint-Simonian doctrine is a vision of history as a purposive, unfolding process between 'organic' and 'critical' epochs (the former characterized by the kind of social and religious cohesion present in the medieval world, the latter by nonconformity and dissent, as represented by the philosophy of the Enlightenment). To understand the reasons for the structural transition from one such epoch to the next was to grasp their latent imbrication and to deduce the subsequent course of History.[11]

This aspect helps us to understand how Liszt's extensive studies of the music of the past could inform his progressive outlook on the development of music rather than cultivating a conservative one. Göran Blix, however, describes how Saint-Simonians were distinctive in how they refined their method of dividing History into 'organic' epochs:

> The Romantic era did not invent historical periods, but decisively transformed and sharpened this ancient concept, seeing the distinct traits of a period as immanent features generated by the historical process itself. The a priori scaffolding of earlier philosophies of history (whether of progress, decline, or the cyclical type) into a series of predetermined stages did not vanish, but was refined into more detailed, supple patterns, in which the unique physiognomy of every period, as defined by its culture, customs, and institutions, occupies the foreground and defines its profile empirically. This internal derivation also had a homogenizing thrust, in which the selected blocks of time, in principle arbitrary, were totalized as whole, organic, and internally coherent entities-zones bounded in time as countries were in space. Simultaneously, they acquired a legitimacy of their own as unique life-worlds, regardless of their title to possess.[12]

These two elements are seen combined in Liszt's preface to the 1842 collection *Album d'un voyageur*:

> As instrumental music progresses, develops, and emerges from its early limitations, it will tend more and more to bear the impress of this ideality which con-

---

[10] Ralph P. Locke, *Music, Musicians, and the Saint-Simonians* (Chicago and London: University of Chicago Press, 1986), pp. 101–6.

[11] Greg Kerr, 'Utopia and Iconicity: Reading Saint-Simonian Texts', *Word and Image*, 28:3 (2012), 324–5.

[12] Göran Blix, 'Charting the "Transitional Period": The Emergence of Modern Time in the Nineteenth Century', *History and Theory*, 45:1 (Feb. 2006), 51–71 (p. 52).

stitutes the perfection of the plastic arts. It will cease to be a mere combination of sounds and will become a poetic language more apt than poetry itself, maybe, at expressing that within our souls which transcends the common horizon, all that eludes analysis, all that moves in the hidden depths of imperishable desire and infinite intuition.

Convinced of this and with this tendency in mind, I undertook the work which is published today. It is written for the few rather than for the many – not ambitious of success, but of the approval of that minority which conceives art as having other uses than beguiling of idle hours and asks more from it than the futile distraction of a passing entertainment.[13]

What is significant about the preface is that it clearly shows that Liszt believed music as an art to have a higher purpose and to be undergoing a process of development and progression in both aesthetic and technical terms. Similarly, Liszt's review in 1855 of A.B. Marx's book *Die Musik des neunzehnten Jahrhunderts und ihre Pflege*, entitled 'Marx und sein Buch', shows that he was consistent on the matter:

Instead of regarding old art as an indispensable stirrup for the present, it [i.e., pedagogy] behaves like Dante's false fortune-teller. It turns its head around on its shoulder in order to aim its eyes backward and to listen as its steps [history's] fade out, and thus not hearing, nor wanting to hear, nor capable of hearing either the voice of the future or the prophecies of destiny's young messengers. Its inner nature was too desiccated to perceive the echoes of these voices.[14]

And similarly:

From now on art must strive to study the past and its masterpieces, rather than imitate in a servile manner the forms that are forever changing and vanishing as time itself forever changes and vanishes – from now on a specialized education [involving] one-sided knowledge and skill is no longer be enough for an artist, because the whole human being, not just the musician, must be elevated and educated.[15]

Either through direct contact with major figures in the movement such as Abbé Félicité Lamennais or as part of the wider intellectual milieu that made up the Paris of his formative years in the early 1830s, Liszt seems highly influenced by Saint-Simonism. An especially relevant musical figure in this respect is François-Joseph Fétis.[16] Fétis's theories on the past and future development of music especially in terms of harmony had a profound effect on Liszt's musical outlook that

---

[13] Franz Liszt's preface to *Album d'un voyageur* (Vienna: Haslinger, 1842), cited in Maurizio Giani, 'Music and the Social Conscience: Reconsidering Liszt's Lyon', in Michael Saffle and Rossana Dalmonte (eds), *Liszt and the Birth of Modern Europe: Music as a Mirror of Religious, Political, Cultural, and Aesthetic Transformations* (Hillsdale, NY: Pendragon Press, 2003), pp. 105–14 (p. 114). Giani cites the translation by F. Copeland, revised by M. Roberts, found in Karen Sue Wilson, 'A Historical Study and Stylistic Analysis of Franz Liszt's Années de Pèlerinage' (PhD diss., University of North Carolina, 1977), p. 311.

[14] Quoted in Cornelia Szabó-Knotik, 'Tradition as a Source of Progress: Franz Liszt and Historicism', in *Liszt and the Birth of Modern Europe*, pp. 143–56 (p. 150).

[15] Ibid., p. 152.

[16] A formative influence on Fétis was the philosopher Victor Cousin.

would last well into his later years.[17] Relevant figures with connections to Saint-Simonism whom Liszt either knew personally or was well-acquainted with through their writings include Pierre-Simon Ballanche, Alfred de Musset, François-René de Chateaubriand, and Jules Michelet.

With this in mind, Liszt's early Lieder can be seen as a manifestation of the composer's desire to develop and progress the genre of the Lied by introducing new elements into it. These elements included stylistic traits from the operatic aria, the dramatic scene, Italianate and French melodic inflection, increased virtuosity, tone painting, and a large variety of innovative piano textures. Liszt can be seen attempting to emulate Schubert and Beethoven, not by imitating their compositional style, but rather by endeavouring to be similarly progressive and push past the boundaries of the genre. Through the introduction of these elements Liszt sought to take the Lied from its origins in a semi-private or domestic setting and transform it into a genre that could occupy the stage of the concert hall. He was well aware of the pre-existing conventions of the genre and, as we shall see, his choosing to subvert them had a profound effect on the reception of these works. The contention is that the overwhelmingly negative contemporaneous reception of the early Lieder in turn exerted an influence or at least significant pressure on the direction that Liszt's revisions would eventually take, even if he would be loath to admit it.

Liszt's industriousness in the art of transcription, apart from enriching the repertoire of the pianist with music from a diverse array of genres, has left the musicologist with a demonstrable and invaluable record of works that came under Liszt's fingers and which he undoubtedly studied closely. The true extent of Liszt's studies may never be known, although it can be assumed to be much larger than simply the list of his transcriptions; nevertheless, the list of his transcriptions provides a solid foundation – if not an exhaustive record – on which to base any assertions or arguments contingent on Liszt's knowledge of a particular repertoire. In fact, before Liszt had penned any of the Lieder published in his first collection, the *Buch der Lieder*, he had already completed and published fifty-six transcriptions of Schubert's Lieder. Again, even though the number of Lieder by Schubert that Liszt studied before 1843 may be unknowable, it will have been greater than the number of published transcriptions – not an insignificant proportion, especially for the period. Given Liszt's tremendous output in transcriptions, it is easy to fall into the belief that he could transcribe in a quick and efficient manner whatever repertoire he wished to. However, this was not the case; for example, for a time he wrestled with the idea of transcribing Beethoven's string quartets for solo piano, but found the task to be beyond him, stating that the results would either be unplayable or move too far from the originals to be true transcriptions.[18] The point to be taken from this is that Liszt may well have studied many

---

[17] Franz Liszt, *The Collected Writings of Franz Liszt*, vol. 2: *Essays and Letters of a Traveling Bachelor of Music*, ed. and trans. Janita R. Hall-Swadley (Lanham, MD: Scarecrow Press, 2012), pp. 18–19.

[18] Alan Walker, *Reflections of Liszt* (Ithaca and London: Cornell University Press, 2011), pp. 26 and 71. Incidentally, Liszt's star pupil, Carl Tausig, did complete transcriptions of six movements from various string quartets of Beethoven, which were published

more Schubert Lieder than those for which he produced transcriptions – and that those merely represented the Schubert Lieder most suited to transcription.

Review of *Buch der Lieder*, Volume 1, in *Neue Zeitschrift für Musik*

Volume 1 of Liszt's *Buch der Lieder* was reviewed by Oswald Lorenz in the *Neue Zeitschrift für Musik* (hereafter NZfM) on 28 December 1843.[19] A close associate of Robert Schumann, Lorenz regularly reviewed Lieder for NZfM and briefly took over as editor in 1844 when Schumann resigned.[20] Before the publication came under the more pro-Liszt direction of Franz Brendel in 1845, the NZfM was, in general, less than full-throated in its praise of Liszt's compositions while still respecting transcendental virtuosity.[21]

One of the most striking aspects of Lorenz's overwhelmingly negative review is that the criticisms levelled at the *Buch der Lieder*, in general, stem from the judgement that the works therein failed to conform in any meaningful way to their nominal genre. From the outset, Lorenz embarks on a critique whose main purpose is to deny the songs' status as Lieder proper. After initially deigning to refer to the six Lieder as such, Lorenz quickly qualifies this by correcting himself and referring to them as vocal pieces or showpieces (*Gesangsstücke* and *Paradestücke* respectively).[22] Lorenz adopts a mocking tone and engages in a form of parody as criticism. He inundates the review with an overabundance of lofty language with chains of adjectives no doubt meant to parody, and in turn ridicule, the perceived overabundance of Liszt's virtuoso piano accompaniments, harmonic language, and his rhetorical and dramatic style. Indeed, Liszt's harmonic language is the butt of jibes such as 'What the good old-timers used to call "the key" sounds like a half-forgotten fairy tale from childhood'.[23]

---

posthumously. Carl Tausig, *Sechs Sätze aus Streichquartetten von L. van Beethoven für Klavier übertragen* (Leipzig: C.F. Peters, 1916).

[19] Oswald Lorenz, *Neue Zeitschrift für Musik*, 19:52 (28 December 1843), 205–6. The translations of all the reviews in this chapter are my own. Transcriptions and translations of the reviews in their entirety can be found in the appendices.

[20] Michael Abu Hamad, 'True Interpreters of Words: Tonal Distances in Franz Liszt's Early Songs' (PhD diss., Brandeis University, 2005), pp. 10–11.

[21] Brendel purchased the journal from Robert Schumann on 1 July 1844, but only took over as editor on 1 January 1845. This explains why the journal remained unenthusiastic about Liszt's compositions during the first months of Brendel's ownership.

[22] There is an apparent inconsistency in Lorenz's numbering, moving from six Lieder to nine *Gesangsstücke/Paradestücke* at the start of the review. However, Lorenz may be referring to Liszt having provided two of the Lieder with extended *ossias* (namely 'Am Rhein' and 'König von Thule') and that 'Englein du mit blondem Haar' is printed in both German and the original Italian. Thus, Liszt may be said to have created nine different versions from six poems.

[23] 'Was die guten Altvordern Tonart nannten, das klingt uns hier nur in träumerischen Undeutungen wie ein halbvergesnes Mährchen aus der Kindheit an.' Oswald Lorenz, *Neue Zeitschrift für Musik*, 19:52 (28 December 1843), 205–6.

Of more interest, though, is that Lorenz finds the harmonic language employed by Liszt to be completely unacceptable in terms of genre, regardless of the nature of the poetic content of the Lied in question. Indeed, evoking a 'half-forgotten fairy tale from childhood' would seem most apt for both 'Loreley' and 'König von Thule'.[24] Although not a genuine folktale or myth, the Lorelei story could be termed a pastiche of either genre; likewise, 'Es war ein König in Thule' evokes fairy tale-like connotations merely from the use of the name 'Thule'. Its origins are attributed to the Greek explorer Pytheas (*c.* 300 BC) who described a land six days' sail north of Britain.[25] By Virgil's time (70–19 BC) 'Thule' or 'Ultima Thule' came to mean 'faraway island realm', and as Sharon R. Roseman writes: 'In Medieval Geography … *Ultima Thule* referred to any faraway place positioned beyond the borders of the "known world". Medieval poets also imagined Thule as a place of awe-inspiring mystery.'[26] Therefore, the opening line of 'Der König in Thule' could be read as analogous to 'Once upon a time, in a far-off distant land …'.

Throughout the review, Lorenz finds Liszt's harmonic trajectories unpalatable, like being swept up in 'unpredictable comet trails through boundless space'. The only exception to this is 'Angiolin dal biondo crin'/'Englein du mit blondem Haar', which – despite being based on an Italian text – Lorenz finds to be the closest to respecting the true character of the Lied in both form and conception. Lorenz elaborates by citing the song's 'simple sweet melody and equally clear harmonisation'. Indeed, the qualities of simplicity and clarity are of utmost importance to Lorenz. Whenever Liszt gives an option to the performer of harder or easier music such as in the more difficult accompaniment to 'Am Rhein', or the heavily chromatic étude-like piano texture during the 'sinking of the cup' section in 'Es war ein König in Thule,' Lorenz prefers the simpler accompaniment. Regarding the two accompaniments in 'Am Rhein' Lorenz writes: 'Here, too, the easier accompaniment is the more beautiful one.'[27] Here Lorenz seems to be using 'beautiful' to mean 'more closely conforming to the received aesthetic' rather than relating to an intrinsic sonic beauty. Lorenz's position on 'König in Thule' is telling, as initially he is quite sympathetic to Liszt's setting of the poem's opening. However, when the chromatic tone painting in the piano accompaniment appears towards the end of the song, this is where Liszt strays into the territory of 'aesthetic sin'. Another aspect that Lorenz finds unsuited to the Lied is the dramatic nature of Liszt's settings, with 'Mignon' and 'Der du von dem Himmel bist' being the worst offenders. Interestingly, even when Lorenz admits that a dramatic setting may be supported by the content of the poem, as in the case of 'Die Loreley', he is of the opinion that a composer should avoid such settings as they fall beyond the boundaries of what is acceptable in Lied composition.

---

[24] I use 'Lorelei' to denote the actual rock on the banks of the Rhine and the myth associated with it. I use 'Loreley' when referring to Liszt's Lied.

[25] Sharon R. Roseman, *The Tourism Imaginary and Pilgrimages to the Edges of the World* (Bristol: Channel View Publications, 2015), p. 122.

[26] Ibid.

[27] 'Bei dem letzteren Gedichte, dem einzigen, ist übrigens der Liedcharakter im Ganzen in Form und Auffassung respectirt', and 'Auch hier ist gewiss die leichtere Begleitung die schönere', *Neue Zeitschrift für Musik*, 19:52 (28 December 1843), 205.

Notices in the *Allgemeine Musikalische Zeitung* and *Gazette Musicale de Paris*

That the *Allgemeine Musikalische Zeitung* chose not to review this first foray into song composition by a composer of Liszt's profile and status is a telling omission. Nevertheless, although the *Allgemeine Musikalische Zeitung* carried no review of the first volume of the *Buch der Lieder*, it was advertised in several successive issues in the *Neue wertvolle Musikalien* section between December 1843 and March 1844. However, it is worth noting that the volume significantly dropped in price from a high on 13 December 1843 of 2½ Thalers to ½ Thaler by 27 March 1844. This was perhaps an indication that the *Buch der Lieder* was not nearly as commercially successful as initially envisaged and was on its way to the proverbial bargain bin.[28] In the 4 February 1844 edition of the *Gazette Musicale de Paris* under the news section, a brief reference was made to the *Buch der Lieder*:

> The songs which Liszt recently published in Berlin under the title Le Lione [*sic*] des Lieder, have elicited fervent enthusiasm when *he* [my italics] accompanies them. The Lieder, Loreley by Heine, Mignon by Goethe, are delightful. The second volume of this collection contains six lyric poems by Victor Hugo, which are impatiently anticipated.[29]

It should be stated that the *Gazette Musicale de Paris* can hardly be accorded the status of impartial arbiter regarding Liszt's newly published music. Liszt had been a major contributor to the journal since the early 1830s and is even listed on the cover of the issue in question as a contributing writer. Moreover, the editor and owner of the *Gazette*, Maurice Schlesinger, was the older brother of Heinrich Schlesinger, the director of the Berlin A.M. Schlesinger that published the *Buch der Lieder*.[30] Nevertheless, this snippet should not be dismissed as merely partisan publicity. The inclusion of the caveat 'when he accompanies them', to describe the enthusiasm created by the Lieder, is noteworthy. It suggests that Schlesinger acknowledged that a successful performance of the Lieder was reliant on the availability of a charismatic performer of the highest calibre. As will be discussed later, this seems to point to the idea that the failure of Liszt's Lieder to resonate with the public, performers, or critics was in part due to a miscalculation on Liszt's part about the nature of the genre, which in turn is also revealing about Liszt's attitudes to the notion of genre in general.

---

[28] *Allgemeine Musikalische Zeitung*, 50 (13 December 1843), 920; *Allgemeine Musikalische Zeitung* (13, 27 March 1844), 231.

[29] *Gazette Musicale de Paris*, 5 (4 February 1844), 39. 'Les airs que Liszt a publiés à Berlin sous le titre le Lione de Lieder, excitent fanatisme quand il les accompagne. Ses Lieds, Lurley de Heine, Mignon de Goethe, sont délicieux. Le second volume de cet ouvrage, contenant six poésies lyriques de Victor Hugo, est attendu avec impatience.'

[30] A.M. Schlesinger was founded in Berlin in 1810 by Adolph Martin Schlesinger. His eldest son Maurice founded his own firm in Paris, M. Schlesinger, in 1821. Adolph Martin's third son, Heinrich, would eventually take over the Berlin firm.

Reviews of *Buch der Lieder*, Volume 2, and *Vierstimmige Männergesänge*

Volume 2 of the *Buch der Lieder* was reviewed again by Lorenz in NZfM on 23 May 1844. Similar criticisms abound in this review, as once more Lorenz calls into question the validity of terming the works Lieder: 'The six Lieder (? –) contained within are likewise, all glittering magnificence and showpieces.' Indeed, Lorenz's objections to Volume 2 are so similar to the previous volume that he saw fit to recycle his opening remarks from that review almost verbatim. This time, Lorenz is even more forceful, declaring that the purchaser/audience of these songs will be severely disappointed if they seek works that conform to the true nature of the Lied.[31] Rather helpfully however for this book, Lorenz goes on to outline some of the characteristics that he felt made up 'the true nature of the Lied':

> if the expression of the melody corresponds exactly to the content of the words, if the accompaniment is only the support of the latter, although it is permissible to enhance the expression occasionally, to stand out in a characteristic way, when with a word in the song, alongside beautiful simplicity, certainty of feeling and truth of expression prevail![32]

The notion that Liszt spectacularly fails to meet these characteristics forms the main thrust of the review. Lorenz continually takes exception to the impudence of Liszt designating his songs Lieder: 'Book of Lieder? We do not know from which seat of judgement (throne) Liszt is able to christen the children of his muse as such.' As with Volume 1, Lorenz finds the songs' technical demands unacceptable, referring to the accompaniment having fingering throughout, and highlighting the harmony as being particularly unpalatable:

> Has anyone ever seen a song composed in which the fingering is interspersed line by line with the accompanying notes? Here you can find it. Along with an unrestrained mass of the double sharps and double flats, the enharmonic confusions, the gnawing chords, in short with this virtuoso accompaniment.[33]

Lorenz seems to imply here that accompaniments should be playable at first sight without the need to refer to fingering to explicate the required technique. Although some concessions are afforded to Liszt given that the songs were based on French poems, Lorenz is still quite damning of the text/music relationships: 'This excuses the many inconsistencies, even the absurdities, in some things that our eyes encounter when we compare the underlying German words with the melody … for exam-

---

[31] Review of Volume 1: 'Er enthält sechs Lieder – neun Gesangsstücke, glänzende Pracht- und Paradestücke, ausgestattet mit allen Würzen und Reizen einer virtuosenmätzigen Begleitung und einer schwelgerischen, alle Gebiete durchschweifenden Harmonik.' Review of Volume 2: 'Die sechs Lieder (? –), die er enthält, sind ebenfalls glänzende Pracht- und Paradestücke, ausgestattet mit allen Würzen und Reizen einer virtuosenmäsigen Begleitung und einer schwelgerischen, alle Gebiete durchschweifenden Harmonik.' *Neue Zeitschrift für Musik*, 20:42 (23 May 1844), 165.

[32] *Neue Zeitschrift für Musik*, 20:42 (23 May 1844), 165.

[33] Ibid.

ple the word 'König' is written as an iamb.' A final aspect of this review worth considering is Lorenz's drawing attention to the newly published transcriptions of the *Buch der Lieder* for solo piano. Lorenz ends his review rhetorically by questioning the importance of this second version. That Lorenz questions which version is the more important, rather than simply valuing each publication on its own terms, is indeed telling – the implication being that Liszt's adaptation of the Lieder so idiomatically for solo piano confirms the reviewer's opinion that the 'originals' were unsuitable for their designated genre.

Liszt's collection of *Männergesänge* (songs for male-voice choir) was reviewed in *NZfM* on 26 September 1844.[34] And similarly, the unnamed critic of this review (Michael Abu Hamad suggests that it may also have been Oswald Lorenz) was also unenthusiastic about Liszt's essays in this genre.[35] Interestingly, however, Liszt here avoids the criticism levelled at his Lieder that called their generic designation into question. There is even some qualified praise: while the style of the music is well-suited, the harmonic changes are said to 'make no sense'.

Review of *Sechs Lieder* in *Neue Zeitschrift für Musik* and *Allgemeine Musikalische Zeitung*

The third volume of Liszt's Lieder, entitled simply *Sechs Lieder*, was reviewed in the *Neue Zeitschrift für Musik* on 10 October 1844 (by Lorenz) and in the *Allgemeine Musikalische Zeitung* in January 1845 (by Julius Schladebach).[36] Michael Abu Hamad has acutely highlighted several ways in which this volume diverges from its two predecessors; moreover, he proposed that Liszt made these changes in order to avoid the type of criticism that the first two volumes received.[37] Firstly, even though this volume undoubtedly represents the projected third volume of the *Buch der Lieder* that was announced in 1843, when the first volume was published, Liszt dropped the *Buch der Lieder* title no doubt in order to distance this new collection from the much-maligned previous volumes. Secondly, Liszt included no ballad texts, or non-German-language texts, only lyric poems, which at that time were considered the more traditional fit for 'true' Lieder. And finally, Liszt structured this collection differently by placing the most adventurous Lied ('Vergiftet sind meine Lieder') inconspicuously in the middle of the collection, in contrast with the first two volumes of the *Buch der Lieder* which located them at the start ('Loreley' in Volume 1, and 'Oh Quand je dors' in Volume 2). Unfortunately for Liszt, in the main, none of these strategies managed to assuage his harshest critics.

In the *NZfM* review Lorenz's views remain largely unchanged. This is not very surprising as a mere ten months had elapsed since his review of the first volume of *Buch der Lieder* and so Liszt's 'aesthetic sins' were still fresh in the critic's mind. This

---

34 *Neue Zeitschrift für Musik* 20:26 (26 September 1844), 102–3.

35 Hamad, 'True Interpreters of Words', p. 14.

36 *Neue Zeitschrift für Musik*, 30 (10 October 1844), 117–18; *Allgemeine Musikalische Zeitung* (1 January 1845), 5–6.

37 Hamad, 'True Interpreters of Words,' pp. 12–13.

is made clear by Lorenz's opening remarks, which reference his own reviews of the previous volumes:

> In contrast with the Buch der Lieder, especially its 1st Volume (see Vol. 19, No. 52. and Vol. 20. No. 42. d., Bl.), these songs have a rather plain and peaceful appearance. However, on closer inspection their true essence does not at all seem so plain and peaceful, but instead, is almost hostile to the true nature of the Lied.[38]

Lorenz's criticisms are again directed at Liszt's failure to comply with the genre's conventions. Lorenz is particularly scathing of Liszt's poor taste, wandering harmonic trajectories, and idiosyncrasies in the declamation. Even when Lorenz praises an initial concept or first verse, he argues that Liszt's poor taste prevails and destroys the initial impression. Lorenz's comments on 'Morgens steh' ich auf und frage' are representative of those found throughout the review:

> 'Morgens steh' ich auf und frage' is, in the first verse, so beautifully written, especially the silent renunciation during the soft conclusion in C sharp minor … the accompaniment then picks up the first sentimental motif and the whole thing concludes in an anodyne fashion – the overall impression being ruined, the song – botched. What a pity! The song would not only have been one of the best of the six, but rather a good one, if not for this poor taste.[39]

One song does emerge in a positive light: 'Die Zelle in Nonnenwerth'. Although Lorenz is 'not spared the ordeal of passages with strong harmonic changes', he finds it the most well-rounded and constructed in the collection and that there is 'in parts so much true songfulness and melodiousness that singers will get their money's worth'.[40]

Julius Schladebach, writing under the pseudonym 'Wise' in the *Allgemeine Musikalische Zeitung*, expressed similar views to Lorenz regarding Liszt's *Sechs Lieder* and his works for male-voice choir.[41] Schladebach's reviews of both collections appeared in the same edition of the *Allgemeine Musickalische Zeitung* on 1 January 1845.[42] In his review of the *Männergesänge*, Schladebach draws attention to Liszt's lack of consideration for the physical limitations of the voice. Indeed, the unidiomatic nature of the vocal writing forms the main part of the criticism levelled at the choral works. Schladebach asserts that the writing is too instrumental, and that Liszt is striving to recreate orchestral effects. In fact, the harmonic language and the

---

[38] *Neue Zeitschrift für Musik*, 30 (10 October 1844), 117.

[39] Ibid.

[40] Ibid.

[41] Schladebach, a Lied composer in his own right, would himself fall foul of criticisms that his songwriting was not in the true style of the Lied. Schladebach was known rather as a composer of part songs, his collection *Sieben Gesänge Dichtungen* reviewed by Otto Lange (Dr. L.) in the *Neue Musikalische Zeitung für Berlin* on 27 April 1847. The vocal writing of his Lieder was found to be more like the tenor part in a choral composition than a melody in its own right. Likewise, the accompaniment was considered unsuitable to the Lied style as it was too intricate; it also overwhelmed the vocal part as it contained most of the harmonic and polyphonic interest.

[42] *Allgemeine Musikalische Zeitung*, 1 (1 January 1845), pp. 5–6.

perceived orchestral nature of the writing lead Schladebach to declare that these works 'could have been written by Berlioz'.[43] Interestingly, a comparison is made with the earlier volumes of the *Buch der Lieder*; Liszt is deemed to have repeated many of the 'mistakes' contained therein, but to a lesser degree.

Schladebach is much more scathing regarding the *Sechs Lieder*. His review is full of criticisms which are just as harsh as those levelled at the previous volumes of the *Buch der Lieder* in the NZfM. Again, the strategy is to call into question the validity of terming the songs Lieder. Schladebach uses the phrase *lucus a non lucendo*, in essence, to claim that these songs are in fact the very opposite of what one would or rather should describe as Lieder. Schladebach suggests that 'fantasies' or 'fantastic rhapsodies' would be more apt terms. While Schladebach recognises that the Lieder 'do not lack a certain poetic inwardness', Liszt's means of expression are deemed completely inadequate. Schladebach remarks that the accompaniments to this collection were not as difficult as expected, but he deplores the constant tone painting in which Liszt indulges. The vocal writing is considered 'strangely clumsy or awkward', but he opines that it could perhaps be tolerable if played on a clarinet. By drawing attention to the instrumental nature of the vocal writing, Schladebach seeks to make the case that these are not Lieder. The entire review is in fact structured around the concept of genre and finishes with a parting shot consistent with the rest of the review: 'We recommend these songs for study to those who would like to learn from illustrative examples how not to do it.'

Review of the Schiller and Goethe Lieder in *Neue Zeitschrift für Musik* in 1849

Liszt's *Drei Lieder aus Schillers 'Wilhelm Tell'* and *Drei Gedichte von Göthe* were reviewed by Karl Emanuel Klitzch in NZfM on 17 May 1849.[44] The editorship of the journal had at that stage been taken over by Franz Brendel. As one might expect of an editor who coined the term 'New German School' to describe the music emanating from Weimar—and who together with Franz Liszt would also become a founding member of the *Allgemeiner Deutscher Musikverein* in 1861—the reception of Liszt's Schiller and Goethe Lieder in the NZfM was much more sympathetic than it had been under Schumann's or Lorenz's stewardship.

The review by Klitzch highlights many of the features of Liszt's Lieder style that had caused such opprobrium in earlier reviews but, in contrast, they are presented now as virtues rather than evidence of a faulty style or aesthetic. Moreover, Klitzch even uses similar language to that found in Schladebach's review of the *Sechs Lieder*, in reference to their lack of genre conformance. Klitzch makes the point of emphasising that 'the composer does not want to serve up compositions in the usual sense of the word', but rather 'free fantasies of the imagination that have been documented in the most distinctive and precise way'. Klitzch's review is in fact at pains to point out how Liszt's Schiller Lieder are radically different from more traditional

---

[43] Ibid.

[44] *Neue Zeitschrift für Musik*, 30:40 (17 May 1849), 217–18.

conceptions of the genre. For example, Klitzsch declares that the composer creates a poem upon a poem, and highlights for high praise the unusual harmonic turns, and the reflection of the poet's words in the smallest details in the accompaniment. Klitzsch mentions the many alpine features, such as cow bell imitations, the *Ranz des Vaches* style melodies of the second song 'Der Hirt', and the storm effects of the third song 'Der Alpenjäger'. This is far removed from the notion of Lied accompaniments merely reflecting the overall mood of the poem. Klitzsch's review of the Goethe poems also draws attention to this point: Liszt is felt to follow Goethe's intentions closely, although it may be more accurate to say that Liszt follows Goethe's content more closely. Klitzch remarks that the vocal writing is more prominent in the Goethe Lieder than in the Schiller Lieder; interestingly, however, his one quibble is that certain passages have a marked Italian influence, which is found to disturb the overall effect, perhaps reflecting more than a little nationalistic possessiveness over this most German of genres. Clearly, then, Klitzsch's concept of genre is at odds with that of Schladebach and Lorenz. By highlighting many of the non-traditional features of Liszt's Lieder as virtues, he articulates a viewpoint that sees genre not as a fixed set of attributes that compositions are measured against in order to make aesthetic value judgements, but rather as a concept with fluid boundaries that allows the traditional attributes of the genre to be challenged or extended by compositions of a more 'progressive' bent.

The collection of reviews gathered here is not meant to be exhaustive but rather representative. I focused on the reviews contained in the *Neue Zeitung für Musik* and the *Allgemeine Musikalische Zeitung* as they were the most prestigious and widely circulated music periodicals of the time, and as such the negative reviews can legitimately be considered a significant force of opposition to Liszt's early Lied aesthetic. Other negative reviews of Liszt's Lieder (such as those found in Herrmann Hirschbach's *Musikalisch-kritisches Repertorium*) have been omitted for considerations of space and repetitiveness; criticisms contained therein are largely of a similar nature.[45] What should be clear from examining the reviews is that a quite specific set of attributes is readily discernible that can approximate Lorenz's and Schladebach's Lied aesthetic, and consequently their horizon of expectations: simple, easily sung melodies with an unobtrusive and playable accompaniment, a close adherence to the natural prosody of the poem, an avoidance of the dramatic, little or no tone-painting, and, finally, that the setting should evoke the overall mood, not slavishly follow

---

[45] Hermann Hirschbach, review, *Franz Liszt, Buch der Lieder, Musikalisch-kritisches Repertorium*, 1:1 (January 1844), 231; Ign. Lewinsky, *Wiener Allgemeine Musik-Zeitung*, 116 (27 September 1845), 462; Dr. L (Otto Lange), 'Francesco Liszt', *Neue Musikalische Zeitung für Berlin*, 35 (1 September 1845), 293. These reviews were not included as they were not as widely circulated as the *Neue Zeitung für Musik* or the *Allgemeine Musikalische Zeitung*, and, as is the case with Lewinsky and Lange, their reviews date from considerably after the initial publication date and may be taking their cues from Lorenz and Schladebach.

every detail of the text. These characteristics align quite closely with the aesthetic often ascribed to the second Berlin *Liederschule*.[46] It is surprising that these characteristics were still so highly valued when one considers the changes in the Lied that had already been instigated by Schubert. E.T.A. Hoffmann eloquently set out these characteristics in a review of Wilhelm Friedrich Riem's op. 27 *Zwölf Lieder*, in the *Allgemeine Musikalische Zeitung* in 1814:

> The inner poet … expresses in his own magical way what normally appears inexpressible; thus a few simple notes often contain the profoundest meaning of the poem. Lieder of the earlier composers were extremely simple, without ostentation or ornament and without contrived modulation, often remaining in the tonic throughout; compact in scale, usually with no ritornello and only accommodating one stanza; singable, that is to say, without wide leaps and only covering a limited compass. *But it should be obvious that these characteristics proceed from the very nature of the Lied* [my italics]. To stir the innermost soul by means of the simplest melody and the simplest modulation, without affectation or straining for effect and originality: therein lies the mysterious power of true genius, such as that commanded by those excellent composers of the past, and by Reichardt and Zelter among the present generation.[47]

Zelter, who is often considered the leading figure of that style, believed, according to Rufus Hallmark, that 'simplicity and sing-ability were the essence of song; anything too elaborate, in voice or piano, would overload a basically simple genre'.[48] That Liszt's Lieder failed to conform to these critics' expectations of genre is clear, but more importantly, what emerges from surveying these reviews is that the concept of genre itself was central to the method of criticism prevalent at the time. This is evident when Lorenz declares that the dramatic nature of Liszt's settings may be supported by the content of the poem, but is not justified. The implication is that while the origins of or rationale behind Liszt's dramatic settings can be easily traced back to the poem and may in fact suit adaptation into another genre, they are not acceptable in a Lied setting. They are contrary to the 'true nature of the Lied'. The dramatic and extrovert nature of many of Liszt's early songs would seem to be ideal for the concert hall. This seems especially relevant to the Schiller Lieder where the goal seems to have been to expand the boundaries of the song genre and create a hybrid of the tone-poem or concert *étude* but for voice and piano. However, as

---

[46] 'The German art song of the latter part of the 18th century, … in reaction to the alleged artificiality of the coloratura aria [G. *Kunstlied*], reverted to a somewhat affected simplicity of expression and style approximating folk music. Representative composers of such songs include J.A.P. Schulz (1747–1800) J.F. Reichardt (1752–1814), K.F. Zelter (1758–1832), F. Silcher (1789–1860).' Willi Apel, *Harvard Dictionary of Music*, 2nd edn (Cambridge, MA: The Belknap Press of Harvard University Press, 1969), p. 482 and p. 920.

[47] E.T.A. Hoffmann, *E.T.A. Hoffmann's Musical Writings: Kreisleriana; The Poet and the Composer, Music Criticism*, ed. David Charlton, trans. Martyn Clarke (Cambridge: Cambridge University Press, 1989), p. 379.

[48] Rufus E. Hallmark, ed., *German Lieder in the Nineteenth Century* (New York: Routledge 2010), p. 193.

Jennifer Roynak has demonstrated, at least up to the 1830s, even in large-scale concerts, the Lied, in contrast to the other works on the programme, would be used as a public vehicle with which to express *Sehnsucht*, interiority, and intimacy.[49]

Liszt was far from the first composer to have suffered the form of censure described above and, indeed, the two predecessors he most revered – Beethoven and Schubert – faced similar criticisms. Václav Tomášek recalls a meeting with Goethe where the poet criticised Beethoven (along with Spohr) for not keeping to the poem's strophic form in their respective settings of 'Kennst du das Land?':

> It seems strange to me that both Beethoven and Spohr so completely misunderstood the song when they composed it. The distinctive mark in the same place in each verse, I would think, was enough to tell composers that what I expect from them is simply a song [Lied]. Evidently, Mignon by her very nature could not sing an aria, but only a song.[50]

Clearly Goethe felt that both Spohr and Beethoven had overcomplicated things, but more tellingly Goethe's feeling that the Lied was an inherently simple genre is also apparent, and one that is simpler than an aria. This is further evidenced, as Carl Dahlhaus points out, by Goethe's belief that it was the performer's task to add variety to each strophe of a Lied, and not the composer's.[51] Similarly, concerns about the suitability of terming Schubert's Lieder as such were raised on 24 June 1824, when his *Sämtliche Lieder* were reviewed in the *Allgemeine Musikalische Zeitung*: 'Herr F.S. does not write Lieder in the accepted sense, nor does he wish to … Instead, he composes free songs [*Gesänge*], sometimes so free that we were better advised to call them capriccios or fantasias.'[52]

There are two points to take from this. Firstly, that there was a well-defined set of attributes which critics associated with what they would term Lieder proper, and were in contrast with other vocal genres that employed terms such as *Gesänge*, which had different connotations; and secondly, that Schubert's Lieder did not conform to this set of attributes. The reviewer here cites examples where Schubert deviates from strophic form. That the correct use of generic terms by composers was still felt to be important by critics in the 1840s can be gleaned not only from the umbrage heaped upon Liszt's works due to his insistence on using the term Lieder, but also, somewhat paradoxically, from our examining the reception of songs where composers decided to eschew heavily loaded terms. A comparison with the critical

---

[49] Jennifer Roynak, 'Performing the Lied, Performing the Self: Singing Subjectivity in Germany, 1790–1832' (PhD diss., University of Rochester, 2010), pp. 224–75.

[50] Lorraine Byrne (ed.), *Goethe: Musical Poet, Musical Catalyst* (Dublin: Carysfort Press, 2004), p. 170.

[51] Carl Dahlhaus, *Nineteenth-Century Music*, trans. J. Bradford Robinson (Berkeley and Los Angeles: University of California Press, 1989), p. 98. It should be noted that plenty of recent research has shown that Goethe was not as musically conservative in his views as formerly acknowledged. See Lorraine Byrne Bodley, *Schubert's Goethe Settings* (Aldershot: Taylor and Francis, 2003), pp. 3–24; and also Byrne Bodley, 'In Pursuit of a Single Flame? On Schubert's Settings of Goethe's Poems', *Nineteenth-Century Music Review*, 13:1 (2016), 11–33.

[52] Ibid., p. 98, citing *Allgemeine Musikalische Zeitung*, 26 (24 June 1824), 426.

reception that greeted Schumann's early Lieder is illuminating and demonstrates how other composers also came up against notions of generic suitability. Several of Schumann's song collections were reviewed in the *Allgemeine Musikalische Zeitung* on 19 January 1842.[53] Like Liszt's Lieder, although in not as harsh terms, those songs of Schumann that contained unusual harmonic turns or an increased prominence in the piano writing were also the object of much criticism. Jon W. Finson encapsulates this by contrasting *Liederkreis*, op. 24, and *Myrthen*, op. 25:

> It becomes clear from the collections and individual songs censured or praised by the reviewer that his conception of the Lied entailed cantabile melody predominating over a subordinated accompaniment with predictable figuration (the Schubertian model that Schumann hoped to move beyond). For this reason, the Heine *Liederkreis* generally does poorly in comparison with *Myrthen*.[54]

Louis Köhler's *Sechs Gesänge*, op. 2, were reviewed in the same edition of the *Allgemeine Musikalische Zeitung* as Liszt's *Sechs Lieder* on 1 January 1845. The contrast in reception between Liszt's collection and that of Köhler, one of his followers and most ardent supporters, is significant:

> In the present two songbooks L. Köhler reveals a decided talent, which we welcome gladly. … From these songs speaks a poetic mind. … They rub shoulders in a dignified manner with the best, with what has recently come to our mind in this genre. We wish, with all sincerity, to acknowledge the beautiful, deepfelt melody, clear, flowing, and interesting harmony, and independent and polished accompaniment … We are happy to have made the acquaintance of the young, talented composer under such favourable circumstances, and wish to continue the same in the same way.[55]

Although by no means as progressive or as radical a composer as Liszt, Köhler was nevertheless closely associated with Liszt and his circle. Therefore, it would be natural to assume that his works would have received similar criticism to Liszt. However, I contend that by avoiding the term *Lieder* and using *Gesänge* instead, Köhler prepared his audience suitably to assuage any misgivings about the novelties contained within his collection. Indeed, the innovative features of Köhler's op. 2 are largely met with approval in the review. However, while the reception of Köhler's op. 2 was not universally positive (for example, in Herrmann Hirschbach's *Musikalisch-kritisches Repertorium* his songs are found wanting in many respects), they are never attacked on an existential level. Their right to exist is never called into question in

---

53 *Allgemeine Musikalische Zeitung* (19 January 1842), 58–63. The review was in two instalments and examined the Heine *Liederkreis*, op. 24, *Mythren*, op. 25, the Geibel *Gedichte*, ops. 29–30, Duets *Liedereihe*, ops. 34–5, and *Zwölf Gesänge aus Rückerts Liebesfrühling*, op. 37.

54 Jon W. Finson, *Robert Schumann: The Book of Songs* (Cambridge, MA: Harvard University Press, 2007), p. 151. Finson is suggesting that by using the term 'Myrthen' as the title, Schumann had better prepared his audience.

55 *Allgemeine Musikalische Zeitung* (1 January 1845), pp. 8–9.

the way Liszt's Lieder are, and in this respect terming the songs *Gesänge* instead of *Lieder* may have been crucial.[56]

The notion that composers were aware of the genre expectations of their audiences seems a given. Liszt himself, even though most of his compositions do not bear standard generic designations, was always careful when designating his works. For example, in his adaptations of orchestral and operatic works, Liszt used a wide variety of terms: *Fantasie über/sur …*; *Grande Fantaisie sur …*; *Réminiscences de …*; *Illustrations de …*; *Konzertparaphrase*; *Stücke aus der …*; *Phantasiestücke über …*; *Partitions de Piano*; and *Transcription*, to name a few. He was obviously sensitive to the fact that each of these terms conveys a different process of adaptation that has its own psychological implications for the listener or critic. Indeed, one of the ways in which composers have navigated the treacherous business of releasing works to the public has been the conscientious use of generic titles to help prepare audiences' expectations. Michael Vaillancourt makes a convincing case that Brahms, by composing and presenting his Serenade, op. 11, to the Viennese public in 1862 – rather than a symphony after the disastrous performance of his Piano Concerto no. 1, op. 15 – was able to create a reputation for himself as a serious young composer of modernist classicism.[57] Vaillancourt argues that the serenade allowed Brahms to differentiate himself from virtuoso-composers who were primarily keyboard-based, and he even suggests that the piece was of vital importance in securing Brahms's position as director of the *Wiener Singakademie*. Vaillancourt writes:

> As a genre, the serenade of the eighteenth and nineteenth centuries encompassed a complex network of overlapping types that included songs, character pieces, and multi-movement ensemble works. Moreover, many nineteenth-century serenades exemplified a process of historicization in which a genre was employed to evoke a type that was broadly accepted as representative of an earlier era. Indeed, Brahms's choice of the serenade genre was an attempt to reassert the values of an idealized Viennese Classical style, and his choice of that genre was the pivotal factor in contemporary reception of the work.[58]

Regardless of the merit of the composition, Vaillancourt believes that Brahms's choice of genre, his knowledge of it, and his ability to gauge correctly his audience's reaction to it were vital in making the composer's first foray into large-scale orchestral composition a success. By side-stepping the weight of expectation that would precede a first symphony, Brahms was able to present himself in a sympathetic light and begin creating a reputation for himself that initially would be unburdened by direct comparison with Beethoven. The importance of the notion of genre in criticism of the period should not be understated. It was a pervasive idea that remained prevalent well into the early twentieth century, as evidenced by Eduard Hanslick's reviews of Mahler's Lieder and his symphonies. Hanslick's review in the *Neue Freie Presse* on 16 January 1900 of the Philharmonic concert in Vienna, which had included

---

[56] Herrmann Hirschbach, *Musikalisch-kritisches Repertorium*, pp. 310–11.

[57] Michael Vaillancourt, 'Brahms's "Sinfonie-Serenade" and the Politics of Genre', *The Journal of Musicology*, 26:3 (Summer 2009), 379–403.

[58] Ibid., p. 381.

three orchestral Lieder from Mahler's *Des Knaben Wunderhorn* and two from his *Lieder eines fahrenden Gesellen*, devoted a significant portion of the review to a discussion of these orchestral songs. As David Kasunic points out, the fact that Hanslick termed these songs collectively in the review as *Fünf Gesänge mit Orchesterbegleitung* is significant.[59] Mahler himself had termed the songs Lieder, but Hanslick refers to them as *Gesänge*. Hanslick's justification for doing so rests on his belief that Mahler's songs contain too many elements that are foreign to the 'true nature of the Lied':

> In the songs we heard yesterday, too, he proclaims himself an enemy of the conventional and the customary, a 'chercheur', as the French would say, without implying any derogatory criticism using the term. The new 'songs' [Gesänge] are difficult to classify, neither lied nor aria, nor dramatic scene, they possess something of all these forms. More than anything, their form recalls that of Berlioz's songs with orchestral accompaniment, 'La captive', 'Le Chasseur danois', and 'Le[jeune] pâtre Breton'.[60]

Likewise, when discussing Mahler's first symphony, Kasunic points out that Hanslick was frustrated by the knowledge that the work had at one point had a programme which was then subsequently removed. 'For Hanslick, this meant that Mahler was calling a "symphony" a piece that really should not be called a symphony at all, for it was "the kind of music which for me is not music at all".'[61]Again, one of the most striking aspects of Hanslick's engagement with these works is how fundamental the notion of genre is to his understanding of them and consequently how it informs his aesthetic judgements.

Even though this discussion on genre in German-language criticism has been necessarily brief, it should suffice to establish that genre, as a concept, was of the utmost importance to composers, critics, and audiences throughout the nineteenth century. And moreover, that it framed many discourses surrounding musical works in the German-speaking world. How modern musicological studies view the development of those genres during the nineteenth century in retrospect is not the main point, which is rather that contemporaneous critics had their own personal conceptions of how genres functioned. And furthermore, these conceptions—even though they may or may not have borne a close resemblance to the activities of composers of the time—nevertheless informed the critical analyses. In actuality, the Lied as a genre had evolved hugely throughout the nineteenth century, and indeed the changes between the settings of Reichardt and Zelter and those of Strauss, Wolf, and Mahler are enormous; despite this, we still detect in Hanslick in 1900 an idealized view of the Lied and its folk-like qualities, particularly apparent when he highlights

---

59 David Kasunic, 'On Jewishness and Genre', in Nicole Grimes, Siobhán Donovan, and Wolfgang Marx (eds), *Rethinking Hanslick: Music, Formalism, and Expression* (Rochester, NY: University of Rochester Press, 2013), pp. 311–38, at p. 325.

60 Ibid., p. 325. Citing Eduard Hanslick, 'Theater und Kunstnachrichten', *Neue Freie Press*, 16 January 1900. Translation is from Donald Mitchell, *Gustav Mahler: The Wunderhorn Years* (Boulder, CO: Westview Press, 1975), Appendix G.

61 Kasunic, 'On Jewishness and Genre', p. 327.

the 'contradiction, a dichotomy, between the concept of the "folk song" [Volkslied] and this artful, superabundant orchestral accompaniment'.[62]

In this way, the extremely negative reception of Liszt's early Lieder can be viewed as a misjudgement, on Liszt's part, as to how far he could challenge or expand his audiences' and critics' respective horizons of expectations. In effect, we have the diametrically opposite result to that experienced by Brahms with his Serenade, op. 11, where the positive reception of that piece can, at least in part, be attributed to Brahms correctly understanding his audience's perception of and associations with genre. Liszt's misjudgement, however, should not be interpreted as evidence of his lack of understanding of the Lied as a genre. As has been discussed earlier, by the time Liszt composed the Lieder for his *Buch der Lieder*, he had already undergone an extensive period of close study of Schubert's Lieder, and likewise had significant performing experience of them as both an accompanist and in their transcribed forms. Instead, Liszt's misjudgement could be attributed to how different his method of engagement with Lieder was from that of his prospective audience in Germany. It was a miscalculation as to what his audience would find acceptable.

The most significant transgression seems not to have been the technical challenges in and of themselves, but that those technical challenges represented an outward public virtuoso persona, which was antithetical to the notion of a Lieder composer revealing inward poetic feeling and expression. That Liszt's move into Lieder composition was part of the composer's conscious effort to create a German-friendly public image in the early 1840s seems clear. However, as is to be expected—but in fact contrary to many of the common myths surrounding Liszt—his touring years in Germany, especially the early years, were not an unbroken succession of spectacular triumphs. Rather, they involved a period of trial and error as Liszt familiarised himself with the various and varying musical tastes that existed in German-speaking lands. An extended discussion of how Liszt's performance experiences influenced his Lieder style will be found in Chapter 4. A major factor in the overwhelming success, in terms of sales that some of Liszt's virtuoso solo piano works enjoyed, was that the works had, in their composer/performer, an advocate of the highest calibre.

As the *Gazette Musicale* pointed out, the Lieder were enthusiastically received when Liszt accompanied them. It is also worth noting that the reviews above were of the publications of Liszt's Lieder and not of how they were received at concerts when he performed them. The medium through which one engages with a musical work is a hugely influencing factor when making an aesthetic judgement on a work. Liszt's Lieder needed singers that could act as champions for them – as he had done for his own solo piano works – so that the difficulties, so conspicuous when confronted with the score, could be bypassed through the experience of encountering the Lieder in performance first. And although one of their earliest advocates, Franz Götze, had a fine reputation, it was an undertaking beyond the tenor to captivate the public's imagination to the degree that a figure such as Maria Malibran might have done. There is some irony in suggesting that Liszt's early Lieder need a

---

[62] Ibid., p. 326.

transcendental virtuoso singer to save them from their own excesses of virtuosity, but that is in fact the point of transcendental virtuosity: to *transcend* and go beyond the difficulties of a work and illuminate the expressive qualities that lie obscured to those less able. Indeed, the highest mark of virtuosity is often the appearance of no difficulties on the part of the performer, and it is this that allows the audience finally to see/understand the work, the virtuoso acting as a conduit in an act of communion between the composer and their audience.

In Part III (Chapters 5, 6, and 7) when examining the revisions that Liszt undertook of his early Lieder, we will see how he chose to address some of their generic transgressions, but not others. In part these revisions can be understood as part of a process of becoming more familiar with his audience's expectations and addressing those aspects of the early Lieder which Liszt believed he could alter or refine to make them more palatable to his audience, while also updating them – that is, bringing them in line with his evolving aesthetic. The virtuosity necessary to perform the Lieder was the biggest obstacle to them functioning as a semi-private art form for domestic music-making, and so a major barrier to their widespread adoption. It is arguable that the early Liszt Lieder are even more demanding in the vocal parts than in their accompaniments. Liszt understood this and believed that they demanded performers endowed not only with rare natural gifts, but also a high degree of musical sophistication and a sincerity of temperament.[63]. Other objections, such as the advanced harmonic language, dramatic and outward character, choice of texts, and the correctness of the settings' prosody, are aspects which were only aesthetic barriers. However, with aesthetic and technical barriers combined, Liszt's early Lieder proved too inaccessible and acquired only a few proponents. These proponents, however, such as Louis Köhler (who included a favourable discussion of Liszt's early Lieder in his book *Die Melodie der Sprache*) and tenor Franz Götze, were musicians of a progressive bent.

The reception of Liszt's early Lieder can be seen as a clash of two opposing conceptions of genre. On one side, as evidenced by the above reviews, we have a stance that viewed genre, style, and forms as largely static concepts, with models that were to be strictly emulated with only minor concessions permitted. In contrast, Liszt felt that the study of the past was to be used as a springboard for future developments, rather than imitated 'in a servile manner'. [64] Given that Liszt's views on genre and historicism can be perceived as being highly influenced by the Saint-Simonian view of history, it is easy to see how his progressive bent would be at odds with a critical stance that viewed the Lied genre as expressing a simpler idealised past and unsuited to radical development. Jauss's 'horizon of expectations' is a useful framework with which to view this clash of conceptions, as it helps in understanding that Liszt's own 'horizon of expectations' would have been radically different from those

---

[63] Michael Short (ed. and trans.), *Liszt Letters in the Library of Congress* (Hillsdale, NY: Pendragon Press, 2003), letter 125, p. 118.

[64] Interestingly, Schumann, like Liszt, believed in the need to progress the genre. 'Underlying this passage, like the rest of his criticism, is the central theme of Artistic progress. In Schumann's view, music and musical style should develop in an orderly way.' Jon W. Finson, *Schumann: The Book of Songs*, p. 4.

of his critics, especially on account of his unique background and temperament. The critical rejection of his early Lieder was so forceful in nature that it may well have contributed to Liszt's abandoning any serious effort in song publication for nearly a decade, no doubt affecting his 'horizon of expectations' with respect to the Lied as a genre. Consequently, this reception can be considered a factor in the formulation of the Lieder style of his Weimar years. In Chapter 4 this concept will be further developed, as Liszt's changing performance experiences and interactions are explored as influencing factors.

CHAPTER 4

The 'Virtuoso Period' and 'Weimar Years' in the Development of Liszt's Lieder Style

∾

This chapter is itself divided into two parts. The first part explores the role that Liszt's performing experiences during his virtuoso years (1830–47) had on the development of his early Lieder. The second part focuses on Liszt's time in Weimar (1848–61) and investigates how his musical life in the principality may have shaped the nature of the revisions of his early Lieder as well as the development of his overall musical aesthetic and song style. The chapter takes the form of a series of brief biographical sketches of the singers and musicians with whom Liszt came into contact during these periods. Where possible, the repertoire that was sung, the venues, and the type of performance that took place are also given, along with any contemporary reception that is related either to the singer in question or to any specific performances. This information is assembled in an attempt to recreate the cultural milieu of the composition of the early Lieder along with the external forces that came to bear on Liszt and may have directed his revisions.

Liszt is often credited with establishing several innovations in concert life: turning the piano side-on to the audience, regularly playing whole programmes mostly composed of other composer's works from memory, being the solo performer for entire concerts, and thus adopting and popularising the term 'piano recital'.[1] However, Liszt's performing activity went far beyond the confines of solo piano performance. He also regularly shared the stage with other performers. During his career he conducted orchestral music and operas and performed a wide variety of chamber music, from piano duets to larger ensembles.[2] This diverse range of performing activity also extended into regularly accompanying singers. The extent of vocal repertoire performed was varied, ranging from selected arias of Italian and French opera to Lieder

---

[1] Alan Walker cites Václav Tomášek as his source when crediting Jan Ladislav Dussek as the first pianist to play with the piano sideways on the stage, however, Walker states that Dussek did not always do this consistently and it had no lasting impact on piano performance practice. Walker believes that Liszt was unaware of Dussek's innovation, but through experimentation with different possibilities, he settled on placing the piano at a right angle to the audience, with the open lid projecting the sound into the auditorium – the position favoured today in practically every concert hall. Alan Walker, *Franz Liszt*, 3 vols, rev. edn (Ithaca, NY: Cornell University Press, 1987–97), vol. 1, p. 283.

[2] Beethoven's 'Kreutzer' sonata, op. 47, 'Archduke' piano trio, op. 97, and Hummel's septet were Liszt's most frequently performed chamber works.

(most regularly Schubert and Beethoven, but also more recently composed works) to arranged folk material to comic *buffa* songs, such as those of John Orlando Parry, with whom Liszt toured extensively throughout Britain and Ireland in 1840–41.[3]

This first part of the chapter focuses on Liszt's activities as an accompanist before 1848. From early accounts it can occasionally be difficult or impossible to determine the precise repertoire in which Liszt accompanied singers, as the titles of vocal pieces were often not mentioned in programmes or press reports of the time. And first-hand accounts from the period are also often vague in this regard, frequently only mentioning scant details such as that an unspecified aria or a Schubert Lied was sung. Yet despite the relative paucity of precise details pertaining to vocal performances compared to those of instrumental works, enough detail survives to allow some conclusions to be drawn about the type of repertoire (if not always the exact works) that Liszt performed, the types of singers he accompanied, and in what sort of venues. By examining the singers he frequently accompanied – their voice type, the variety of roles with which they were associated, their dramatic skills, and performing persona – it can be inferred what types of singers Liszt was attracted to, and by extension what types of voices and venues Liszt may have had in mind when he composed his first Lieder.

The Singers of the 'Virtuoso Period' (1830–47)

Caroline Unger (1803–1877)

Caroline Unger's connection to Liszt (she is more commonly associated with Beethoven and Schubert) goes back to 1 December 1822 when she appeared on stage at Liszt's debut concert in Vienna. She sang an aria from Rossini's opera *Demterio e Poblibio*. In 1824 she would perform in Beethoven's Mass in D major, under the composer's baton, and was also the alto soloist at the premiere of Beethoven's Ninth Symphony. One of the earliest advocates of Franz Schubert's Lieder, she was even coached by the composer.[4] She later moved to Naples and became one of the most celebrated *bel canto* singers of her age, comparable in stature and success with Maria Malibran. Unger was an alto with a wide range from low a to d''', able to sing soprano roles as well, and numerous composers wrote roles specifically for her. The following table of roles she created between 1825–1839 compiled by Klaus Martin Koptiz gives an indication of the breadth of her talent and the esteem in which she was held by Italian *bel canto* composers of the period (table 4.1):

---

3   John Orlando Parry would in general accompany his own singing; however, Liszt was known to have accompanied Parry's performance of one of his more serious songs, 'The Inchcape Bell', in Bury in two concerts in September 1840. David Allsobrook, *Liszt: My Travelling Circus Life* (London and Basingstoke: The Macmillan Press, 1991), p. 87.

4   Klaus Martin Kopitz, 'Caroline Unger', *Musik und Gender im Internet*, Musikvermittlung und Genderforschung: Lexikon und multimediale Präsentationen, hg. von Beatrix Borchard und Nina Noeske, Hochschule für Musik und Theater Hamburg, 2003 ff. Stand vom 25. April 2018, online verfügbar unter <https://mugi.hfmt-hamburg.de/receive/mugi_person_00000837 >[accessed 14 May 2022]. This occurred when Unger was performing in a production of *Così fan tutte* at the Vienna Court Opera in 1821. Schubert worked as a repetiteur for a brief period during this time.

Table 4.1. Caroline Unger's operatic performances, 1825–39.

Role	Opera	Composer	Date	City	Type of Performance
Matilde	*Sapienti Pauca*	Pietro Raimondi	Winter 1825	Naples	World premiere
Asteria	*Niobe*	Giovanni Pacini	19 November 1826	Naples	World premiere
Tacia	*Tacia*	Giuseppe Balducci	Winter 1826	Naples	World premiere
Giacinda	*Giacinda ed Ernesto*	Julius Benedict	31 March 1827	Naples	Premiere
Celestina	*Un cestellino di fiori*	Pietro Raimondi	6 July 1827	Naples	Premiere
Marietta	*Il borgomastro di Saardam*	Gaetano Donizetti	19 August 1827	Naples	World premiere
Ramiro d'Elva	*I cavalieri di Valenza*	Giovanni Pacini	11 June 1828	Milan	World premiere
Alessio	*L'Orfano della Selva*	Carlo Coccia	15 November 1828	Milan	World premiere
Isoletta	*La straniera*	Vincenzo Bellini	14 February 1829	Milan	World premiere
Gli Illiensi	*Gli Illiensi*	Feliciano Strepponi	20 November 1829	Trieste	World premiere
Enrico	*Bianco di Belmonte*	Luigi Rieschi	26 December 1829	Milan	World premiere
Selene	*I saraceni in Catania*	Giuseppe Persiani	29 July 1832	Padua	Premiere
Parisina	*Parisina*	Gaetano Donizetti	17 March 1833	Florence	World premiere
Elisa	*Il colonnello*	Luigi Ricci	24 March 1835	Naples	World premiere
Giovanna I	*Giovanna I*	Antonio Granara	26 December 1835	Venice	World premiere
Antonina	*Belisario*	Gaetano Donizetti	4 February 1836	Venice	World premiere
Rosmonda	*Rosmonda di Ravenna*	Giuseppe Lillo	26 December 1837	Venice	World premiere
Maria	*Maria Rudenz*	Gaetano Donizetti	30 January 1838	Venice	World premiere
Bianca	*Le due illustri rivali*	Saverio Mercadante	10 March 1838	Venice	World premiere
Donna Isabella	*La sposa di Messina*	Nicola Vaccai	2 March 1839	Venice	World premiere
Leonora di Guienna	*Rosmonda d'Inghilterra*	Otto Nicolai	26 November 1839	Trieste	Premiere
Emilio	*Furio Camillo*	Giovanni Pacini	26 December 1839	Rome	World premiere

Source: Klaus Martin Koptiz, 'Caroline Unger', *Musik und Gender im Internet* <https://mugi.hfmt-hamburg.de/receive/mugi_person_00000837 > [accessed 14 May 2022].

With her virtuosic talents, a wide vocal range, and a strong connection to two of his most beloved composers, it is not difficult to understand how Liszt would be attracted to Unger's voice. While it is not clear whether or not the original meeting in 1822 made an impression on the young Liszt, when they met again in Florence in 1838 Liszt sent an effusive letter to his publisher Maurice Schlesinger soon afterwards (November of that year).

> Miss Unger, endowed with deep feeling, remarkable intelligence, and the will-power to guard against over strain, has, as a result of ten years of continuous study, emerged as the most beautiful dramatic talent that has appeared on stage since Mme(Giuditta) Pasta and (Maria) Malibran. Unger's voice is extensive, pure and flexible … a consummate musician, she comprehends all roles with facility. She is as familiar with the comic repertoire as she is with the tragic, and the all-roundness of her talent is as extraordinary as it is deepening.[5]

In 1839 Liszt spent two weeks, beginning on October 26, with Unger in Trieste. During this period, they performed together at least twice: firstly, in a concert at the Mario Faliero Theatre in Trieste, and, secondly, at a private party in Count Alberti's house – after a dinner in honour of Unger's thirty-sixth birthday – where Liszt and Unger performed a non-specified Mozart aria and three Schubert Lieder; 'Erlkönig', 'Trockne Blumen', and 'Der Einsame'.[6] In February 1842 Liszt also accompanied Unger at the piano in a *concertante* performance of Meyerbeer's *Les Huguenots* at the Prussian court. They appeared together several times in Berlin during this period, most notably in a prestigious soirée hosted by Amalie Beer, the mother of Meyerbeer, where Unger premiered Liszt's 'Loreley'.[7] In 1855, as he was making the final preparations for the publication of the first revised editions of his Lieder, Liszt disclosed in a letter to Heinrich Schlesinger that he had had in mind exceptional voices, such as Caroline Unger's and Josef Tichatschek's, when composing his early Lieder.[8] This point should not be understated, as it reveals that Liszt viewed his early Lieder as akin to operatic arias – that is, vocal works written for an exceptional and professionally trained voice rather than for amateur performance, and even tailoring the vocal writing to the specific talents of a particular singer.

1830s Paris

During the early to mid-1830s Liszt regularly accompanied Maria Malibran and Adolphe Nourrit in public performances. They represented the uppermost echelons of the Parisian opera world of the period. Liszt's musical association with Nourrit is particularly significant as Christopher Gibbs notes that 'Liszt's performances of

---

[5] La Mara, *Liszt und die Frauen*, 2nd edn (Leipzig: Breitkopf & Härtel, 1919), pp. 75–6. Translation is my own.

[6] Michael Short (ed. and trans.), *Correspondence of Franz Liszt and the Countess Marie d'Agoult* (Hillsdale, NY: Pendragon Press, 2013), p. 114.

[7] La Mara, *Liszt und die Frauen*, p. 80.

[8] Michael Short (ed. and trans.), *Liszt Letters in the Library of Congress* (Hillsdale, NY: Pendragon Press, 2003), letter 125, p. 118.

"Erlkönig" with Nourrit, considered the foremost French tenor of the time, had an important impact on the reception of Schubert Lieder in France'.[9]

Maria Malibran (1808–36)

Maria Malibran was a Spanish mezzo-soprano, the daughter of Manuel Garcia and older sister of Pauline Viardot (*née* Garcia).[10] Malibran was known to have been associated with the Saint Simonians and was even forced to deny rumours that she had become a priestess of the movement. As Liszt was well-known for having a strong sympathy for Saint-Simonian ideas, to the extent of regularly attending their meetings, it can be inferred that they were kindred in more than musical matters.

One of the earliest mentions of Liszt as an accompanist is found in Joseph d'Ortigue's biographical sketch of the composer that appeared in the *Gazette Musicale de Paris* on 14 June 1835. As part of a short episode, d'Ortigue merely mentions that Liszt had accompanied Maria Malibran in a performance of an unspecified aria to great acclaim in a concert that took place in 1831 in the hall of the Saint-Simonians. The purpose of including this passage in d'Ortigue's biography was not to associate the young pianist with a singer of Malibran's distinction: rather, it was to show the mutual affection between Liszt and the ageing General Lafayette who was still seen as a revolutionary figure and a supporter of the Polish cause, and thus to situate Liszt's politics in similar territory to Lafayette's. As Liszt was walking Malibran back to her dressing room, the composer recognises Lafayette, and they embrace. Ralph P. Locke considers that the anecdote may have been a fabrication of Ortigue's, but regardless, Ortigue's emphasis lay in associating Liszt with Lafayette and not Malibran. This is merely one of the earliest of several accounts of Liszt performing with Malibran, but is worth noting, since it asserts that Liszt, only nineteen at the time, was already accompanying an artist of the highest calibre and profile.

Trained by her father, Manuel Garcia, Malibran was known to have extraordinary flexibility and power, and both Bellini and Donizetti adapted roles for her voice, which encompassed g to e'''. According to Robert Schumann, Liszt acknowledged that he had learned the most from Malibran, along with Paganini.[11] This frustratingly vague assertion leaves us to speculate as to what exactly he learned from the singer. As Malibran is mentioned in the same breath as Paganini, it may indicate that Liszt learned the transcendental limits of vocal execution. On the other hand, the intended purpose may have been to contrast Malibran with Paganini – to indicate that Liszt had learned from Malibran a seriousness of purpose, interpretive insights, or another form of stagecraft. Malibran was known to have innovated arrhythmical gestures for her performances of the title role of Bellini's *Norma*, that is, gestures

---

9   Christopher Gibbs, 'The Presence of *Erlkönig*: Reception and Reworkings of a Schubert Lied', (PhD diss., Columbia University, 1992), p. 231.

10   The less common terms *assoluta* voice or *soprano-sfogato* may be a more accurate description than mezzo-soprano. More common in the *bel canto* era, they describe a female voice that is naturally low, but that has the range and flexibility to sing coloratura soprano roles.

11   Robert Schumann, *On Music and Musicians*, ed. Konrad Wolff, trans. Paul Rosenfeld (University of California Press, 1983), p. 158.

that were not in time with the music. This is in contrast with her great contemporary Giuditta Pasta (1797–1865), whose gestures were performed in time to the music. According to Susan Rutherford, Malibran 'created a character that stepped out from the music into contemporary reality; if Pasta's performance had the *sentimento del bello*, Malibran's had the *sentimento del vero*'.[12] As Liszt was also known during his virtuoso years for incorporating expressive gestures into his performances, it may have been that he learned from Malibran to make those gestures more authentic, spontaneous, and unaffected.

Adolphe Nourrit (1802–39)

Adolphe Nourrit, active in the Paris Opera from 1826 to 1836, was described as having a mellow but powerful voice, great dramatic skills, and excellent control of vocal timbre. Like Malibran, he had associations with the Saint-Simonian movement and so shared an affinity with Liszt that went beyond the purely musical.[13] Although Nourrit was known as a leading exponent of the 'head voice', Evan Walker has stated that his voice must also have had considerable power as the orchestration in many of his roles would have necessitated it. This is also corroborated by Liszt, who writes to Adolphe Pictet in 1837 that 'Nourrit captivated us with his powerful singing of Erlkönig'.[14] Nourrit is now probably most famous for his rivalry with Gibert-Louis Duprez, which would eventually drive Nourrit to suicide.[15]

In their reminiscences Louis Marie Quicherat and Joseph d'Ortigue concede that Duprez was the greater singer from a purely vocal perspective, but Nourrit was the greater artist. Duprez sang sounds whereas Nourrit sang feelings, sentiments, and ideas.[16] In his later years Liszt would state that he still viewed Nourrit as an ideal singer for his Lieder, suggesting that it was not Nourrit's vocal qualities he most admired, but rather his interpretive qualities and temperament as an artist. Nourrit's first encounter with Liszt goes back to 1825 when he performed in the young composer's only completed opera *Don Sanche*.[17] It was this youthful Liszt who introduced Nourrit to Schubert's Lieder and to 'Erlkönig' in particular. A colourful

---

[12] The sense or feeling of beauty versus that of truth. Susan Rutherford, '"La cantante delle passioni": Giuditta Pasta and the Idea of Operatic Performance', *Cambridge Opera Journal*, 19:2 (2007), 107–38, at p. 131.

[13] Ralph P. Locke, 'Liszt's Saint-Simonian Adventure', *19th-Century Music*, 4:3 (Spring 1981), 209–27.

[14] Franz Liszt, *The Collected Writings of Franz Liszt*, vol. 2: *Essays and Letters of a Traveling Bachelor of Music*, ed. and trans. Janita R. Hall-Swadley (Lanham, MD: Scarecrow Press, 2012), p. 260.

[15] Mary Ann Smart, 'Roles, Reputations, Shadows: Singers at the Opéra, 1828–1849', especially the subsection 'Tenors as Trumpets', in David Charlton and Jonathan Cross (eds), *The Cambridge Companion of Grand Opera* (Cambridge: Cambridge University Press, 2003), pp. 108–31 (pp. 117–22).

[16] J.Q. Davies, *Romantic Anatomies of Voice* (Berkeley, Los Angeles, London: University of California Press, 2014), p. 125.

[17] It only ran for four performances and was considered lost until the 1970s.

episode from Louis Marie Quicherat's 1867 biography of the singer describes this encounter:

> It was at the house of a friend of Liszt, a Hungarian banker named M. Dessauer. The artist [Liszt] was at the piano playing Erlkönig when Nourrit entered. All the more reason to continue. Nourrit was all ears. As he became aware of this dramatic music, he showed deep emotion and his face lit up. When the piece ended, he requested that it be played again, but Liszt replied that it would be better if he sang it. Nourrit excused himself on the grounds that he did not know German. When Liszt explained the text to him, the singer agreed to vocalize the melody, which he did with the expressiveness of an inspired interpreter; lonqumque bibebat amorem. From that day on, he was taken with an intense passion for those songs; at his request a certain number were translated, and he became their indefatigable propagator.[18]

A review in *Le Courrier de Lyon* of a concert in the Grand-Théâtre of Lyon on 3 August 1837 that had met with extraordinary success singled out the performance of 'Erlkönig' by Liszt and Nourrit for special attention:

> Liszt's accompaniment in the Erlkönig, notably, swept the hall with a passion, which was in some way magnetic. In order to understand all the pathos, terror, and fantasy in Erlkönig, one must hear Liszt and Adolphe Nourrit perform this famous ballad by Goethe. Who else but Nourrit would be able to make us hear in so clean-cut and distinct a manner the three entirely different voices of the Father, the Child, and the Erlkönig? Who else but Nourrit could excite those feelings of pity and terror which so deeply moved the audience? And at the same time who else but Liszt could thus follow the singer in all the shadings of his song, and lend his playing that energy and power which doubled the apprehension experienced by the listener upon hearing the cries of the unhappy child? Those scales, so numerous and so rapid, whose rolling, like the thunder, made the listeners tremble with terror, who else but Liszt, in order to increase their sonority, would have dared to play them in octaves.[19]

Several important observations can be gleaned from this account. Firstly, that Liszt's conception of the accompaniment was that it was in no way subservient to the vocal line, especially in this sort of Lied/Ballade. Indeed, as the account states, he is able not only to support but also to comment on the vocal melody through his piano playing. In addition, he alters the piano part, with the single-note passages now played in octaves. Obviously, this brings to mind his own transcription of 'Erlkönig' for piano solo. And from the account given above, it would not be a

[18]   Frits Noske, *French Song from Berlioz to Duparc*, trans. Rita Benton (New York: Dover Publications, 1970), p. 28, citing Louis Marie Quicherat, *Adolphe Nourrit: Sa vie, son talent, son caractère, sa correspondance* (Paris: L. Hachette et Cie, 1867), p. 32.

[19]   Ibid., p. 232, citing Henri Girard, *Emile Deschamps, dilettante: Relations d'un poète romantique* (Paris: Paris É. Champion, 1921), p. 108. It was a large miscellany concert with orchestral works, opera arias, choral works, and two virtuoso paraphrases by Liszt. For the full programme of the concert see Antoine Sallès, *Liszt à Lyon,* (Paris: E Fromont, 1911) p.19.

stretch to imagine Liszt adding the type of embellishments found in his transcription to a performance when accompanying a singer. From the transcription it can be inferred that Liszt looked to display the qualities of the three separate characters in 'Erlkönig' to their extreme.[20] And a larger performance space such as the Grand Théâtre de Lyon would have been better suited to this increase and variety in sonority than a smaller salon, taking the song into almost symphonic proportions.

Eight Concerts in Vienna in 1838: Ludwig Tietze and Benedikt Randhartinger

In 1838 Liszt returned to Vienna after an absence of almost fifteen years. According to Alan Walker, Liszt's initial motivations for returning to the city were to raise funds for the victims of the recent floods in Pest, and though the first concert on 18 April was indeed a charitable event, it also gave Liszt the opportunity to reconnect with the city associated with two of his most beloved of composers: Beethoven and Schubert. It proved a watershed moment in Liszt's life: following this seven-week stay in Vienna he embarked on a series of concert tours in which he would almost ceaselessly criss-cross Europe for nearly ten years. Indeed, this initial series of concerts can be said to have inaugurated Liszt's virtuoso tours. The first concert on 18 April was, in Liszt's own words, 'an enormous success' and he needed to add concerts continually to keep up with the unprecedented demand, extending his stay until the end of May.[21] Between 18 April and 25 May, Liszt appeared on stage at least fourteen times in Vienna; for eight of these concerts he was the headline performer in the old *Musikverein* hall.[22] During these concerts Liszt began to move away from the standard format of the miscellany concert, and only the first concert (18 April) featured an orchestra. In the other seven concerts Liszt performed and contributed to the performance of more pieces than was typical at the time.[23] Liszt participated in chamber music (Hummel's Septet) and accompanied singers, in Lieder by Beethoven, Schubert, and the contemporaneous composer Johann Vesque. 'Erlkönig' was featured prominently and appeared in both original and transcribed form, and two of the singers Liszt accompanied in these concerts, Ludwig Tietze and Benedikt Randhartinger, were associated with Schubert. This was in contrast with the concert programmes of virtuosos Sigmund Thalberg and Clara Wieck, both of whom had also recently given a series of concerts in the city.[24]

---

[20] Franz Liszt, *12 Lieder von Franz Schubert*, S. 558 No.4/ LW A42 No.4 (Vienna and Paris: Diabelli and Richault, 1838).

[21] Christopher Gibbs, '"Just Two Words. Enormous Success": Liszt's 1838 Vienna Concerts', in Christopher H. Gibbs and Dana Gooley (eds), *Liszt and His World* (Princeton: Princeton University Press, 2006), pp. 167–230 (pp. 182–5).

[22] Ibid. This is not to be confused with the current *Musikverein*. In 1838, the *Saal der Geschellschaft der Musikfreunde* was in Tuchlauben. Demolished in 1885, the old hall had a capacity of around 700. By comparison, the current capacity of the *Musikverein* is 1,744 seated with a further 300 standing.

[23] Gibbs, '"Just Two Words. Enormous Success"', pp. 216–19.

[24] Ibid., pp. 212–15.

Ludwig Tietze (1797–1850)

Ludwig Tietze was a popular Viennese tenor who was a member of the Imperial Chapel and the *Tonkünstler-Societät*.[25] Tietze sang tenor solos in Handel's *Solomon*, *Athaliah, Jephthah*, and *Messiah* and Haydn's *Creation* and *Seasons*. However, he was mostly associated with the performance of Schubert Lieder in numerous soirées of the *Gesellschaft der Musikfreunde*, presenting at least sixteen of Schubert's works for the first time. Tietze was even accompanied by Schubert and a French horn player in 'Auf dem Strome' on 26 March 1828.[26] According to Carl Ferdinand Pohl in the first edition of Grove's *Dictionary of Music and Musicians*, Tietze was possessed of a 'sympathetic and highly-trained tenor voice with a very pure style of execution'.[27] Liszt accompanied Ludwig Tietze on 29 April 1838 in the *Musikverein* in a performance of two Schubert Lieder: 'Erlkönig' and 'Liebesbotschaft', and on 25 May 1838 also in the *Musikverein* in two works by Johann Vesque, 'Stänchen' and 'Ermunterung'.[28]

Benedikt Randhartinger (1802–93)

Benedikt Randhartinger was a prolific Austrian composer, tenor, and conductor. He studied composition with Salieri and was a friend of Schubert.[29] Liszt and Randhartinger first met while Liszt was studying in Vienna in the 1820s, and both Sacheverell Sitwell and Jonathan Kregor believe that Randhartinger introduced Liszt to many of Schubert's Lieder.[30] Therefore, it was natural that their reunion in 1838 would be based around performances of Schubert's Lieder. Three were presented in a concert, on 14 May 1838 in the *Musikverein*: 'Das Fischermädchen', 'Der Kreuzzug', and 'Die Forelle', with the last one being encored. Later in the same concert, Liszt was also the accompanist in two of Randhartinger's own compositions, 'Elfengesang' and 'Mannestrotz'.[31]

By accompanying two singers so closely related to Schubert to great public and critical acclaim in Schubert's home city, Liszt received a degree of authority in performance from the Viennese public, who were considered among the most discerning and cultivated in Europe at the time. It was an ideal start to his touring career, and it served him well especially during his German tours of 1840–45. A key point to take away from these concerts is Liszt's greater participation in the miscellany concert. That is, that he would participate in more items on the programme than was customary at the time. He could perform as soloist, soloist with orchestra, as

---

[25] C.F. Pohl, 'Titze, or Tietze, Ludwig', *A Dictionary of Music and Musicians (A.D. 1450–1879)*, ed. George Grove, 4 vols (London, Macmillan & Co., 1898), vol. 4, p. 129.

[26] Ibid.

[27] Ibid.

[28] Gibbs, '"Just Two Words. Enormous Success"', pp. 216–19.

[29] George Grove, 'Randhartinger, Benedikt', *A Dictionary of Music and Musicians*, vol. 3, pp. 73–4.

[30] Sacheverell Sitwell, *Liszt* (London: Cassell, 1955), p. 133; Jonathan Kregor, *Liszt as Transcriber* (Cambridge: Cambridge University Press, 2010), p. 103.

[31] Gibbs, '"Just Two Words. Enormous Success"', pp. 216–19.

accompanist, and, on exceedingly rare occasions at this point, as conductor all at the same concert. This is in marked contrast to the view that sees Liszt, instigator of the piano recital, as moving away from this form of concert.

Virtuoso Tours (1839–47)

Wilhelmine Schröder-Devrient (1804–60)

Wilhelmine Schröder-Devrient, with whom Liszt was associated during the 1840s, also had a strong connection to Schubert. Schröder-Devrient was a German soprano, dubbed the 'Queen of Tears', who was noted for her dramatic skill.[32] She was one of the earliest advocates for Schubert's Lieder and, in a performance accompanied by Eduard Genast, had won over Goethe to Schubert's setting of his 'Erlkönig', which he had initially not warmed to. Her vocal qualities were not universally praised, however, with both Berlioz and Henry Chorley finding deficiencies with her singing. Chorley did curb his criticism by praising her acting and stating that 'her voice was a strong soprano … with an inherent expressiveness of tone which made it more attractive on the stage than many a more faultless organ'. Robert Schumann also praised her performance of 'Erlkönig' in Dresden in 1840 with Liszt accompanying her, stating that she was 'almost the only artist capable of asserting herself in such company'.[33] Given that she was known to have vocal deficiencies with a powerful but occasionally unruly instrument, it must be assumed that her successful performances were built on a captivating stage persona, charisma, and keen interpretive and acting abilities. Like Nourrit, Schroder-Devrient's influence on Liszt would most likely not have been founded on the physical qualities of her voice but rather on these aspects of her performance style.

There is an interesting parallel here with how Liszt himself performed. An account by Liszt's pupil William Mason dating from the 1850s contrasts Liszt's playing with that of the composer-pianist Jules Schulhoff.[34] The extract is worth reproducing in full as it identifies several important aspects of Liszt's performance style. And moreover, it demonstrates that even though Liszt is still widely held to have been one of the greatest piano virtuosos of any age, the qualities that may have been most highly valued by his contemporaneous audiences differ from those of modern audiences:

> The difference between Liszt's playing and that of others was the difference between creative genius and interpretation. His genius flashed through every pianistic phrase, it illuminated a composition to its innermost recesses, and yet his wonderful effects, strange as it must seem, were produced without the advantage of a *genuinely musical touch*. [my italics]

[32] Louisa M. Middelton, 'Schröder-Devrient, Wilhelmine', in *A Dictionary of Music and Musicians*, vol. 3, pp. 315–18, at p. 316.

[33] Schumann, *On Music and Musicians*, p. 156.

[34] Julius Schulhoff (1825–98), a Bohemian composer who, according to William Mason, wrote piano compositions which 'were very effective, but more appropriate to the drawing-room than to the concert-hall'. William Mason, *Memories of a Musical Life* (New York: The Devine Press, 1901), p. 71.

> I remember on one occasion Schulhoff came to Weimar and played in the drawing-room of the Altenburg house. His playing and Liszt's were in marked contrast. He [Schulhoff] has been mentioned in an earlier chapter as a parlour pianist of high excellence. His compositions, exclusively in the smaller forms, were in great favour and universally played by the ladies.
>
> Liszt played his own *Bénédiction de Dieu dans la Solitude*, as pathetic a piece, perhaps, as he ever composed, and of which he was very fond. Afterwards Schulhoff, with his exquisitely beautiful touch, produced a quality of tone more beautiful than Liszt's; but about the latter's performance there was intellectuality and the indescribable impressiveness of genius, which made Schulhoff's playing, with all its beauty, seem tame by contrast.[35]

It is interesting that Mason believed Liszt's performance to be such that it transcended the need for a beautiful or even musical tone. It was instead founded on intellectuality and what Mason terms the 'indescribable impressiveness of genius'. We may interpret this perhaps as a combination of incisive charisma, creativity, and vitality. What Mason values is not a supreme technical polish, but rather playing that resuscitates a composition in a real act of creation.

Josef Tichatschek (1807–86)

Josef Tichatschek was a Bohemian opera singer who was based from 1837 to 1870 at the Royal Court Theatre in Dresden, where he was the principal tenor there. In a wide range of roles, his repertoire during his time at the theatre included parts for lyric tenor, *Spieltenor*, and *Heldentenor*. On 20 October 1842 he sang the role of tribune Cola Rienzi at the premiere of Wagner's *Rienzi*.[36] The opera in its original form lasted over six hours, and Tichatschek felt that this performance was one of his greatest artistic successes.[37] The performance was also the start of a close relationship between the tenor and Wagner. Tichatschek would go on to perform two more title roles in Wagner's operas *Tannhäuser* and *Lohengrin* under Liszt's baton.[38] As stated above, Tichatschek was one of the exceptional voices Liszt had had in mind when composing his early Lieder. A letter from Liszt to Baron Wolf August von Lüttichau, dated 23 February 1844, demonstrates how Liszt viewed Lieder (or at the very least his own Lieder) as sitting comfortably in a large miscellany concert to be performed alongside various orchestral and instrumental works. In the letter Liszt proposes the following programme to take place at the Hoftheater in Dresden (see Table 4.2).

It is unclear whether this programme was performed, but it is evident that Liszt in the 1840s saw his Lieder as well-suited to forming part of a larger multi-genre concert. This type of concert was still common at the time, and I believe that Liszt

---

[35] Mason, *Memories of a Musical Life*, pp. 112–13.

[36] Wilhelmine Schröder-Devrient sang the role of Adriano at this performance. Barry Millington, *Wagner*, rev. edn (Princeton: Princeton University Press, 1992), p. 28.

[37] Richard Wagner, *My Life*, ed. Mary Whittall, trans. Andrew Gray (New York: Da Capo Press, 1992), pp. 223–33; first published as *Mein Leben* (Munich: Paul List Verlag, 1963).

[38] Tichatschek sang the title role in the premiere of *Tannhäuser* in Dresden on 19 October 1845, although not to Wagner's satisfaction. Wagner, *My Life*, pp. 303–6.

Table 4.2. Programme proposed by Liszt for Dresden concert in 1844.

Composer	Composition	Performer
Unknown	Overture	Orchestra
Beethoven	Concerto in E flat	Orchestra with Liszt as soloist
Liszt	'Die Loreley'	Tichatschek with Liszt
Bellini/Liszt	Réminiscences de la Sonnambula/di Norma	Liszt
Unknown	'Some vocal or orchestral work, the first to be determined by M. Tichashek [*sic*] and the second by M. Wagner.'	
Liszt	Hungarian Melodies and March	Liszt
Unknown	'Some song or other'	Tichatschek
Weber	*Aufforderung zum Tanz*	Liszt

wrote his early Lieder specifically with this type of musical event in mind. This is in stark contrast with other central figures in the genre. Even Schubert and Schumann, whose performance experiences were radically different from those of Liszt, in general, seem to not have envisaged this type of performance environment with regard to their Lieder. Indeed, the songs found in Liszt's first *Buch der Lieder* or his *Drei Lieder aus Schillers Wilhelm Tell* might even sound out of place in a domestic/private or semi-public performance in a smaller salon.

On this point, the mammoth programme under Liszt's direction of 12 November 1848 in Weimar is worth considering. The first half of the concert consisted of the overture to Wagner's *Tannhäuser*, the ballade 'Des Sängers Fluch' by Heinrich Esser for voice and piano, the Andante movement from Henselt's piano concerto with Liszt at the keyboard, a duet by Donizetti, the dramatic scene for tenor and orchestra entitled *Lovelace* by Franz Kroll, and finally the *Tarantelle di bravura d'après la tarantelle de La Muette de Portici* by Liszt for piano solo, which the composer performed. The second half [!] of the concert was a performance of Act 4 of Meyerbeer's *Les Huguenots*.[39] Not only is there a wide variety of genres, but the scale of the works leans heavily towards the grand and virtuosic. In this context it becomes clear that a Lied of the scale of 'Erlkönig' would be necessary to sit comfortably in this sort of programme. This concert comes at the start of Liszt's tenure in Weimar, and he did indeed make serious efforts to reform the concert practices of Weimar during his time there. Nevertheless, it seems reasonable to assume that at this point, in the

---

[39] *Les Huguenots* by Meyerbeer is arguably the most demanding of the works programmed. Apart from large orchestral forces, it requires seven virtuoso singers to fill the seven lead roles. An indication of its reputation as a singer's opera is that during the 1890s the Metropolitan Opera in New York billed its famous performances of the work as 'les nuits des sept etoiles' (the Nights of the Seven Stars). Robert Ignatius Letellier, *Meyerbeer's Les Huguenots: An Evangel of Religion and Love* (Newcastle: Cambridge Scholars Publishing, 2015), pp. xxii and 132.

late 1840s, Liszt still conceived of his Lieder in terms of the massive, multi-genre, miscellany concert.

Liszt collaborated with a diverse array of singers of various profiles during the period 1835–47.[40] These included Benedict Gross (voice type and dates unknown), bass Joseph Staudigl (1807–61), soprano Hortense Duflot-Maillard (1808–58), soprano Adelaide Kemble (1815–79), tenor Luigi Pantaleoni (d. 1872), soprano Jenny Lutzer (1816–77), and tenor Giovanni Battista Rubini (1795–1854). In this discussion it may seem strange to omit a detailed description of Liszt's relationship with a singer of Rubini's stature, and indeed, Liszt and Rubini performed together numerous times to great acclaim in 1841–2. However, the collaboration was, in Alan Walker's words, an 'uneasy alliance', and there are a few surviving anecdotes that reveal some degree of mutual dissatisfaction. None of these concerns artistic issues, but rather the practicalities and small vanities surrounding performances.

The composition of Liszt's early Lieder (1839–47) coincided with his most hectic touring years in German-speaking lands. During this period, it is estimated that Liszt performed an average of one concert every three days.[41] While we might assume that Liszt composed a certain amount on the move or in hotel rooms, a closer examination of his schedule reveals several extended stays in a variety of locations which were used as bases from which he continued concertizing. The most pertinent of these, for this study, took place during the summer of 1841, when Liszt spent a few weeks on the island retreat of Nonnenwerth on the Rhine. The seclusion of Nonnenwerth no doubt provided a welcome respite to his otherwise crowded schedule and, according to Alan Walker, Nonnenwerth afforded Liszt the opportunity to 'compose, practise, and plan the next phase of his concert tours in tranquillity'.[42] And it was during his stay, from August to October 1841, that some of his earliest Lieder were composed, namely 'Mignon' and 'Loreley'. During this same period, however, Liszt also performed in at least twenty concerts, which took him to Frankfurt, Baden-Baden, Aachen, Bonn, Koblenz, and Cologne.[43] Therefore, any notions of a tranquil existence for Liszt during this period should be taken in relative terms. Instead, Liszt's virtuoso years could be characterised as being comprised of extended periods of travelling and concertizing, interspersed with brief periods of intense compositional productivity. These brief sojourns from almost constant touring are in marked contrast to the more stable environment Liszt would later find in Weimar.

'Erlkönig' as a Compositional Model

When examining Liszt's repertoire for voice and piano that he performed with singers in the 1830–40s, Schubert's 'Erlkönig' featured most regularly, even in compar-

---

[40] Liszt's relationships with these singers, to whom he was less connected than those already described, have not been detailed here due to considerations of space.

[41] Michael Saffle, *Liszt in Germany: 1840–1845: A Study in Sources, Documents, and the History of Reception* (Stuyvesant, NY: Pendragon Press, 1994), p. 3.

[42] Walker, *Franz Liszt*, vol. 1, p. 366.

[43] Saffle, *Liszt in Germany*, pp. 234–8.

ison with his own solo piano works. From surviving programmes it is not always possible to discern if Liszt performed the song solo or with a singer. Nonetheless, its regularity far outstripped that of any of his own Lieder. Dana Gooley, in both *The Virtuoso Liszt* and his chapter in *The Musician as Entrepreneur, 1790–1910*, has suggested that Liszt's use of the music of Beethoven and to a lesser extent the vocal music of Schubert in concert performances was part of a cynical strategy to transform his public image from that of a virtuoso to a serious artist. 'Liszt will emerge as a brilliant strategist, mobilizing the resources of his contemporary environment to stage an artistic profile and win the audience's approval', a sentiment that takes Heine's withering assessment of Liszt as its starting point: 'No one in this world knows how to organise his successes so well, or much more, their *mise-en-scène*, than our Franz Liszt.'[44] While there is much merit in Gooley's thesis, it is overly censorious in tone and disregards Liszt's lifelong commitment and the promotion of both composers' music.

As with many aspects of Liszt, it is possible that both points of view are true, namely that Liszt may indeed have seen in the music of Beethoven and Schubert a vehicle with which to forward his own personal ambitions, while also being sincerely committed to the promotion and dissemination of their music. Liszt's affinity with and admiration for the music of Schubert was lifelong and his association with Schubert goes back to his time in Vienna (for a brief period, less than two years, Liszt was the pupil of Salieri, who had also taught Schubert). The young Liszt may have been aware of Schubert, as both composers did submit a variation on Diabelli's Waltz theme at the invitation of the publisher, although there is no evidence that they ever met.[45] Liszt was an important figure in the early reception of Schubert and instrumental in popularising Schubert's works outside of Vienna. Christopher Gibbs asserts that:

> When Liszt played 'Erlkönig' and other Lieder during the 1830s and 1840s, he was frequently presenting the audience with their first exposure to Schubert's music. For many listeners outside of Vienna, in fact, Liszt provided the initial exposure even to Schubert's name.[46]

Indeed, Liszt promoted Schubert's Lieder through not only his performances of them with singers, but also his transcriptions, which were to become staples of his concert touring years. 'Erlkönig', 'Stänchen', and 'Ave Maria' were the most frequently performed, in both original and transcribed versions, during his tours

---

[44] Dana Gooley, 'The Virtuoso as Strategist', in William Weber (ed.), *The Musician as Entrepreneur, 1700–1914: Managers, Charlatans, and Idealists* (Bloomington: Indiana University Press, 2004), p. 143; Dana Gooley, *The Virtuoso Liszt* (Cambridge: Cambridge University Press, 2004), pp. 53–4; Rainer Kleinertz, 'Heinrich Heine on Liszt', in Christopher Gibbs and Dana Gooley (eds), *Franz Liszt and His World* (Princeton: Princeton University Press, 2006), p. 461.

[45] This collaborative work was published as *Vaterländischer Künstlerverein*. Liszt's variation (no. 24 in part II) was his first published composition. Even though it is a tantalising possibility, it is unlikely that they ever met. Liszt himself was adamant that they had not and listed it among his major regrets.

[46] Gibbs, 'The Presence of *Erlkönig*', p. 213.

of Germany in 1840–45.[47] Eduard Hanslick evaluated Liszt's contribution to the promotion of Schubert Lieder thus:

> Liszt's transcriptions of Schubert Lieder were epoch-making. There was scarcely a concert in which Liszt did not play one or two of them; even when they were not listed on the program they would have to be played. Far be it from me to praise the artistic value of these transcriptions or even to see a glorification of Schubert in them. When one takes away the words and voice from Schubert Lieder, one has not glorified them, but rather impoverished them. Still, the fact remains incontestable that Liszt, through these paraphrases, did a great deal for the dissemination of Schubert Lieder. Printed concert programs prove that since the appearance of Liszt's transcriptions of Schubert songs, the originals have been publicly sung more frequently than before: the power of virtuosity proves itself once again and this time served a good cause.[48]

Leaving aside Hanslick's faulty logic (it is not clear whether transcriptions and performances were a driving force in the upsurge in Schubert Lieder performance or merely coincided with it), Liszt's effort in the promotion of Schubert was clearly tremendous and sustained over a significant length of time. As has been mentioned, the numerous transcriptions of Schubert's Lieder – more than fifty – leave us with an invaluable record of Liszt's close study of another composer's work. This is especially interesting as Liszt would not attempt song composition until 1839. Therefore, these transcriptions could be seen to be serving as a form of apprenticeship in song writing. Liszt had some previous experience of vocal writing, having composed his only completed opera, *Don Sanche*, in 1825 at just fourteen years of age. The work, while remarkable as juvenilia, sticks close to the opera conventions of the time; Liszt may have been aided in its composition by his teacher Ferdinando Paer.[49]

Of the three Schubert Lieder which Liszt performed most frequently, 'Erlkönig' is perhaps where we can most readily see Schubert's influence on Liszt, as many of the characteristics of this Lied are present in Liszt's early songs. Firstly, and most evidently, there is the virtuosity required for both pianist and vocalist. The piano part of 'Erlkönig' is often cited as one of the most difficult in the Lieder repertoire, if the written score is adhered to. Phenomenal stamina is needed to maintain the right-hand octaves. This was made even more difficult by Liszt in performance, with his adding octave doublings to the left-hand part. Secondly, the piano writing contains a compositional device, the use of a distinctive opening piano figuration which serves, to use Alfred Brendel's phrase, to 'distil the essence' of the entire composition, as is

---

[47] Saffle, 'Appendix C: Sources and Evidence for Individual Concerts', in *Liszt in Germany*, pp. 237–78.

[48] Eduard Hanslick, in Susan Youens, 'Tradition and Innovation: The Lieder of Hugo Wolf', in James Parsons (ed.), *The Cambridge Companion to the Lied* (Cambridge: Cambridge University Press, 2004), p. 357 n. 5. Originally in Eduard Hanslick, *Geschichte des Concertwesens in Wien* (Vienna: William Braumüller, 1869), p. 336.

[49] The one-act work *Don Sanche*, S.1 / LW O1, was premiered by the Paris Opera in Salle Le Peletier on 17 October 1825, and received only four performances on its initial run. Considered lost for many years, it was rediscovered in 1903 and revived in London on 20 October 1977.

also the case in 'Gretchen am Spinnrade'.[50] In fact, Liszt adopted this compositional device in both his solo piano writing and his own Lieder – in the first versions of 'Am Rhein, im schönen Strome', 'Kling leise, mein Lied', 'Drei Lieder aus Schillers Wilhelm Tell', and is extremely common among Liszt's French songs as well. It is also present in the first versions of 'Mignon', 'Loreley', and 'Der du von dem Himmel bist', but to a lesser degree as the distinctive accompaniment figurations are not a feature throughout most of the song. Thirdly, the vocal part calls for the singer to shade their voice to distinguish clearly between the three main characters and the narrator of the ballad, and to bring out the work's dramatic possibilities. This need for the singer to shade their voice subtly is also common in Liszt's Lieder, which are often peppered with performance instructions for the singer to alter the tonal quality of their voice, especially in the later Lieder. Finally, two aspects of Schubert's 'Erlkönig' that appear to have had a far-reaching impact on Liszt are how Schubert uses form and modulation to reflect the poem's content – his use of chromatic harmony, his alternation between major and minor modes, and the structural importance given to mediant-related harmonies.

Schubert's 'Erlkönig' as a through-composed setting of a strophic text seems to have appealed to Liszt greatly, as in his own settings he rarely composed in regular song forms or slavishly mirrored the form of the poetic text. Instead, most of Liszt's Lieder are either through-composed or in a type of modified ternary form, with a returning A section that has been heavily transformed. This is even the case when the text would more obviously lend itself to a strophic setting, such as in 'Mignon'. Schubert's use of modulation as a means of expression in closely mirroring the development of the text's poetic content can also be found in many of Liszt's Lieder, for example 'Der Fischerknabe'. That Liszt was conscious of this aspect of Schubert's works is undeniable, as he cited it in an essay on Robert Franz whom he perceived to be following Schubert's example in this regard. Liszt called these types of modulations the 'true interpreters of words.'[51]

Taken as a whole, this group of dimensions – the virtuosity (of both performers), distinctive piano figurations, the necessity for vocal shading, vacillation between major and minor modalities, distinctive modulations to mediant keys and use of a through-composed form – show that Schubert's influence via 'Erlkönig' on Liszt was profound and multifaceted. It should be noted, however, that some of the features listed above were atypical for Schubert; for example, through-composed form is rare in his oeuvre compared to the number of strophic and modified strophic settings. The main argument is that it was Schubert's 'Erlkönig' rather than his whole body of work that exerted a massive influence on Liszt. This does not mean that the rest of Schubert's oeuvre had little influence on Liszt, but rather that 'Erlkönig' – as

---

50 Alfred Brendel, 'Liszt's *Années de pèlerinage* I and II', in Brendel, *On Music: Collected Essays* (London: JR Books, 2007), p. 257. Brendel cites this quality in relation to 'Au lac de Wallenstadt', but it is a compositional device which Liszt used throughout his career from the early *Apparitions no. 1* to the late *Jeux d'eaux à la Villa d'Este* and which is also noticeable in such Lieder as 'Es war ein König in Thule'.

51 Michael Abu Hamad, 'True Interpreters of Words: Tonal Distances in Franz Liszt's Early Songs' (PhD diss., Brandeis University, 2005), p. 32.

the work that Liszt performed more than any other (including his own) during his virtuoso years – exerted an exceptional influence on the composer.[52] It should also be noted at this point that, by associating himself with the music of Schubert and performing with singers who were either directly related with Schubert himself, his circle, or known as leading exponents of his Lieder in Vienna, Liszt was receiving a form of tacit endorsement as an artist. It could be argued that Liszt's choice of repertoire and his accompaniment of these singers formed part of a strategy to create a more German-friendly image for himself as he embarked on his tours of *Vormärz* Germany, as it would allow him to distance himself from the image of a superficial virtuoso, and simultaneously validate his credentials as a serious artist.[53]

Liszt's Musical Life in Weimar

When Liszt took up his position on a full-time basis as *Kapellmeister extraordinaire* in Weimar in 1848, he was walking away from one of the most successful performing careers in history, while at its zenith.[54] On the face of it, this was a strange decision, but Liszt had in fact long yearned for such an appointment to afford him the opportunity to complete the large-scale orchestral works which he had envisaged as far back as the mid-1830s. Liszt had shown interest in similar positions in both Paris and Vienna; however, as Kenneth Hamilton and Joanne Cormac have discussed, neither aspiration was likely to be realised.[55] Liszt's estranged lover, and mother of his three children, Marie d'Agoult, resided in Paris, which made Parisian society life hostile to Liszt. His embrace of the Hungarian national cause and his concert success there were likewise received with hostility in Paris. In Vienna, Donizetti

[52] Beethoven's *Adelaide*, op. 46, is also worth citing as a possible formative influence on Liszt from a songwriting perspective. And indeed, Liszt created three versions of the song for solo piano. Like 'Erlkönig', it is an atypical Lied. It is through-composed even though it is based on a strophic text. Beethoven signalled its unconventional nature by terming it a 'cantata for voice with keyboard accompaniment'.

[53] Gooley, *The Virtuoso Liszt*, pp. 52–8. Gooley argues that Liszt employed a similar strategy to differentiate himself from Thalberg in Paris in the 1830s. Liszt attempted this, Gooley argues, not by performing his own works, but by performing Beethoven's op. 106 and organising a series of four chamber music concerts in Paris in 1837 which Liszt termed séances. These séances were a mix of virtuoso works for piano solo, vocal selections (which Liszt accompanied), and more standard chamber works such as Beethoven's 'Archduke' piano trio. In this respect 'Erlkönig' could be seen to perform an analogous function to Beethoven's op. 106 in Liszt's performing repertoire.

[54] Liszt had been initially appointed on a part-time basis in 1842; from 1848 onwards, the duties of *Kapellmeister* were divided between him and the existing *Kapellmeister*, André Hyppolyte Chélard. Chélard took charge of the dramatic performances, while Liszt was primarily concerned with concerts. This division, however, does not adequately capture the shifting and *ad hoc* nature of Liszt's duties in Weimar. For a fuller discussion see Joanne Cormac, *Liszt and the Symphonic Poem* (Cambridge: Cambridge University Press, 2017), pp. 1–68.

[55] Kenneth Hamilton, '"Not with a Bang but a Whimper": The Death of Liszt's *Sardanapale*', *Cambridge Opera Journal*, 8:1 (1996), 45–58; Cormac, *Liszt and the Symphonic Poem*, pp. 4–5.

occupied the post *Kapellmeister* to the Chapel of the Royal Court, which Liszt coveted; by the time of Donizetti's death in 1848, Liszt had taken up his position in Weimar. Moreover, as Liszt was primarily known at that time as a virtuoso with no significant experience as either a conductor or composer of successful operatic works, he would have been deemed underqualified to fill a role such as Donizetti's in the Vienna opera. The small provincial city of Weimar did however have a number of advantages that were not immediately obvious and that were attractive to Liszt. As Alan Walker elucidates:

> Weimar was one of the cultural centres of Germany; already the city of Goethe and Schiller could boast of a century's unbroken association with the arts. It had a theatre and an orchestra, its own poets and painters, and an academy of scientists. The nearby city of Jena possessed a university. Most important of all, Weimar enjoyed the benign patronage of Grand Duchess Maria Pawlowna the sister of Tsar Nicholas I of Russia. This triple alliance of court, theatre, and academia was difficult to resist. Moreover, Weimar was small and appeared to offer a quiet harbour from the storms of the outside world. ... And there were other advantages. The arrival in the city of its first railway line in 1846 gave Liszt ready access to all parts of Germany ... what this meant to Liszt in pursuit of his artistic goals cannot be overestimated.[56]

Walker even asserts that Liszt intended to revive the cultural life of all of Thuringia, which included the towns of Jena, Erfurt, Eisenach, and Sondershausen.[57] He made connections throughout the domain of Thuringia and was able to call on the musical resources of the entire area when he put on the large Wagner and Berlioz festivals of the mid-1850s. He was even involved in the restoration of the old castle of Wartburg, which according to Walker 'symbolised Old Germany' to Liszt. Walker suggests that Liszt viewed the regeneration of Thuringian culture and the restoration of the old castle as inextricably linked.[58] The locality also afforded Liszt the opportunity to study the organ tradition, and in turn Liszt promoted the old kingdom's most distinguished musicians, Bach and Handel. Liszt even conducted full performances of Handel oratorios, which was not standard practice at the time.[59]

Liszt's time in Weimar is commonly held to be his most productive, when the inspired but flawed works of his youth would be moulded into their mature forms. Weimar was the city where Liszt embarked on a series of grand orchestral compositions and where he began his career as a conductor in earnest. He conducted the premieres of many notable operas and orchestral works, and revived many masterworks there, while instituting many reforms in conducting, concert, and theatre practice. Weimar was the city where he and his followers gathered to produce the avant-garde

---

[56] Walker, *Franz Liszt*, vol. 2, p. 6.

[57] Ibid.

[58] Ibid.

[59] Liszt conducted Handel's *Messiah* four times between 1850 and 1857. In 1859, to mark the hundredth anniversary of the composer's passing, Liszt conducted the Weimar premiere of *Judas Maccabeus* on 20 May 1859, followed by *Messiah* on 21 May 1859. Walker, *Franz Liszt*, vol. 2, pp. 286–93, and p. 510.

music of the nineteenth century, which in time would come to be referred to as the 'New German School'. It was also in Weimar that Liszt introduced the concept of the masterclass, where the finest young pianists from all over the world would gather for instruction. The Weimar period is subject to arguably as many legends as the virtuoso period; often depicted as a halcyon age, it is only more recently that scholars have begun to examine Liszt's activities during the period critically and in detail. As Alan Walker and, later, Wolfram Huschke, and Joanne Cormac illuminated, Liszt's time in Weimar, like his virtuoso years, was far from an unbroken chain of triumphs and successes. His day-to-day activities often brought him into conflict with 'Old Weimar' and there were many members of the court and theatre establishment whose views and competing interests stymied Liszt's artistic efforts.[60]

Lieder composition and publication seems to have been only an intermittent concern of Liszt during his time in Weimar. Until 1858, performances at the Weimar Court Theatre and the ducal palace would have been the foremost concerns of Liszt's musical activity. As late as 1856 – when the first revised version of the *Buch der Lieder* appeared – we can see that Liszt still grouped his songs more by topic than poet.[61] However, by the time the first volumes of Liszt's thoroughly revised (third) version of the songs appeared in 1859 he had settled on a division by poet and/or language.[62] The date is significant as it comes after Liszt had conducted the disastrous premiere of Peter Cornelius's *Der Barbier von Bagdad*.[63] From this date onwards Liszt no longer conducted any works at the theatre and concerned himself only with the palace concerts. It can therefore be inferred that, with his resignation from theatre activities, Liszt then had the time to attend to his Lieder revisions.

Liszt's Weimar Salon as a Musical Laboratory

After Liszt arrived in Weimar, he quickly set up his own salon in the Altenburg, the house where his companion Princess Carolyne had taken up residence. Musical gatherings took place on Sunday afternoons and Liszt was helped in the administration of his salon by Carolyne's daughter (Marie de Hohenlohe-Schillingsfürst, *née* de Sayn-Wittgenstein), who had travelled with her from Ukraine. Together they created an artistic environment that would have held its own with any of the

---

[60] Wolfram Husche, *Franz Liszt, Wirken und Wirkungen in Weimar* (Weimar: Weimarer Verlagsgesellschaft, 2010), pp. 116–57; Cormac, *Liszt and the Symphonic Poem*, especially pp. 32–68; Walker, *Franz Liszt*, vol. 2, pp. 74–167.

[61] Franz Liszt, *Buch der Lieder*, 2nd version (Berlin: Schlesinger, 1856).

[62] Franz Liszt, *Gesammelte Lieder*, 6 vols (Berlin: Schlesinger, 1859), vol. 1.

[63] Peter Cornelius, *Der Barbier von Bagdad*, comic opera in two acts on a libretto by Cornelius himself. Composed between 1855 and 1858, it was premiered in Weimar's Hoftheater with Liszt conducting. James Deaville, 'Cornelius, (Carl August) Peter (i)', *Grove Music Online*, 2001, < https://www.oxfordmusiconline.com/grovemusic/view/10.1093 /gmo/9781561592630.001.0001/omo09781561592630-e-0000040631> [accessed 29 August 2018].

salons in Paris at the time.[64] During his time in Weimar Liszt took advantage of the skills present there to consult on such diverse matters as orchestration, instrumental writing, and, more pertinently to this study, vocal writing. Liszt used the musical resources available to him at Weimar to inform his compositional process. William Mason leaves a colourful description of one such occasion when Liszt was in the process of composing his symphonic poem *Tasso: lamento e trionfo*:

> Liszt was in earnest, however, and availed himself of every means of preparation for the work. Frequently upon his request the best orchestral players came to the Altenburg, and he asked them about their instruments, their nature, and whether certain passages were idiomatic to them. About the time I came to Weimar to study with him he had nearly finished 'Tasso', and before giving it the last touches he had a rehearsal of it, which we attended. We went to the theatre, and he took the orchestra into a room which would just about hold it. Imagine the din in that room! The effect was far from musical, but to Liszt it was the key to the polyphonic effects which he wished to produce.[65]

This passage is instructive as it shows Liszt's willingness to seek advice and use the expertise of specialists. Indeed, it was not just on musical matters that Liszt availed of the talents that were within easy reach. He also valued the linguistic skills of those in his circle. The composer Peter Cornelius became Liszt's private secretary for a year in 1853, and Cornelius translated several of Liszt's song texts into German, as well as his essays and articles from their original French. Therefore, it is not unreasonable to assume that he would have also consulted the exemplary vocal talents that were at his disposal in Weimar, most especially the von Mildes (Hans Feodor and Rosa) and the Genasts (Eduard and his daughter Emilie).

It was not just Liszt's works that were performed at the Altenburg. Liszt's protégées would also often try out their works in his salon. Cornelius, also being an esteemed composer of Lieder, is noteworthy, as Liszt was never too proud to be influenced by a younger composer:

> Shortly afterwards he [Cornelius] turned to the Lied and composed his set of nine songs *Vater unser* (op.2) and the cycle *Trauer und Trost* (op.3), which, by common consent, reveal a mature hand. A stream of songs poured from his pen during the Weimar years. Many of them were first performed in the Altenburg by Rosa von Milde, the gifted young soprano of the Weimar theatre, accompanied by Liszt.[66]

As the following lengthy extract from William Mason's memoir clearly illustrates, Weimar – under Liszt – became a hive of musical activity that was both tremendously varied and in an unceasing flow. Mason claimed that this extract from his diary was chosen at random and was therefore not exceptional but, rather, representative of the time he spent with Liszt in Weimar:

[64] Pauline Pocknell, Malou Haine, and Nicolas Dufetel (eds), *Lettres de Franz Liszt à Marie de Hohenlohe-Schillingsfürst, née de Sayn-Wittgenstein* (Paris: Vrin, 2010), pp. 17–20.

[65] Mason, *Memories of a Musical Life*, p. 121.

[66] Walker, *Franz Liszt*, vol. 2, p. 194.

As an illustration of some of the advantages of a residence at Weimar almost en famille with Liszt during 'die goldene Zeit', a few extracts from my diary are presented, showing how closely events followed one upon another:

Sunday, April 24, 1853. At the Altenburg this forenoon at eleven o'clock. Liszt played with Laub and Cossman two trios by César Franck.

This is peculiarly interesting in view of the fact that the composer, who died about ten years ago, is just beginning to receive due appreciation. In Paris at the present time there is almost a César Franck cult, but it is quite natural that Liszt, with his quick and far-seeing appreciation, should have taken especial delight in playing his music forty-seven years ago. Liszt was very fond of it.

May 1. Quartet at the Altenburg at eleven o'clock, after which Wieniawski played with Liszt the violin and pianoforte 'Sonata in A' by Beethoven.

May 3. Liszt called at my rooms last evening in company with Laub and Wieniawski. Liszt played several pieces, among them my 'Amitié pour Amitié'.

May 6. The boys were all at the Hotel Erbprinz this evening. Liszt came in and added to the liveliness of the occasion.

May 7. At Liszt's, this evening, Klindworth, Laub, and Cossmann played a piano trio by Spohr, after which Liszt played his recently composed sonata and one of his concertos. In the afternoon I had played during my lesson with Liszt the 'C Sharp Minor Sonata' of Beethoven and the 'E Minor Fugue' by Handel.

May 17. Lesson from Liszt this evening. Played Scherzo and Finale from Beethoven's 'C Sharp Minor Sonata.'

May 20, Friday. Attended a court concert this evening which Liszt conducted. Joachim played a violin solo by Ernst.

May 22. Went to the Altenburg at eleven o'clock this forenoon. There were about fifteen persons present – quite an unusual thing. Among other things, a string quartet of Beethoven was played, Joachim taking the first violin.

May 23. Attended an orchestral rehearsal at which an overture and a violin concerto by Joachim were performed, the latter played by Joachim.

May 27. Joachim Raff's birthday. Klindworth and I presented ourselves to him early in the day and stopped his composing, insisting on having a holiday. Our celebration of this event included a ride to Tiefurt and attendance at a garden concert.

May 29, Sunday. At Liszt's this forenoon as usual. No quartet to-day. Wieniawski played first a violin solo by Ernst, and afterward[s] with Liszt the letter's duo on Hungarian airs.

May 30. Attended a ball of the Erholung Gesellschaft this evening. At our supper-table were Liszt, Raff Wieniawski, Pruckner, and Klindworth. Got home at four o'clock in the morning.

June 4. Dined with Liszt at the Erbprinz. Liszt called at my rooms later in the afternoon, bringing with him Dr. Marx and a lady from Berlin, also Raff and Winterberger. Liszt played three Chopin nocturnes and a scherzo of his own. In the evening we were all invited to the Altenburg. He played 'Harmonies du Soir', No. 2, and his own sonata. He was at his best and played divinely.

June 9. Had a lesson from Liszt this evening. I played Chopin's 'E Minor Concerto'.

June 10. Went to Liszt's this evening to a bock-beer soirée. The beer was a present to Liszt from Pruckner's father, who has a large brewery in Munich.

Sunday, June 12. Usual quartet forenoon at the Altenburg. 'Quartet, Op. 161', of Schubert's was played, also one of Beethoven's quartets.

The last entry may not seem to be particularly important, but it may be as well not to end the quotations from a musical diary with a reference to a bock-beer soirée.[67]

The extract makes clear that Liszt's musical activity was far-reaching, performing not only a wide range of piano compositions, but facilitating and partaking in chamber, orchestral, and vocal compositions. Furthermore, the works were not solely those of Liszt's immediate circle, but included works from as far back as the Baroque era. It is worth noting that the unidentified string quartet by Beethoven mentioned in the 22 May entry was performed by musicians of the highest calibre: 'Ferdinand Laub, the leader of the quartet, was about twenty-one years of age, and already a violinist of the first rank. Wieniawski and Joachim, young men of the age of twenty-two and nineteen years respectively, were among the most welcome visitors to Weimar: Joachim, already celebrated as a quartet player, was regarded by some as the greatest living violinist. The playing of Wieniawski appealed to me more than that of any other violinist of the time, and I remember it now with intense pleasure.'[68]

The Weimar Singers

By the time the first volume of Liszt's *Gesammelte Lieder* was published in 1859, he had been in Weimar for over a decade – his musical activity vastly different from the early 1840s, when he was in the midst of the most persistent touring of his career. During his Weimar years he interacted with a whole range of voice types, from the virtuosos who visited Weimar, to the established and professional court singers who performed in the operas, concerts, rehearsals, Sunday matinées, soirées, and other less formal occasions, to the members of the Weimar chorus, who were mostly actors, not famed for their vocal ability. Although the large-scale project of revising his entire Lieder catalogue would not begin in earnest until the end of the decade, we can clearly see in a letter to his publisher Heinrich Schlesinger from 18 December 1855 how his Lied aesthetic had developed substantively and contrasted with that of

---

[67] Mason, *Memories of a Musical Life*, pp. 122–6.

[68] Ibid., p. 128.

his earlier Lieder. Here is the already-mentioned reference to Liszt's having composed his earlier Lieder with 'exceptional voices' in mind:

> Enclosed is the manuscript of the first five Lieder, which I would ask you to publish *as soon as possible* in a second edition (with the wording 'edition revised and facilitated by the composer') ... In this guise the Lieder are accessible to most singers, male and female, and accompanists, while presumably you will obtain a wider circulation than has been the case thus far, for in composing them I thought of some quite exceptional voices (such as, especially, Mme Ungher-Sabatier and Tichatschek). Fräulein Wagner might be so obliging as to champion a couple of them – *Mignon* and *Der König in Thule* suit her voice completely – perhaps also the Loreley, which has now become human in its accompaniment, without losing any of its effect.[69]

Pauline Viardot (1821–1910)

> It has been a long time since this great artist has appeared on our stages. For the many of us who have heard her earlier performances, we can attest to how captivating and enchanting her performances can be. They have remained a long-lasting memory in our minds. More than all other artists, she is endowed with a unique tonal quality and vocal pitch ability. She renders tones beautifully and much better than other celebrities who have attempted the same subject matter.[70]

With these remarks, Liszt began his glowing character sketch of Pauline Viardot which first appeared in *Neue Zeitschrift für Musik* on 28 January 1859. Born into the Garcia musical dynasty, Pauline Viardot (*née* Garcia) was the youngest daughter of Manuel del Popolo Garcia (1775–1832) and Joaquina Garcia Stitchès, the sister of Maria Malibran and Manuel Patricio Garcia (1805–1906).[71] It is therefore not surprising that she would have been endowed with exceptional vocal talent.[72] However, as Liszt would go on to expound, Viardot's musical talents went far beyond vocal ability, to encompass composition, arrangement, virtuoso pianism, highly accom-

---

[69] Short, *Liszt Letters in the Library of Congress*, letter 125, p. 118.

[70] Franz Liszt, 'Pauline Viardot-Garcia', in *The Collected Writings of Franz Liszt*, vol. 3, part 1, ed. and trans. Janita Hall Swadley (Lanham, MD: Rowman & Littlefield, 2014), p. 202. The reference to her earlier performances is perhaps suggestive of the fact that Viardot's voice was beginning to show signs of wear due to the gruelling nature of her excessive touring schedule as referenced by contemporary reviews of several of her 1858 performances in Hungary. Klára Hamburger, 'Liszt et Pauline Viardot-Garcìa (dans l'optique de sept lettres inédites)', *Studia Musicologica Academiae Scientiarum Hungaricae*, T. 34, Fasc. 1/2 (1992), p. 195.

[71] I have used Viardot throughout this book, as this is how she referred to herself after marriage, often going by 'Mme Viardot'.

[72] Beatrix Bochard, 'Viardot [*née* García], (Michelle Ferdidnande) Pauline', *Grove Music Online*, 2001 [accessed 30 August 2018].

plished organ playing, rare feats of sight reading, artistic interpretation of the high-est calibre, and pedagogy.[73]

Liszt's series of character sketches, of which Viardot's is the last, are worth con-sideration as, instead of following a simple biographical line, he often used these sketches to elucidate his own views on a wide range of topics. Therefore, they give us a useful window into Liszt's aesthetic principles regarding both performance and composition.[74] Several facets of the Viardot character sketch are specifically relevant to Liszt's Lieder. The sketch was penned contemporaneously with Liszt's first volume of *Gesammelte Lieder*, and as Liszt used Viardot as an example of his ideal artist, the qualities that he highlights in this article are a useful lens through which to view his revised Lieder. Indeed, Elisabeth Perten states with respect to Liszt's essay on Viardot: 'As the culmination of so many strands of Liszt's life and career, the examination of this character portrait proves essential to an analysis of Liszt's Weimar works.'[75] Perten goes on to link this portrait with Liszt's earlier essay from 1835, 'On the Situation of Artists', making the case that it can be used to trace the development of Liszt's ideas over a twenty-five-year period on a whole range of topics, including contemporary opera, the need for an educated audience, and the role of the artist in society.[76] Liszt's connection to Viardot goes back to Paris in the 1830s, when she studied piano with him. They became friends and maintained an active correspondence until Liszt's death. Viardot initially harboured ambitions of becoming a concert pianist and appeared on stage professionally as a pianist before making her vocal debut. However, after the sudden death of her sister Maria Malibran in 1836, her mother persuaded her to pursue a career as a singer. Initially, the remarkable aural resemblance to Malibran worked to create an aura of excite-ment around Viardot. However, as Barbara Kendall-Davies explains, in contrast with her sister, Viardot's eschewing of the large gesture and her attention to nuanced

---

[73] Franz Liszt, *Neue Zeitschrift für Musik* (28 Jan 1859), cited in *The Collected Writings of Franz Liszt*, vol. 3, part 1, p. 209. Liszt on Viardot's musicianship: 'Unlike many other songstresses, she makes use of a golden chain of virtuosic runs, cadenzas, and embellishments, all for the sake of music drama, which always compliments our interest for the character being performed and enhances our feeling for the work's compositional Idea. She is a splendid pianist, who can play full orchestral scores with the most difficult accompaniments prima vista, and even better than many concertizing virtuosos.' The last quality listed above, pedagogy, is perhaps not so surprising given that her older brother, Manuel Patricio Garcia, is considered the father of modern vocal pedagogy, described as 'the leading theoretical writer of Rossini vocal school'. Rodolfo Celletti, *A History of Bel Canto* (Oxford: Clarendon Press, 1996), p. 172. The qualities listed above are all also closely associated with Liszt, and perhaps in Viardot Liszt saw a 'keeper of the flame'. After all, in her youth Viardot had studied piano with Liszt and composition with one of Liszt's own teachers Anton Reicha. Furthermore, like Liszt, Viardot was sympathetic to Saint-Simonism and was associated with several charitable endeavours.

[74] The other figures honoured by Liszt in this series were John Field, Clara Schumann, Robert Schumann, A.B. Marx, Hector Berlioz, Robert Franz, and Eduard Sobolewski.

[75] Elizabeth Perten, 'Liszt as Critic: Virtuosity, Aesthetics, and the Artist in Liszt's Weimar Prose (1848–1861)' (PhD diss., Brandeis University, 2014), p. 159.

[76] Ibid., p. 154, citing Franz Liszt, 'On the Situations of Artists', *Gazette Musicale de Paris* (May–June 1835).

detail in performance may have in fact worked against her on the opera stage in the early phase of her career:

> a flamboyant, extrovert creature such as Malibran was preferred to Pauline with all her subtlety. They wanted their operatic heroines drawn on a large canvas, not in exquisite miniatures, and this is a reason why, in her early career, Pauline was sometimes seen to greater effect in the salon or concert hall than on the opera stage. Many people remarked that to observe her at close range with the wide variety of expression at her command was to see her at her best.[77]

Viardot focused not only on the aural aspect of vocal performance, but also the dramatic and the visual. In reviews of her performances, comparisons were often made with the leading dramatic actresses of the time as well as with other singers, and her attention to visual detail went as far as costume design. She immersed herself in the historical and literary background of a work, making sure that her characters were dressed in a historically accurate way.[78] In her attention to a performance's visual aspect, there is a strong parallel with Liszt, who was known for his expressive performance gestures; as Robert Schumann famously wrote, 'If Liszt were to play behind a screen, a great deal of poetry would be lost.'[79] And Viardot's refinement of a performance style for the smaller venue – with more subtle gestures than her sister's – perhaps influenced Liszt in his own vocal compositions.

Liszt describes in his essay how Viardot can weave these various threads into an all-encapsulating performance. This setting up of Viardot as an ideal artist also allowed Liszt to tackle the then-thorny subject of virtuosity. The critical backlash against instrumental virtuosity in the German-language press in the nineteenth century was such that Dana Gooley has dubbed it 'the battle against instrumental virtuosity'.[80] Therefore, it is interesting to examine the thoughts of one of the foremost virtuosos of the era on the matter. Liszt uses the article to expound his own views regarding interpretation and virtuosity, and how the two are inextricably linked:

> As it is with all great performers who are inflamed with the sacred poetic fire, Madame Viardot uses virtuosity only as a means to express the Idea – the thought and character of a work or role. Virtuosity exists only so that the artist is able to reproduce everything that is expressive in Art. For this purpose, it is indispensable, and for this purpose only; I cannot stress this enough. Once you learn this, you will appreciate these types of works, especially when you see them performed by artists who do not use virtuosity as a spectacle, but rather as an expression of feeling. Virtuosity allows the artist to express the fullness and richness of the [musical] language.[81]

---

[77] Barbara Kendall-Davies, *Life and Work of Pauline Viardot Garcia*, 2 vols, 2nd edn (Newcastle: Cambridge Scholars Publishing, 2013), vol. 1, p. 107.

[78] Ibid., p. 104.

[79] Schumann, *On Music and Musicians*, p. 156.

[80] Dana Gooley, 'The Battle against Instrumental Virtuosity in the Early Nineteenth Century', in *Franz Liszt and His World*, pp. 75–112.

[81] Liszt, *The Collected Writings of Franz Liszt*, vol. 2, p. 304.

Liszt enumerated Viardot's numerous qualities, and not only from a technical standpoint. He praised her knowledge of languages, visual art, literature, her good nature, charm, wittiness, and how she was able to put all these qualities in the service of her art.[82] In an extract that highlights their shared cosmopolitanism, Liszt also draws attention to Viardot's ability, due to her extensive education, travels, and background, to master any national style:

> Her performances always communicated the beauty of her soul and an enticing sense of intellectual nobility. She is admired in every land, and she glows with unanimous success on every stage. ... Because of her Spanish nature, her French upbringing, and her German sympathies, she is able to combine the idiosyncrasies of different nationalities in such a way that no land can claim her decisively or exclusively; instead, for her, art is 'the Fatherland of freedom and love'. This very great artist has an innate talent to arouse the most perfect and Ideal form of the national element, and her endeavours are received enthusiastically. Pauline Viardot has the ability to comprehend every comparable Ideal; she understands its secretive and hidden meaning. This offers her the opportunity to continually explore and internalize its forms, take hold of them, and master them.[83]

Interestingly, Liszt later in the sketch humanises Viardot by mentioning the strain that her voice has undergone in recent years from the demands of her performing career. But rather than seeing this as a fault, he goes on to praise her, seeing it as further evidence that she is a mature artist who has worked for her art.[84] The key point is that artistry is not something that one is naturally endowed with, but rather a question of temperament, and it is acquired through persistent work. In this regard there are parallels with both Adolphe Nourrit and Wilhelmine Schröder-Devrient, in that their artistry derives from the spirit or temperament and not a physical characteristic.

In an extract that reveals an understanding of Hegel's *The Phenomenology of Spirit*, Liszt frames Viardot as an example of a true artist. He sees their 'exceptional abilities' to synthesise different strands in a composition into an intelligible whole to arouse the higher feelings in the audience:

> A true artist is someone who is richly endowed with the most exceptional abilities and personality. He or she is able to conquer seemingly overwhelming obstacles and acquire equal amounts of expressiveness in two artificial languages with essentially different contents, take possession of both living principles, affirm their very different points of origin and tendencies, become conscious of the intense passions for which humans strive, duplicate their momentary sensual wishes and brief mortal joys, and at the same time, find a way to escape from other contradic-

---

[82] Viardot was fluent in Spanish, French, Italian, German, English, and Russian. She is credited as the first major singer to visit Russia and perform in Russian. She was instrumental in promoting the works of Glinka and Dargomizhsky..

[83] Liszt, *The Collected Writings of Franz Liszt*, vol. 3, part 1, p. 192.

[84] Ibid.

tory forces, passionate influences, and transient desires so that we can experience only the pure joys of the higher and more refined feelings.[85]

We can see how Liszt presented Viardot as the exemplary artist, in his praise of not only her vocal dexterity but, more importantly, her deep interpretive insights – insights only attainable from a thorough understanding of a work in its musical context as well as from its relation to other works of art across genres and the history of ideas.

Emilie Genast (1833–1912)

Emilie Genast was born into a theatrical family. She was the daughter of Weimar-based singer, actor, and stage manager/director Eduard Genast (1797–1866) and singer, actor, and pianist, Karoline Christine Böhler (1800–60). Emilie was possessed of a fine voice, by all accounts, but not imbued with qualities that would make her a natural fit for the opera stage; instead, she made her reputation as a singer of oratorio and Lieder.[86] La Mara (Ida Marie Lipsius) writes that 'Her voice, a soft mezzo-soprano, was not large, but with a noble and sympathetic richness of tone; her recitation was thoroughly full of poetic magic'.[87]

Liszt held her in high esteem and was very appreciative of her performances of his own Lieder. Liszt performed with Genast in both concert and salon settings, in Weimar, Berlin, and Leipzig, during the late 1850s. Particularly notable was a performance in Berlin: after Hans von Bülow's conducting of a performance of Liszt's symphonic poem *Die Ideale* in Berlin in 14 January 1859 experienced a hostile reception, he arranged for Liszt and Genast to perform at a second concert on 27 February, when *Die Ideale* would be presented once more, but this time with Liszt conducting. Liszt and Genast also performed two Schubert Lieder and Liszt's 'Mignon' at the concert, which was considered a success.

In his memoirs, composer and conductor Wendelin Weißheimer (1838–1910) left an account of his attendance at the *Tonkünstler-Versammlung* which took place in Leipzig over the first days of June 1859:

> The artistic highlights of this first Tonkünstler-Versammlung were … at a concert given on the stage of the Old City Theatre; the recitation of Liszt's melodrama on Burgers' Lenore; and the first public performance of his glorious Loreley, in the hall of the riflemen's club-house. It will be difficult for any of those present ever

---

[85] Ibid., p. 203. In *The Phenomenology of Spirit*, Hegel describes a dialectical process, using the terms abstract, negative, and concrete. See Georg W.F. Hegel, *The Phenomenology of Spirit*, ed. and trans. Terry Pinkard (Cambridge: Cambridge University Press, 2018), pp. 339–65. In the excerpt above, with 'two artificial languages with essentially different contents', Liszt is presenting the Italian and German schools as opposites that have been mastered and synthesised into a concrete whole by Viardot.

[86] La Mara, *Liszt und die Frauen*, pp. 207–8; Klára Hamburger, 'Emilie (Merian)-Genast, Liszt's Confidante', *The Hungarian Quarterly*, 189 (2008), 163–9 (p. 163).

[87] 'Ihre Stimme, ein weicher Mezzosopran, war nicht groß, doch von edler, sympathischer Klangfarbe; ihr Vortrag durch und durch beseelt voll poetischen Zaubers.' Ibid., p. 209. Translation is my own.

to forget that performance: Liszt at the piano and in front of him, interpreting the 'Loreley', Emilie Genast, one of the finest Lieder singers of the time![88]

Liszt dedicated 'Die drei Zigeuner' and the fourth version of 'Die Zelle in Nonnenwerth' to Genast as well as orchestrating the accompaniments of three of his Lieder ('Mignon', 'Die Loreley', and 'Die drei Zigeuner') and three of Schubert's with performances by her in mind. Genast called on Liszt at the Altenburg regularly during his last years in Weimar before he moved to Rome in 1861, and for a brief time during this period they were lovers. He thought highly of her musicianship, as his letters to her often go into detail on musical matters, and he regularly consulted her regarding vocal issues. For example, when revising his oratorio *Die Legende von Heiligen Elisabeth* he asked Genast for her help, writing on 23 March 1861:[89]

> In the past weeks I have worked only on ancillary tasks (revisions, arrangements, and corrections), which always put me in a very bad mood. Before long, I shall return to *Elisabeth* to re-write and complete it. I would once again like to ask for your helpful assistance with the final scene, taking it upon myself to relentlessly probe you with different versions to try out. I hope you will grant me this friendly service, for which I will repay you to some extent by writing the conclusion to your satisfaction.[90]

Genast performed the title role of the work at its premiere and was a champion of the work for many years. 'Die Loreley' also became somewhat of a speciality for her, and she performed it in Berlin in 1860 to great acclaim. According to Liszt:

> At the last Court concert in Berlin Fraulein Genast selected the 'Loreley' as her concluding song, and the Frau Princess Victoria expressed herself very favourably about it, remarking that a Schubert spirit breathed in the composition. One of these days Fraulein Genast is again singing the 'Loreley' at the Philharmonic Concert in Hamburg. Otten has specially begged her to do so. The same gentleman wrote about eighteen months ago to Frau von Milde that he must beg to

---

[88] Adrian Williams, *Portrait of Liszt: By Himself and His Contemporaries* (Oxford: Clarendon Press, 1990), p. 356. For a fuller account, see Wendelin Weißheimer, *Erlebnisse mit Richard Wagner, Franz Liszt und vielen anderen Zeitgenossen nebst deren Briefen* (Stuttgart: Deutsche Verlags Anstalt, 1898), pp. 35–9.

[89] *Die Legende von Heiligen Elisabeth*, S.2/ LW I4, sacred oratorio composed by Liszt in 1857–61.

[90] 'In den letzten Wochen habe ich nur mit Nebenarbeiten – revisionen, arrangemens und Correcturen – zu thun gehabt, was mich immer in sehr schlechte Stimmung versetzt. Nächstens aber soll endlich wieder die Elisabeth vorgenommen und fertig geschrieben sein. Zur Schluß Scene erbitte ich mir abermals Ihren hilfreichen Beistand – und behalte mir vor Sie mit dem probiren verschiedener Versionen schonungslos zu belästigen. – Hoffentlich gewähren Sie mir diesen Freundschafts-Dienst den ich damit vergelten mochte diese Schluß Scene einigermaßen zu Ihrer Zufriedenheit herzustellen.' Klára Hamburger, 'Franz Liszts Briefe an Emilie Merian-Genast aus den Beständen des Goethe-und Schiller-Archivs, Weimar Teil 2', *Studia Musicologica*, 49:1/2 (March 2008), pp. 143–92 (p. 147). Translation is my own.

remark 'that in regard to the choice of compositions to be performed, Robert Schumann is the extreme limit to whom his programme could extend!'[91]

Emilie Genast may therefore have been another of Liszt's model interpreters when he was revising his Lieder. Indeed, as we have seen when Liszt composed his first Lieder, he had specific voices in mind, interpreters with 'exceptional voices'. So it is possible that Liszt kept to the practice of having a particular voice in mind when revising his Lieder but simply modelled the revisions around a voice that was less physically exceptional. Moreover, as it is well documented that Genast was consulted by Liszt with regard to the vocal parts not only of *Die Legende von Heiligen Elisabeth* but also his Lieder, it would not be unreasonable to assume that they were tailored, at least to some degree, to her voice.[92] And since she was renowned as a singer of Lieder and oratorio rather than opera, and she embodied many of the qualities that Liszt highly valued in a performer, it would not be surprising if he did see her as an ideal interpreter of his works. In addition, as Liszt was able to witness her performances of his Lieder he could then refine them accordingly.

Franz Götze (1814–88)

Franz Götze was a celebrated German lyric tenor. Initially a first violinist in the Weimar court orchestra (he had been a pupil of Louis Spohr), Götze was the principal tenor in the Weimar theatre between 1836 and 1852. Interestingly, Götze was self-trained as a singer, but after finding some initial success in Weimar and taking on students including Rosa Agthe (later von Milde) he consulted with Manuel Garcia, the famous vocal pedagogue and brother of Maria Malibran and Pauline Viardot.[93] Götze found that his own ideas were in accordance with Garcia's and that he had independently developed a similar approach to the training of the voice. Götze also believed that roles he had studied with Wilhelmine Schröder-Devrient when she performed in Weimar were important to his development. Indeed, he credited her with improving his acting and dramatic singing.[94] During his time in Weimar Götze performed numerous roles in works by Gluck, Mozart, Beethoven, and, under Liszt, Wagner's *Lohengrin* and *Tannhäuser*. In 1853 Götze left Weimar, joined the Leipzig Opera, and began a successful teaching career at the Leipzig Conservatory. Götze

---

[91] Letter to Franz Brendel, 25 January 1860, in *Letters of Franz Liszt*, ed. La Mara, vol. 1, letter 232, p. 423.

[92] Hamburger, *Franz Liszts Briefe an Emilie Merian-Genast*, pp. 146–8; Klára Hamburger, 'Emilie (Merian)-Genast, Liszt's Confidante', *The Hungarian Quarterly*, 189 (2008), 163–9 (pp. 164–6).

[93] Johann Christian Lobe, 'Ein deutscher Gesangsmeister', *Die Gartenlaube*, 20 (1880), 324–7 (pp. 324–5).

[94] Ibid., pp. 324–7. The article does not state when Götze performed with Schröder-Devrient; however, she performed several roles in Weimar between 1842 and 1843 so it is assumed that this is when the collaborations took place. Roles performed by Schröder-Devrient in Weimar during the period included Desdemona in Rossini's *Othello*, Leonore/Fidelio in Beethoven's *Fidelio*, Iphigenia in Gluck's *Iphigenia in Aulis*, Lucrezia Borgia in Donizetti's *Lucrezia Borgia*, Maria in Grétry's *Raoul Barbe-bleue*, Rebecka in Marschner's *Der Templer und die Jüdin*, and Romeo in Bellini's *I Capuleti e i Montecchi*.

was the first singer of note to support Liszt's songs publicly and the composer in return was highly appreciative. Furthermore, he entreated Götze to perform two of his songs at a concert in Leipzig in 1857:

> Dear Friend,
>
> In consequence of an invitation of the directors, I shall have the honour of having several of my works performed at the concert on the 26th February for the Orchestral Pension Fund in Leipzig, and very much wish that you would do me the kindness of singing two of my songs ('Kling leise, mein Lied' and 'Englein du mit blondem Haar'), to rejoice the public with your ardent and beautifully artistic rendering of these little things. Fraulein Riese is so good as to bring you the new edition of my six first songs (amongst which is the 'Englein' in A major) – a couple more numbers will shortly follow. Grant me my request, dear friend, and rest assured beforehand of the best thanks, with which I remain,
>
> Yours in most sincere friendship,
>
> F. Liszt.[95]

It is worth noting that Liszt made a point of keeping Götze up to speed with new editions of his Lieder. Later in 1860, near the publication of the first edition of the *Gesammelte Lieder*, Liszt was anxious to make sure that Götze received a copy of the revised versions (no doubt so that he could continue to champion the songs in their most recent incarnations). As Götze was by this stage an influential teacher at the Leipzig Conservatory, Liszt may have also hoped that Götze would pass on his enthusiasm for his Lieder to subsequent generations of talented singers:

> I cannot quite remember whether I sent Götze a copy of my songs. Please ask him, and if I have not yet done so let me know. Götze has a special claim to them, for in earlier years he had the courage to sing several of my nonentities – and I will see that he has a copy at once.[96]

Although there are surprisingly few accounts describing Götze's voice in any detail, from the esteem in which he was held, and substantial number and variety of roles he performed, he must have been a tenor of the first rank. A retrospective on the singer written by composer and theorist Johann Christian Lobe published in *Die Gartenlaube* in 1880 offers one brief description. Götze's voice is described as 'not powerful, but as pleasant as I have ever heard in lyric roles or soulful Lieder recitals'.[97] Rena Charnin Mueller claims that 'much of the Heft VII of the *Gesammelte Lieder* is tailored to the superior vocal qualities of Franz Götze'; therefore, a few

---

[95] Letter to Franz Götze, 1 February 1857. *Letters of Franz Liszt*, ed. La Mara, vol. 1, letter 174, pp. 316–17.

[96] Letter to Franz Brendel, 25 January 1860. *Letters of Franz Liszt*, ed. La Mara, vol. 1, letter 232, p. 423.

[97] Lobe, 'Ein deutscher Gesangsmeister'. 'Seine Stimme gehörte nicht zu den mächtigen, aber zu den sympathischen, wie ich sie im bewunderungswürdigen Cantabile lyrischen Rollen und in seelenvollen Liedervorträgen schöner nie gehört habe.' Translation is my own.

attributes of Götze as a singer can be gleaned by examining the songs within Heft VII. In Charnin Mueller's estimation these songs demand:

> a singer with Bel Canto training and an uncommon ease in changing registers, an ability to summon gradations in tone colour within a phrase, and a fearless top register. Yet more is required than this, for Liszt intended these songs for an interpreter of uncommon talent in savouring the text and delivering the sense of the word, albeit within a small vehicle, as if this were part of an operatic continuum.[98]

Götze was also known to have performed Liszt's *Tre sonnetti di Petrach* to great acclaim. In their first incarnation, these are among the most difficult works for voice in the entire song literature. The later versions were not published until the 1880s, so it can be assumed that Götze performed the first versions of these songs, which were first published in 1846.[99] They demand not only power and flexibility in the voice but also a large range and an ability to manage the contrasts between the dramatic outbursts and beatific lyricism convincingly.

Hans Feodor von Milde (1821–99) and Rosa von Milde-Agthe (1827–1906)

Hans Feodor von Milde and Rosa von Milde-Agthe were husband and wife opera singers based in Weimar. Hans was born in Austria and trained by Manuel Garcia in Paris. In 1845 Hans embarked on an operatic career and moved to Weimar where he would remain for the rest of his forty-year career.[100] Rosa was born into a musical family in Weimar and was trained by Franz Götze. She made her operatic debut in Weimar in 1848 singing the title role in Spohr's *Jessonda*. Hans and Rosa married in 1851 and often performed together in Weimar opera productions. They were associated with performing works of the New German School, especially the works of Wagner. In Weimar, they sang the roles of Tungsten and Elisabeth in *Tannhäuser* and Telamund and Elsa at the premiere of *Lohengrin*. Other joint appearances in Weimar included performances of Berlioz's *Benvenuto Cellini*, the premiere of Schubert's *Alfonso und Estrella*, and Cornelius's *Der Barbier von Bagdad* and *El Cid*.[101] Given that both singers were trained in similar methods, by Manuel Garcia and Franz Götze respectively, and that both were associated with the New German School, it seems that both combined the dramatic requirements of the German school with the vocal flexibility and tone quality of the *bel canto* voice. The von Mildes were also regular performers at Liszt's Sunday matinées, and so would have helped Liszt craft his Lieder either through consultation or by simply affording the composer opportunity to experiment with his works.[102]

---

[98] Rena Charnin Mueller, 'The Lieder of Liszt', in *Cambridge Companion to the Lied*, p. 173.

[99] Franz Liszt, *Tre sonetti del Petrarca*, S. 270/LW N. 14.1 (Vienna: Haslinger, 1846).

[100] Elizabeth Forbes, 'Milde, Hans (Feodor) von', *Grove Music Online*, 2001 [accessed 30 August 2018].

[101] Ibid.

[102] Alan Walker, *Reflections on Liszt* (Ithaca, NY: Cornell University Press, 2005), p. 151; Susan Youens, 'Heine, Liszt, and the Song of the Future', in *Franz Liszt and His World*, p.

It is not possible to make the definitive assertion that the von Mildes had a direct influence on Liszt's compositional aesthetics. And it could be argued, rather than their influencing him, that his aesthetics simply drew him towards those singers whose views and artistic temperament he already shared. Of course, both situations could be true: Liszt was open to influence and regularly acknowledged his debt to many individuals and composers.

✤

Based on the discussion of the singers above, it would be reasonable to surmise that Liszt's early Lieder were, at least in part, a reflection of his own performing experiences. The early Lieder were not composed for a domestic setting or even the semi-public arena of the salon where they would be sung by capable amateurs. Instead, Liszt envisaged a large hall for their performance, by artists of the highest calibre in a programme that could feature music from a wide variety of genres. Viewed in this light, we can see that many of the criticisms which met these early Lieder were a function of Liszt's attempts to expand the boundaries of the genre, as he had done for piano music, rather than a failure to understand its conventions. Indeed, extreme virtuosity had not hampered the sales of his piano music, and so it seems that he simply misjudged the pliability of his audiences' horizons of expectations regarding Lieder.

During his Weimar period, he often collaborated with performers, taking advice from Joachim Raff regarding orchestration, Joseph Joachim when transcribing his works for violin, and, as mentioned, the mezzo-soprano Emilie Genast with regard to the vocal parts when revising many of his Lieder in the 1850s and 1860s – even though it is impossible to pin down where Liszt incorporated this advice. However, it should be noted that these consultations with other artists seem to have been mostly of a technical nature, as Liszt would strive to find the best form for his content.

One important aspect is that Liszt's concert experiences were drastically different from when he took up his position in Weimar. Firstly, monetary concerns no longer formed an integral part of the decision-making process, and therefore the programmes from the Weimar period onwards can be seen to be a greater reflection of Liszt artistic ideals, court theatre restrictions notwithstanding. Secondly, Liszt's activity was more varied, including rehearsing operatic and orchestral works, conducting duties, chamber music, and the administration of his musical salon in Weimar, where musical matinées took place every Sunday.[103] Therefore, it is clear to

---

71 n. 9; Maria Eckhardt and others, 'Franz Liszt', in *Grove Music Online*. These references do not cite the same level of documentary evidence regarding the von Mildes as they do regarding the previous singers highlighted. Due to the proximity and the length of time that the von Mildes were in contact with Liszt (both professionally and personally) there is the common assumption that they must have been an influence on his vocal writing.

[103] Pocknell, Haine, and Dufetel (eds), *Lettres des Franz Liszt à Princess Marie de Hohenlohe-Schillingsfürst, née de Sayn-Wittgenstein* (Belgium: Librairie Philosophique J. Vrin 2011), pp. 17–20. Princess Caroline's daughter, Princess Marie de Hohenlohe-Schillingsfürst, née de Sayn-Wittgenstein, was a key figure in the administration of these Sunday matinées,

see how Liszt's environment in Weimar, so markedly different than that of his virtuoso years, would have had a direct influence on his works.

Interestingly, as late as 1882 Liszt still looked to the example of Nourrit as an ideal interpreter of his songs:

> The same publisher will also publish my 3 Sonnets of Petrarch for voice, to which your charming drawing of the laurel of Petrarch and Laura will serve as an illustration – as it has already adorned the title of the piano version of the same sonnets, published 25 years ago. I endeavoured to complete the canto of these sonnets – and to make it as crystalline, transparent and adequate to poetry, as possible. If they meet a non-vulgar amoroso tenor, gifted with a certain idealism of the heart – perhaps they will find some success. I do not count on it however, knowing how rare such idealism is – especially among tenors, fond of the applause of the theatre. Occasionally, noble exceptions have been found – most notably Adolphe Nourrit and Schnorr. Both died quite young for their trouble![104]

Liszt here does not highlight any physical traits of the voice, but instead, focuses on temperament, as discussed earlier. By also mentioning Ludwig Schnorr von Carolsfeld – often regarded as an exemplar of the *Heldentenor* – in tandem with Nourrit, Liszt makes it clear he was not after a particular voice type, but rather a type of performer. He is implying that ideally singers of his Lieder should be of a sincere and idealistic nature, have intelligence, be cultured, and avoid display of a shallow or vulgar nature.

---

which, according to Nicolas Dufetel, were comparable to the finest Parisian salons of the time – in both the quality of the music and artists, and the elegant atmosphere and serious conversation, which boasted as many notable scientists as artists.

[104] Letter to Princess Carolyne, 15 August 1882. Franz Liszt, *Franz Liszt's Briefe*, ed. La Mara, 8 vols (Leipzig: Breitkopf & Härtel, 1905), vol. 7, pp. 353–4.

PART III

CHAPTER 5

A Selection Box of Fluid Texts: Contrasting Revision Processes in Three of Liszt's Lieder

∽

This chapter examines three of Liszt's Lieder that underwent revision, presenting a selection of the variety of ways in which the composer revised his settings. The three Lieder, 'Am Rhein, im schönen Strome', 'Ich möchte hingehn', and 'Es rauschen die Winde', all underwent revision in the early to mid-1850s. However, each of their individual journeys from initial version/conception to revised version is unique, as are the ways in which Liszt remodels or reuses his music. The revised versions are examined as evidence that Liszt's view of these works had changed in terms of a deeper understanding of their respective poems, as well as in terms of the nature of the genre, along with the intended performers and venue. These changes between versions are viewed as responses to both the reception of the early Lieder, changes in Liszt's personal situation, and as intertextual encounters – in one instance Liszt directly references/quotes the work of Wagner. All these, in turn, would have informed not only Liszt's evolving Lied aesthetic, but also his knowledge of his audience's horizon of expectations, and thus allowed him to gauge his audiences' responses better and tailor his revisions accordingly.

Revisions included those to the piano texture, the technical difficulty of the writing (for both performers), the vocal tessitura, the prosody, harmonic and motivic material, along with changes to the form. By exploring many facets of the textual fluidity between versions, rather than solely focusing on one element, such as the harmony, we are better able to glimpse into Liszt's compositional environment and see how his interactions with his contemporary society affected the development of his works.

A Case for the Surface Level: Parallel Lines in Liszt's 'Am Rhein, im schönen Strome'

'Am Rhein, im schönen Strome', set to a poem by Heinrich Heine (1797–1856) in 1841, is unusual among Liszt's songs and his oeuvre in general, not for existing in more than one published version, but rather because the first edition foregrounds Liszt's comfort with the concept of multiple versions of the same work to an unusual degree. This first edition (1843) contains an extended *ossia* in the piano part, which runs for the entire song's length, creating another version parallel to the first. In addition, the vocal part contains several bars in which the performer is given a second option. Thus, from this first edition alone it would be possible to assemble at least four separate performing versions. Moreover, soon after its initial publication, Liszt transcribed and published the Lied for solo piano.[1] The 1856 version, in contrast, contains only one *ossia* bar in the voice; it is, however, a radical *reworking* of the song that, while maintaining many of the harmonic and melodic elements of the first versions, departs in terms of texture, metre, dynamics, and pedalling – changes that impact the song's aural effect substantially.

This section contrasts two editions of 'Am Rhein, im schönen Strome', and the three versions contained therein. It explores the role that Liszt's use of non-chord tones and piano texture plays in shaping the character and the listening experience of each version. This is examined from a 'sonoristic' perspective, where an emphasis is placed on the work in its sounding form. When considered from this point of view, non-chord tones and changes in texture – features often considered subsidiary – are shown to be of vital importance. The rationale behind these revisions both in terms of performance implications and their relationship to the poem will be considered, along with Liszt's non-traditional attitude to the musical work.

By the time Liszt composed 'Am Rhein, im schönen Strome' in 1841, he and Heine were well-acquainted. They had first met in Paris in June 1831, shortly after Heine's arrival in the city, and although there was a considerable age gap between them (Heine was fourteen years Liszt's senior), they quickly struck up a friendship. During the early 1840s both artists were involved in supporting the drive to complete Cologne Cathedral, which features prominently in the Lied in question.[2] Liszt had also recently published his transcriptions of six of Schubert's Heine settings the previous year (1840). His settings of Heine's poems are among his most celebrated compositions in song form, and according to Susan Youens they are 'some of the best Heine songs of the century'.[3] 'Die Loreley' and 'Du bist wie eine Blume' are just two that have gained some popularity outside of Liszt circles. Liszt set seven of Heine's poems, all of which were published in at least two separate revised versions. 'Am Rhein, im schönen Strome' from 1841 is not only Liszt's earliest Heine setting, but also possibly his first Lied.[4] It was published in 1843, by Schlesinger of Berlin, as part of Liszt's first collection of Lieder, *Buch der Lieder*, whose reception

---

[1] Franz Liszt, *Buch der Lieder für piano allein*, 2 vols (Berlin: Schlesinger, 1844), I, S. 531 No.2/ LW A97 No.2.

[2] Heine would eventually distance himself from the project when he learned of King Friedrich Wilhelm's nationalistic aims. According to Susan Youens, 'Prussian king Friedrich Wilhelm IV had reactionary politico-religious reasons for underwriting the project.' Susan Youens, liner notes to *Liszt: The Complete Songs, Vol. 1*, Matthew Polenzani (tenor), Julius Drake (piano), Hyperion CDA67782, 2010, p. 8.

[3] Susan Youens, liner notes to, *Liszt: The Complete Songs Vol. 3*, Gerald Finley (baritone), Julius Drake (piano), Hyperion CDA67956, 2015, p. 5.

[4] By his own recollection, Liszt believed 'Kennst du das Land?' and 'Die Loreley' to have been written earlier, but according to Susan Youens, and the *Grove* catalogue, Liszt was mistaken in this regard. Susan Youens, liner notes to *Liszt: The Complete Songs, Vol. 1*; Maria Eckhardt, Rena Charnin Mueller, and Alan Walker, 'Liszt, Franz', *Grove Music Online*, 2001 [accessed 29 August 2018]. There is also an argument to consider 'Angiolin dal biondo crin' Liszt's first Lied, its being arguably his first song to conform to many of

was discussed in Chapter 3.[5] Liszt's *Buch der Lieder* draws its title from Heine's collection of poetry bearing the same name.

Heinrich Heine's *Buch der Lieder*

'Am Rhein, im schönen Strome' is a setting of the eleventh poem, from the *Lyrische Intermezzo* section of Heine's *Buch der Lieder*.[6] Heine did not give titles to the poems in this collection; they are simply numbered. The eleventh poem (beginning 'Im Rhein …') was arguably most famously set by Robert Schumann and is the sixth song of Schumann's celebrated *Dichterliebe*, op.48. Schumann's song cycle was composed in 1840, but not published until 1844.[7]

Heine's *Buch der Lieder* is itself an interesting fluid text. After its publication in 1827 there were four further revised editions published during Heine's lifetime, in 1837, 1839, 1841, and 1844.[8] Between the 1827 and the 1837 versions Heine made a small but significant revision to the first line of the eleventh poem: the 1826 version reads 'Im Rhein, im heiligen Strome', whereas the 1837 and subsequent versions read 'Im Rhein, im schönen Strome'. This change which was made by Heine has led more than one scholar to assume, ironically, that both Liszt (who uses 'schönen') and Schumann (who uses 'heiligen') had edited Heine's text. However, it seems more likely that they worked from different editions of the *Buch der Lieder*, or that they simply chose the version of the text that best suited their own purposes.[9]

---

the common attributes of the genre; however, as it was set to an Italian text that was then translated, it would be difficult to sustain the argument that it is a 'true' Lied.

5   Franz Liszt, *Buch der Lieder*: 'Loreley,' 'Am Rhein,' 'Mignon,' 'Der König von Thule,' 'Der du von dem Himmel bist,' 'Angiolin/Englein' (Berlin: Schlesinger, 1843).

6   Heinrich Heine, *Buch der Lieder* (Hamburg: Hoffman und Campe, 1827, 1837, 1839, 1841, 1844).

7   As the relationship between Liszt and Schumann was still cordial in this period it is conceivable that Liszt was acquainted with Schumann's setting before composing his own. For more on the relationship between Liszt and the Schumanns, see Alan Walker, *Reflections on Liszt* (Ithaca, NY: Cornell University Press, 2005), pp. 40–50.

8   While 1826 was the first publication of Heine's *Buch der Lieder*, the poem 'Im Rhein' was first published in 1822 in *Rheinisches Unterhaltungsblatt* under its then title of 'Der Gruß des Engels'. It was later included in *Tragödien nebst einem lyrischen Intermezzo* published in 1823. Given that Liszt named his first collection of Lieder *Buch der Lieder*, he most likely first encountered 'Im Rhein' in its revised edition from 1837.

9   James Jolly, interview with James Gilchrist regarding his recording of *Dichterliebe*, *Gramophone*,<www.gramophone.co.uk> Jan 13th 2016 [accessed 21 December 2020], 'If the first four songs of the cycle maintain a tone of happiness filtered through memory, the second four see despair setting in — in "Im Rhein, im heiligen Strome", as Gilchrist points out, Schumann even changes Heine's words. "Im Rhein, im schönen [beautiful] Strome" is what Heine wrote, as set delightfully by Liszt, but Schumann's has "heiligen [holy] Strome", and this more serious, darker word chimes with the bell-like motifs and gothic architecture of the song — stamping out all hope. As time goes by, my interpretation of this song gets darker and darker'; Alan Walker, 'Liszt and the Lied', in *Reflections on Liszt*, p. 164: 'Incidentally the first line of Heine's poem runs "Im Rhine, im heiligen Strome", a reference to the "holy river." Liszt changed that all-important phrase to "Im Rhein, im

Table 5.1 Heinrich Heine 'Im Rhein, im heiligen/schönen Strome'.

Im/Am Rhein, im (heiligen/schönen) Strome,	In/On the Rhine, in the (holy/beautiful) river,
Da spiegelt sich in den Wellen,	There is reflected in the waves,
Mit seinem großen Dome,	With its great cathedral,
Das große, das heil'ge Köln.	Great and holy Cologne.
Im Dom da steht ein Bildnis,	In the cathedral hangs a picture,
Auf goldnem Leder gemalt;	Painted on gilded leather;
In meines Lebens Wildnis	Into my life's wilderness
Hat's freundlich hineingestrahlt.	It has cast its friendly rays.
Es schweben Blumen und Englein	Flowers and cherubs hover
Um unsre liebe Frau;	Around our beloved Lady;
Die Augen, die Lippen, die Wängelin,	Her eyes, her lips, her cheeks
Die gleichen der Liebsten genau.	Are the image of my love's.

Translation by Richard Stokes.

There is, however, a minor change in the text of Liszt's first editions of the 1843 and 1859 versions (presumably made by the composer). Instead of 'Im Rhein', the song is titled 'Am Rhein' or 'Am Rhein, im schönen Strome', and the first word of the song's first line is also accordingly changed from 'im' to 'am', a seemingly small distinction that most singers ignore when performing the song. The current tradition in both scholarly literature and performance to call the song 'Im Rhein, im schönen Strome' seems not to have originated with Liszt, but may stem from the version edited by Eugen d'Albert that printed both the song's title and opening line as 'Im Rhein, im schönen Strome'.[10] As d'Albert had been a pupil of Liszt, and his edition was published by C.F. Kahnt, who also published Liszt, this edition would have been seen as authoritative. This change, presumably by d'Albert, was adopted by the 1921 Breitkopf & Härtel edition of the songs which printed both the song's title and opening line (in both versions) as 'Im Rhein, im schönen Strome', further cementing the change in title.[11] I have chosen to refer to the song by Liszt's given title in the first editions (Am …) and to the poem by Heine as (Im …). As soon as one hears the opening measures of the *ossia* version its significance becomes clear, as Liszt's intention is to create a tone picture depicting the flowing Rhine and on

schönen Strome", which refers to the "beautiful river." Was this deliberate, or did Liszt's memory play him false? It is almost as if the Catholic Liszt had decided to secularize the poem before allowing Heine to draw his profane connection.' These examples serve as a reminder of the pitfalls that may befall the scholar who fails to consider the textual fluidity of their sources.

[10] Franz Liszt, *20 ausgewählte Lieder*, ed. Eugen d'Albert (Leipzig: C.F. Kahnt, 1908), p. 56.

[11] Franz Liszt, *Musikalische Werke* (Leipzig: Breitkopf & Härtel, 1921), VII.I, pp. 20; Franz Liszt, *Musikalische Werke* (Leipzig: Breitkopf & Härtel, 1921), VII.II, p. 37.

its reflecting surface Cologne cathedral.[12] Liszt's small change may be an attempt to infuse as much meaning as possible in to the Lied by giving the opening two words more than one meaning – as in, 'at the Rhine' or 'on [the banks of] the Rhine,' and quite literally reflecting *on* its surface.

Liszt's 'Am Rhein, im schönen Strome'

Liszt's 1841 setting is in a hybrid of modified strophic and through-composed form, in contrast to the strophic form of three quatrains in the poem. There are minor musical differences between settings of the first and second verse, while the third verse has more dramatic change, through extensive modulations and large crescendos, but a unity is maintained by maintaining the consistent arpeggio pattern and a motivic relationship with the first verse. This creates an AA′ B form with an extended coda for piano solo. Liszt uses this form to reflect the change in mood created by the last line of the poem. The first two quatrains depict the poet's enchantment with the Rhineland, the cathedral, and its art.[13] However, this mood is undercut at the end, as Heine associates the picture of the Madonna with the protagonist's beloved and thus profanes the sublime imagery with more earthly associations. This form is consistent among all three versions of the song – the two from 1841 and one from 1856. Thus, all of Liszt's settings of the poem musically reflect the third stanza's change in mood through their form and texture. They are an example of one of the many ways that Liszt avoided slavishly following the strophic form of a text if the content did not merit such a setting. It is worth stating that, on this point, Liszt diverges sharply from the more traditional aesthetic that maintained it was for the performer to vary the mood of each stanza through subtle inflection and that it was not the composer's task to rewrite the music for every stanza of a strophic text.[14]

The *ossia* of 'Am Rhein' is an unusual feature that needs close examination. Many of Liszt's works contain *ossia* measures or sections, such as in the *Réminiscences de Norma* (LW A77/ S.394) or the first Paganini Étude (LW A52 No.1 /S.140 No.1), though these *ossias* are normally facilitations (easier options) printed in smaller type above the main part (see Figs 5.1 and 5.2). *Réminiscences de Norma*, which is

---

[12] 'Am Rhein', along with 'Loreley', and the song for male chorus he composed that year 'Rheinweinlied,' show Liszt making a concerted effort to create a German-friendly image, in consideration of the Rhineland dispute of the time. 'Rheinweinlied' is especially nationalistic, with the phrase 'der Rhein soll Deutsch verbleiben!' (The Rhine should remain German!) repeated enthusiastically numerous times.

[13] The picture in the poem refers to the retable by Stephan Lochner, situated behind the main altar of the Cathedral. Painted c. 1440–45, it depicts The Adoration of the Magi, when opened, and The Annunciation when closed.

[14] Carl Dahlhaus, *Nineteenth-Century Music*, trans. J. Bradford Robinson (Berkeley, Los Angeles: University of California Press, 1989), p. 98. Dahlhaus maintains that Goethe held the view that the accompaniment should only reflect the poem's overall mood and not follow every twist and turn of the text. Lorraine Byrne has shown that Goethe was, in musical outlook, a much more progressive figure than previously acknowledged. The main point, however, is not whether or not Goethe held this view, but rather that this more conservative viewpoint of the Lied was prevalent at the time.

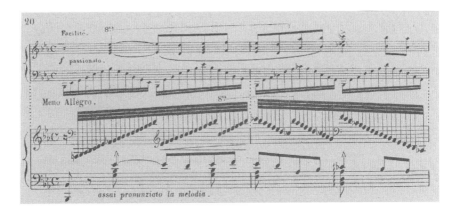

Figure 5.1. *Réminiscences de Norma*, Schott edition 1844 (bars 338–9).

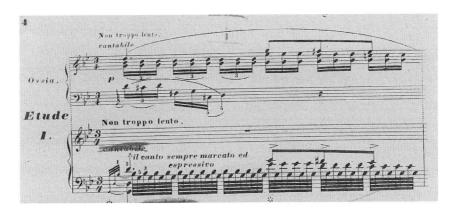

Figure 5.2. *Études d'exécution transcendante d'après Paganini*, no. 1,
Haslinger Edition 1840.

Figure 5.3. 'Am Rhein, im schönen Strome', Schlesinger 1843 (bars 5–8).

contemporaneous with 'Am Rhein, im schönen Strome', presents its *ossia* measures in this more traditional way, with a smaller type placed above the main part. By contrast, in 'Am Rhein' the *ossia* is placed below and in the first edition the size of type was unchanged, if a little more crowded (see Fig. 5.3). On first inspection, the Schlesinger edition of 'Am Rhein, im schönen Strome' may indeed appear to have printed the *ossia* on smaller notes. However, at that time Schlesinger employed a printing convention where shorter note values were printed with smaller note heads, and thus the *ossia* has the appearance of smaller type because of the preponderance of shorter note values. If notes of equal duration are compared between the *ossia* and the 'main version', they are clearly discernible as being the same size.

Other contemporaneous examples published by Schlesinger using this style of reflecting the note lengths with the size of note head include Théodore Kullak's *Grande Sonate* for piano, op. 7 (1842), Alexei Lvov's *Le Duel Divertimento*, op. 8, for piano trio (1842), and Guillaume Taubert's *Tour de Mazourka*, op. 52 (1844). Kullak's *Cavatine de Robert le Diable* (1843) employs it sporadically, but interestingly contains some extended facilitations in the right-hand part which are printed above the main part and in smaller type. This further attests to the proposition that Liszt did not wish to present the *ossia* to 'Am Rhein' as being of lesser importance.

This point of whether an edition uses smaller type or not may seem trivial, but its significance becomes clear when we examine Philip Friedheim's 1984 article on Liszt revisions from the *Music Review*.[15] Friedheim states that what he calls the alternate version (the *ossia*) is 'superior to the original' in terms of evoking both the meaning and the atmosphere of Heine's text even though it has been 'relegated to the small notes of the *ossia* version'.[16] Later editions such as the 1921 Breitkopf & Härtel edition do indeed present the *ossia* in a slightly smaller type, and so it is easy to understand why Friedheim would have considered this version 'relegated'. However, the first edition does not contain an *ossia* in a smaller type, so perhaps the two versions were considered of at least equal importance. Liszt was often concerned with presentation issues in publishing his music, and offered suggestions on these matters regularly, as evidenced by his correspondence with Heinrich Schlesinger. As such, the decision to print the two versions in parallel with the *ossia* below the 'main' version and in an equal-size type, can legitimately be thought of as concordant with Liszt's wishes.

A series of letters from June to September 1843 between Liszt and his publisher, Schlesinger, in the run-up to the publication of the *Buch der Lieder* reveal that both parties were very conscious of the difficulties contained within this collection and that there was a need to prepare some form of facilitation if the songs were to be readily performable to anyone bar seasoned performers. It is interesting to note how Liszt's opinion of this task changes over the course of four months. In June 1843 he wrote: 'I have already replied to you about the facilitation of the accompaniments to

---

[15]   Philip Friedheim, 'First Version, Second Version, Alternative Version: Some Remarks on the Music of Liszt', *The Music Review*, 44: 3/4 (August/November 1983), 194–202.

[16]   Ibid., p. 197.

the Lieder. –Kullak would do it excellently if he would be so kind.'[17] Later in the same letter Liszt gives instructions to add 'a facilitation in the vocal line to "Die Loreley" which you should print on the last page. The accompaniment remains exactly the same. The vocal line does not descend so low – in any case the original must stay as is already printed.'[18] This is important as it demonstrates that while Liszt would agree to add facilitations, his wish was to preserve the original thought. Later, on 11 August that same year, Liszt showed more reluctance to engage with the idea of having to create complete alternate versions for all his Lieder:

> With respect to the accompaniments to the Lieder you are quite right – but I am too lazy lazy [Liszt repeats the word for emphasis] to facilitate them – the most appropriate thing would be to get some pianist, Krüger, Stern or other to attempt an easier accompaniment to be appended as a second version. I have no patience for it.[19]

By 18/19 September Liszt seems to have abandoned the idea altogether: 'I am also now of the opinion to put off once more the facilitation of my Lieder.'[20] Being that 'Am Rhein' was possibly the first Lied that Liszt composed, it may be reasonable to assume that, when preparing to publish the collection, it was the first item to which he returned to create a facilitated version. More pertinently, it would have been the easiest item in the *Buch der Lieder* for which to create a facilitation, as the piano texture is so consistent throughout. It is also reasonable to assume that Liszt perceived the *ossia* version to be superior or at least preferable to the first version; when he came to transcribe the Lied for the solo piano version of the *Buch der Lieder*, he chose the *ossia* version and not the 'first version'. Although I accept the possibility that Liszt felt that the *ossia* version would simply work better as a solo piano piece rather than finding it also superior in song form, I would contend that the *ossia* is not only Liszt's preferred version but also the original version, not a relegation, and that in the first edition it is, at most, merely *presented* as an alternative.

The *ossia* is unusual for several reasons. Firstly, it is not a facilitation of the accompaniment, but rather a more difficult version. Secondly, as mentioned, it is placed below the staff, not above as is more common in Liszt's other *ossias*. Thirdly, it is a radical departure in terms of piano figuration. Finally, and as we will see, its use of non-chord tones along with the different figuration transform the aural experience of listening to the song considerably. Both 1841 versions use arpeggio figurations to depict the flowing water of the Rhine. This, among other things, offers us two separate ways in which Liszt chose to depict the familiar musical topic of a flowing river. However, in the *ossia* version the range and scale of these arpeggios is much wider, going from triplet quavers that span an octave, easily manageable within the hand and necessitating little adjustment of hand-position, to a three-octave range in semiquavers that necessitate

[17] Letter to Heinrich Schlesinger (dated as June 1843 by Michael Short). Michael Short (ed. and trans.), *Liszt Letters in the Library of Congress* (Hillsdale, NY: Pendragon Press, 2003), p. 25.

[18] Ibid., p. 25.

[19] Liszt is presumably referring to Willhelm Krüger (1820–83), a German pianist and composer. Short, *Liszt Letters in the Library of Congress*, p. 27.

[20] Ibid., pp. 28–30.

hand-crossing and quick changes of hand-position.[21] Liszt creates the four-note semi-quaver groups that make up the arpeggio figuration by adding non-chord tones: unaccented passing notes and appoggiaturas. These non-chord tones (NCTs) are mostly 9ths in relation to the root of the chord, but also occasionally appear as 6ths and 4ths. As the passage is undoubtedly intended to be performed while employing the damper pedal, chords with static non-functional 4ths, 6ths, and 9ths are created, a sonority that Susan Youens has likened to Debussy or Ravel.[22]

Sonoristics

Before looking at 'Am Rhein, im schönen Strome' in further detail, the theory or term 'sonoristics' should be more fully introduced.[23] In raising the topic of sono-risitics my aim is not to construct a strictly sonoristic reading of 'Am Rhein', but rather to use Józef Chomiński's concepts to highlight the importance of the difference in surface elements between versions of the song.[24] Not widely adopted in either English- or German-language musicology, sonoristics originated in Poland in the 1950s. It was developed by Chomiński through a series of articles and books as a branch of study that seeks to analyse and understand a work of music in its sounding form.[25] Initially devised as a method for analysing twentieth-century compositions, it has since become widely adopted in Polish musicology, and its concepts have also been applied to music from earlier periods. Chomiński's concept is diametrically opposite to schematic systems that seek to reveal the inner fundamental structure of a work. Instead, Chomiński's analysis of form does not necessarily point to the internal structure of a work but instead it is directed towards the surface.

---

[21] The third verse of the alternative version does contain some increasing difficulty, with hand-crossing, arpeggios of a larger span, and the introduction of tremolos. However, as these are still performed as triple quavers, they are quite manageable and they pale in comparison with the analogous section in the *ossia*.

[22] 'We hear his first setting of these words, composed in 1840, in which Liszt creates cascading water-music half a century before Debussy and Ravel made watery strains a hallmark of Impressionism in music.' Youens, liner notes to *Liszt: The Complete Songs, Vol. 1.*

[23] Sonoristics is an Anglicisation of the original Polish term, 'sonorystyka'. My understanding of 'sonoristics' is based upon Zbigniew Granat, 'Rediscovering "Sonoristics": A Groundbreaking Theory from the Margins of Musicology', in Zdravko Blažeković and Barbara Dobbs Mackenzie (eds), *Music's Intellectual History* (New York: Répertoire International de Littérature Musicale, 2009), pp. 821–33.

[24] Wallace Berry's method for examining texture in music in *Structural Functions of Music* would also meet this need well.

[25] Józef Chomiński, 'Z zagadnień techniki kompozytorskiej XX wieku' (Some Problems of Compositional Technique in the Twentieth Century), *Muzyka*, 1:3 (1956), 23–48; Józef Chomiński, 'Technika sonorystyczna jako przedmiot systematycznego szkolenia' (The Sonoristic Technique as the Subject of a Systematic Training), *Muzyka*, 6:3 (1961), 3–10; Józef Chomiński, 'Wkład kompozytorów polskich do rozwoju języka sonorystycznego' (The Contribution of Polish Composers to the Development of the Sonoristic Language), in E. Dziębowska (ed.), *Polska Współczesna Kultura Muzyczna 1944–1964* (Polish Contemporary Musical Culture 1944–1964) (Kraków: Polskie Wydawnictwo Muzyczne, 1968), 95–119; Józef Chomiński, *Muzyka Polski Ludowej* (The Music of People's Poland) (Kraków, 1968).

The term, which he coined in 1961, itself derives from Chomiński's own dissatisfaction with many of the pre-existing terms used to describe the timbral aspects of music, such as tone colour or colouristics. He maintained that because these terms express a visual aspect, they introduce an extraneous foreign element into the language when discussing elements such as timbre. For Chomiński, using the term 'sonoristics' was significant, as he sought to bring the focus back directly to the sound, and thus moved away from describing twentieth-century music in more conventional terms such as 'atonal', 'athematic', or 'noise' – with their perceived negative connotations of lacking something. Chomiński believed that twentieth-century composers, instead of focusing primarily on the functionality of chords, began to explore their purely timbral or surface qualities. As he said, cited in Zbigniew Granat's 'Rediscovering Sonoristics':

> Although an analyst may still discover in a composition the dominant-tonic relationships, the actual, sounding form of the work contains something more than its external tonal attire. There arise, from the specific elements of the harmonic or melodic type, sonoristic values.[26]

For Chomiński, sonorisitics constituted a new lens with which to view the musical work, one that was not focused on any one particular element of the music in question, but rather was concerned with how the many elements interact together. The list of elements examined in sonoristic analyses include not only timbre, texture, registers, articulation, dynamics and rhythm, but also both melody and harmony. However, to quote from Granat again, 'it is their interaction with other elements that generates sonoristic values.'[27] Chomiński divided sonoristics into the following five categories: sound technology, rationalisation of time, formation of horizontal and vertical structures, transformation of elements, and the formal continuum. Demonstrating how sonoristics can be applied to earlier music, Granat quotes Krzystof Penderecki, who describes a form of 'sonoristic listening':

> listening to a Čajkovskij [Tchaikovsky] symphony, putting aside its harmonic course and specific pitch content and concentrating solely on the development of instrumental sound: its timbre, dynamics, register, durations of individual tones, density, and width of the sound throughout the score, types of figurations in the strings, etc. It will become evident that this trajectory is in itself extremely interesting, rich, and altogether consciously composed. As an artistic value of the piece, it at times significantly surpasses its harmonic content – suffice it to compare it with the piano reduction alone. Of course, in Čajkovskij, these aspects are still closely connected, and the listening I have proposed … is an artificial manipulation. Nevertheless, it allows one to realize that the habits of sonic perception of music were developing long ago, though originally, they were grounded in strictly intervallic progressions.[28]

---

[26] Granat, 'Rediscovering Sonoristics', p. 822. Granat's article cites as its source, Jozef Chomiński, 'Ze studiow nad impresjonizmem Szymanowskiego' (1956) (Studies on Szymanowski's Impressionism), *Studia nad twórczością Karola Szymanowskiego* (Kraków: Polskie Widawnictwo Muzyczne, 1969), p. 193.

[27] Ibid., p.825.

[28] Ibid., p. 832.

Granat describes this type of listening as anachronistic, but equally:

> 'sonoristic hearing' is also highly rewarding, for, by breaking away with the estab-
> lished manner of listening and opening one's ears to the intricacies of a composi-
> tion in its actual sounding form, one becomes capable of discovering an entirely
> new aspect of the music in question.[29]

As stated, in introducing sonoristics, the aim was not a rigid application of the five
categories as outlined by Chomiński. Instead, it was to advocate applying a form of
'sonoristic hearing' to the revisions of Liszt's Lieder – that is, to draw attention to
those intricacies of the composition that are already considered vital in performance
practice but are often relegated to a subordinate position in musicological and analytical studies: dynamics, articulation, and texture. I will, however, use the sonoristic
concepts of 'horizontal and vertical structures'.[30]

With this in mind, it is fruitful to conceive of Liszt's *ossia* to 'Am Rhein' in a sonoristic way, namely, to focus on the difference that the surface elements make to the
experience of listening to a performance of the song. By conceiving of the arpeggios
of 'Am Rhein' in sonoristic terms, the non-chord tones (NCTs) and change of texture assume a much greater importance as their effect on the aural experience of the
listener is significant. Clearly Liszt put a large emphasis on the sound itself, and even
though Chomiński considered the French Impressionists as the first emancipators
of sound, in this capacity we can link Liszt to Debussy and Ravel not only aurally, but
also conceptually. The main point is that, by preparing two versions of the accompaniment where the main differences are textural or surface features, Liszt has created
two versions of the same song of which a comparative analysis solely based on a
traditional method of harmonic reduction would not capture the essence of what
separates the two versions.

The range of notes in the *ossia* is much larger than it is in the alternative version,
which I will refer to as the 'facilitation', and they surround the singer's voice with a
range that extends far above and below the vocal tessitura. The repetition of NCTs
also adds much more harmonic colour, as these are sustained throughout each bar
by the pedal and repeated with every change of octave in the piano part. With that in
mind, it is reasonable to consider the NCTs as actually part of the harmony or, more
accurately, and to employ the sonoristic term, they are part of the vertical structures
and thus have both the traditional ornamental function as well as a sonoristic one.
These differences in the *ossia* version paint a much more vivid tone picture and are
able to imbue each new harmony with more subtle inflections.

---

[29] Ibid.

[30] Chomiński uses this term to define the 'sound objects' that would replace the traditional
harmonic or melodic constructs of the tonal composer. Although these are very general
terms, Granat explains their usefulness with reference to the tone clusters in Penderecki's
Anaklasis. By describing the clusters using these terms versus attempting to use more
traditional descriptions such as chords, which would add the perception of a 'selectivity'
in the pitch material which they do not possess, our attention is drawn to the clusters'
sounding form.

Figure 5.4. 'Am Rhein', 1843 version; vertical structures *Ossia*
and 'facilitation' (bars 5–11).

Indeed, Liszt uses the same NCT addition to each harmony for each change of register, implying that he has chosen each NCT for its specific timbral qualities. For example, at the opening of the song the NCT added is a 9th which creates an instability that is only partly resolved by the end of the first verse, where the chosen NCT is a 6th. Describing the changes between the versions (especially between the two early versions) in a sonoristic way is a more accurate way of depicting the revisions than relying on more traditional methods such as a harmonic reduction or a Schenkerian graph. In a Schenkerian taxonomy, the *ossia* version would not even be considered a separate version, as the first move in any traditional harmonic reduction or preparation of a Schenkerian graph is to remove the NCTs – the very points of interest we are trying to analyse. Clearly then, these are not the correct analytical tools with which to tackle this problem. This is in no way meant to imply that these forms of analysis do not have a value, but rather that for this purpose they are not best suited.

Instead, it is more illuminating to graph the vertical structures of the piece (see Figure 5.4 above). As the music in question is tonal, this bears a close resemblance to a traditional harmonic reduction, but with several important distinctions. Firstly, all the NCTs are included, as this is fundamental to understanding the difference between sounding form and functional harmony. Secondly, the vertical structure graph also preserves the register at which all the notes are sounded, and finally, it does not dispense with notes that have been doubled. When this sort of graph is prepared between the two early versions, more of the huge sonic difference between the versions is preserved (although much information is still lost, such as the rhythmic differences and the varying rates of decay of the individual notes).

Comparison between the 1843 and 1856 versions

The main differences between the two early versions and the 1856 version are in keeping within the general trend of Liszt's revisions in the 1850s, which include a thinning out of the arpeggio textures, the introduction of a counter-motif to the main melody, much more variety of texture, and more passages of solo voice interpolated with subtle piano interjections in the later stages of the song (see Example 5.1). The level

Example 5.1. 'Am Rhein, im schönen Strome' (third version),
Schlesinger 1856 (bars 3–8).

of difficulty in the piano part of the 1856 version has also been greatly reduced when compared to the *ossia* version of 1843, while the piano solo coda has been reduced from 16 bars to just five. Another interesting alteration is the time signature which has been changed from ¾ in the 1843 versions to § in the 1856 version. However, this change looks more drastic on the page than in its actual aural effect, as the earlier versions begin with two-bar hyper-measures, which can give a § feel to the Lied in any case. This, of course, does depend on the sensitivity of the performers to notice the hyper-measures and in turn choose to bring them out in an audible fashion.

Liszt often chooses to depart from the main texture in the 1856 version for the purposes of tone painting. For example, when setting the words 'das große, das heil'ge Köln', Liszt uses large eight-note *ff* chords which are de-synchronized and spread over three octaves, giving a suitable sense of magnitude. Likewise, when setting 'Es schweben Blumen und Englein um unsre liebe Frau' (see Example 5.2), Liszt transfers both hands to the upper register of the piano and introduces a cross-rhythm, which envelopes the vocal line in an ethereal texture, closely matching both the content and mood of the line.

Liszt in the 1856 version used a variety of textures for expressive and illustrative purposes, rather than settling on a texture that would be consistent throughout the setting and relying on modulation as the primary means of expression. He also employs more expression marks, differentiated dynamics between the voice and

Example 5.2. 'Am Rhein, im schönen Strome' (third version),
Schlesinger 1856 (bars 28–32).

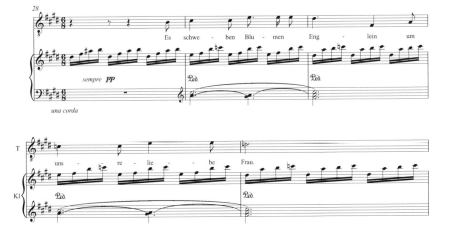

Example 5.3 'Am Rhein, im schönen Strome' (third version),
Schlesinger 1856 (bars 34–43).

the piano part, and introduces descriptions ('etwas zurückhaltend') and commands ('der Stimme folgend').

By comparing the differences between the two 1843 versions and the 1856 version we can see that Liszt employed two different revision strategies. It is not necessary to establish definitively which of the two earlier versions was composed first, the *ossia* or the 'facilitation', to recognise that the relationship between them falls into a grey area between that of a recomposition and a variant. Indeed, although on first appearances one seems to be a recomposition of the other, the relationship could just as accurately be described as that of a variant, albeit an extreme one. As the change in piano texture is significant enough to classify the *ossia* as a separate version and no two bars are the same between the *ossia* and the facilitation, it would seem logical to term the relationship a recomposition. However, there is an element of interchangeability between the versions that brings the relationship back to that of a variant. By using the term interchangeability, it is not the intention to imply that there are not significant differences between the versions and that they should be considered the same version, but rather that it would be possible to substitute music seamlessly from one version to the next. However, this would not be recommended bar to bar, but instead only in large sections – hence my assertion that the relationship between the versions falls into a grey area. An example of this is shown in a performance by tenor Ben Bliss and pianist Lachlan Glen, Bruno Walter Auditorium, 4 April 2014, where the 'facilitation' accompaniment is performed for the first verse of the Lied, after which Glen switches to the *ossia* version for the rest of the performance. By citing this performance, this is not to advocate that performances should switch between versions, but merely to highlight that it is musically feasible to do so without the result descending into farce.

The relationship between the early versions and the 1856 version, on the other hand, is of a different order altogether. By changing the metre, introducing more variety in the piano texture, counter-motifs, and removing some word repetition, Liszt created a version that could in no way be confused with either of the earlier versions, and one in which music from those earlier versions could not be interchanged without the results being much more musically jarring. As will be discussed in Chapter 7 in further detail, the reduction in difficulty between the *ossia* and the 1856 version suggests that Liszt had also changed his perception of who the intended performers of his Lieder should be, and in what type of setting or venue they were to be performed.

In drawing attention to this way of perceiving the surface elements of a piece, the intention is not to reject other perspectives. Rather, it is a call to highlight the importance of elements that have often been considered trivial, but may in fact open up novel avenues of enquiry when considered as vital elements of a work. This approach could be applied to a wide range of the Liszt repertoire and beyond. It is a useful critical approach with which to analyse the differences between versions, as Liszt regularly retains those elements that are often considered defining in single-version pieces, namely, the harmonic outline and melodies. Sonoristic listening reminds us that surface elements inform our reaction to musical works much more than we realise and can be as influential as those elements often considered to be 'fundamental'.

'Ich möchte hingehn'

'Ich möchte hingehn' is an exception in this book, as it was published only once during Liszt's lifetime. So it may seem strange to include it in a study focused on textual fluidity. However, its number in the Searle catalogue (S.296iii) reveals that this published version was in fact only one of at least three versions that Liszt had prepared. By exploring the compositional development of the song and investigating the rationale behind Liszt's insertion of a single bar late into the (re)compositional process, a greater sense of meaning can be derived from the Lied, and thus also highlighting the value of knowing a composition's textual history.

'Ich möchte hingehn' has been the subject of a considerable amount of discussion in Liszt studies. It was composed in 1844 to a poem by Georg Herwegh (1817–75), but not published until 1859 as the final song in the sixth volume of Liszt's *Gesammelte Lieder* by Schlesinger of Berlin.[31] Alan Walker has likened the song, with it its weariness, to a foretaste of the world of Mahler's *Das Lied von der Erde* and 'Ich bin der Welt abhanden gekommen'.[32] Walker proposes that the song's origins lie with Liszt's ill-fated affair with Caroline Saint-Criq, which 'threw the young Liszt into despair and precipitated a nervous breakdown'.[33] And indeed, Liszt's letter to Carolyne Sayn-Wittgenstein on 12 April 1851 shows that there may indeed be a connection: he recounts to Carolyne that he had written in red crayon on the manuscript that 'this Lied is my testament of youth'.[34] The song was composed in 1844, shortly after Liszt and Caroline Saint-Criq met again that year for the first time in fourteen years after their agonising split over ten years previously. It would be the last time that they saw each other.

Unfortunately, most of the discussion surrounding the song has been limited to a single bar (bar 125) out of the 163 that comprise the composition. 'Ich möchte hingehn' had been an extremely obscure song, generally not mentioned in any Liszt scholarship until Peter Raabe claimed in 1931 that Liszt had already presented 'this progression ten years before Wagner had penned a note of Tristan'. The subsequent debate between Liszt and Wagner scholars – determined to answer the question 'who got there first?' – has unfortunately dominated most of the scholarship on the song since.[35] Although it may now seem strange that the relative stature of each composer would depend directly on the outcome of this question, the heated nature of

---

31   Volume 6 of Liszt's *Gesammelte Lieder* was the last to be published by Schlesinger. A further two volumes (7 and 8) were published by Kahnt of Leipzig, along with reissues of Volumes 1–6. 'Ich möchte hingehn', 'strophen aus der Fremde', in *Gedichte eines lebendigen*, 2 vols (Zürich and Winterthur: Verlag des Literarischen Comptoirs, 1841, 1843), vol. 1, pp. 100–101.

32   Walker, *Reflections on Liszt*, p. 153.

33   Ibid.

34   Franz Liszt, *Franz Liszt's Briefe*, ed. La Mara, 8 vols (Leipzig: Breitkopf & Härtel, 1889), vol. 4, p. 89.

35   Franz Liszt, *Franz Liszt Musikalische Werke VII Lieder und Gesänge*, 3 vols, ed. Peter Raabe (Leipzig: Breitkopf & Härtel, 1921), II, p. XII.

Example 5.4. 'Ich möchte hingehn' (first published version),
Schlesinger 1859 (bars 123–6).

the discussion between the camps is testament to the amount of investment scholars on both sides of the debate have had in this notion.

Rena Charnin Mueller's invaluable investigation into Liszt manuscripts has all but conclusively revealed that Liszt could not have penned the bars in question before 1856, as it was a paste-over close to the time of publication and on a type of paper that Liszt did not use before that date (see Example 5.5). Thus, the window of opportunity for Liszt to have anticipated Wagner is much narrower than Raabe claimed.[36] Mueller concluded that it was more likely that the *Tristan* material was a quotation from Wagner, not the reverse, and that Raabe's proclamation was incorrect.[37] However, as Alan Walker points out, if scholars are keen to prove Liszt 'got there first', they would be best served by looking at the opening measures of 'Die Loreley', which did undeniably tread similar musical ground to the opening of *Tristan und Isolde* three years before Wagner.[38] Regardless of who got there first, it was in Wagner's hands that this material created seismic shocks throughout the musical world. That said, it was in Liszt's hands, as we shall see, that the 'Tristan' chord went beyond having a purely musical function and became a personal signifier able to draw intertextual links between Liszt's own life and the works of Wagner, Herwegh, and Schopenhauer.

A most welcome addition to the discussion on this song was Alexander Rehding's article 'TriZtan', which moved matters beyond the textual debate to investigate how these bars function within the song.[39] Indeed, in investigating the origins of these bars and why Liszt inserted them into the song shortly before publication, Rehding

---

[36] Rena Charnin Mueller, 'Liszt's Tasso Sketchbook: Studies in Sources and Revisions' (PhD diss., New York University, 1986), pp. 121 and 382.

[37] Ibid., pp. 122–3.

[38] Walker, *Reflections on Liszt*, pp. 160–61.

[39] Alexander Rehding, 'TrisZtan: Or the case of Liszt's "Ich möchte hingehn"', in Jim Samson and Bennett Zon (eds), *Nineteenth-Century Music: Selected Proceedings from the Tenth International Conference* (Aldershot: Ashgate 2002), pp. 75–97.

focuses on the poet Herwegh, who in the early 1850s was close friends with both Liszt and Wagner. Indeed, it was Herwegh who introduced Wagner to the writings of Schopenhauer.[40] Wagner expressed his newly acquired enthusiasm for the philosopher in a letter to Liszt dated 29 September 1854. Interestingly, in the same letter Wagner mentions that he has just begun to conceive of a work based on the myth of Tristan and Isolde:

> This is Arthur Schopenhauer, the greatest philosopher since Kant, whose thoughts, as he himself expresses it, he has thought out to the end … His chief idea, the final negation of the desire of life, is terribly serious, but it shows the only salvation possible. To me of course that thought was not new, and it can indeed be conceived by no one in whom it did not pre-exist, but this philosopher was the first to place it clearly before me … I have in my head Tristan and Isolde, the simplest but most full-blooded musical conception; with the 'black flag' which floats at the end of it, I shall cover myself to die.[41]

Later, writing in *My Life*, Wagner cites Herwegh as being an important figure for developing his own understanding on several points.

> In the tranquillity and stillness of my house I now became acquainted with a book, the study of which was to assume vast importance for me. This was Arthur Schopenhauer's *The World as Will and Idea*. Herwegh told me about this book … Actually it was Herwegh who made me reflect further on my own feelings with a well timed word. This insight into the essential nothingness of the world of appearances, he contended, lies at the root of all tragedy, and every great poet, and even every great man, must necessarily feel it intuitively.[42]

Rehding explored the 'Schopenhauerian sentiment' that pervades Herwegh's poem and the personal links between Herwegh, Wagner, and Liszt. Therefore, when Liszt inserts a brief 'quotation' from *Tristan und Isolde* into the sixth verse it seems natural.[43] It may also be a case of Liszt discovering the Schopenhauerian origins of the poem after he had composed the first version, and then deciding to include the quotation in order to link the song to a wider set of ideas, as *Tristan* was more widely known to have been inspired by Schopenhauer. Indeed, the quotation serves to make clear the mode of interpretation that explains the unrelenting bleakness of the poem.

There are many 'Tristanesque' elements that were pre-existing in the song before Liszt added the 'quotation', such as the opening yearning-like motif, and the wandering tonality replete with enharmonic changes and chromatic modulations. 'Ich möchte hingehn' is set in a through-composed form, with the yearning motif returning between stanzas, which change key and texture throughout. Interestingly, as Rehding observes,

---

[40] Richard Wagner, *My Life*, ed. Mary Whittall, trans. Andrew Gray (New York: Da Capo Press, 1992); originally *Mein Leben* (Munich: Paul List Verlag, 1963), p. 508.

[41] Francis Hueffer (ed. and trans.), *Correspondence of Wagner and Liszt*, 2 vols (New York: Charles Scribner's Sons, 1897), vol. 2, letter 168, p. 53.

[42] Wagner, *My Life*, pp. 508–10.

[43] As Rehding points out ('TrisZtan', p. 79), Liszt's chord is not in fact an exact copy of the 'Tristan' chord.

Table 5.2. 'Ich möchte hingehn' (1841) – Georg Herwegh (1817–75).

Ich möchte hingehn wie das Abendrot
Und wie der Tag in/[mit] seinen letzten
  Gluten –
O leichter, sanfter, ungefühlter Tod!
Mich in den Schoß des Ewigen verbluten.
	I would like to pass on like the sunset
	And like the day with its last
	  glowing –
	Oh light, gentle, imperceptible death
	To bleed myself out into the bosom of eter-
	  nity!

Ich möchte hingehn wie der heitre Stern, Im vollsten Glanz, in ungeschwächtem Blinken, So still und schmerzlos möchte gern Ich in des Himmels blaue Tiefe sinken.	I would like to pass on like the bright star In the full glow, in undimmed twinkling, So quietly and painlessly would I gladly Sink into the deep blue of heaven!

Ich möchte hingehn wie der Blume Duft,
Die freudig sich dem schönen Kelch
  entringet
Und auf dem Fittig blütenschwangrer Luft
Als Weihrauch auf des Herrn Altar sich
  schwinget.
	I would like to pass on like the scent of a flower
	That joyfully wrings itself from the beautiful
	  calyx,
	And on the wings of blossom-laden breezes
	Swings itself aloft to the Lord's altar as
	  incense.

Ich möchte hingehn wie der Tau im Tal,
Wenn durstig ihm des Morgens Feuer winken;
O wollte Gott, wie ihn der
  Sonnenstrahl,
Auch meine lebensmüde Seele trinken!
	I would like to pass on like the dew of the valley,
	When the fires of morning thirstily signal to it –
	Oh, would God, as the sunbeam drinks the
	  dewdrop
	Also drink my life-weary soul!

Ich möchte hingehn wie der bange Ton,
Der aus den Saiten einer Harfe dringet,
Und, kaum dem irdischen Metall entflohn,
Ein Wohllaut in des Schöpfers Brust
  [v]erklinget.
	I would like to pass on like the timid tone
	That emerges from the strings of a harp,
	And, barely having escaped from earthly metal,
	Already dies away euphoniously in the
	  Creator's bosom.

Du wirst nicht hingehn wie das Abendrot, Du wirst nicht stille wie der Stern versinken, Du stirbst nicht einer Blume leichten Tod, Kein Morgenstrahl wird deine Seele trinken.	You shall not pass on like the sunset, You shall not pass on like the sinking of a star, You shall not die the easy death of a flower, No morning sunbeam shall drink up your soul!

Wohl wirst du hingehn, hingehn ohne Spur,
Doch wird das Elend deine Kraft erst
  schwächen, Sanft stirbt es einzig sich in der
  Natur,
Das arme Menschenherz muß stückweis
  brechen.
	You shall verily pass on, pass on without a trace,
	But wretchedness shall first weaken your
	  vigour; Solely in nature can dying be
	  gentle,
	The poor human heart must break piece by
	  piece!

Liszt's changes to Herwegh's text are given in square brackets.

Translation is by Richard Stokes, *Liszt: The Complete Songs, Vol. V*, Allan Clayton (tenor), Julius Drake (piano), Hyperion CDA68179, 2018.

Example 5.5. 'Ich möchte hingehn' (unpublished early draft) (bars 123–6).

the quotation functions completely differently in Liszt's song. Unlike in Wagner's prelude, where it sets off a long sequence of development which is not resolved until Isolde's death, in Liszt's song it is used to move neatly from F sharp minor into A major. Bar 125 can legitimately be referred to as a quotation not only due to its similarity to Wagner's music, but also because it has a form of musical parentheses surrounding it: a rest separates the beginning of the quote from the previous bar and a fermata separates it from the subsequent music. It seems logical, then, to refer to it as a quotation, as it is both presented and functions as a citation. Indeed, by using these 'musical parentheses', it is as if Liszt has opened a curtain briefly revealing a Wagnerian musical landscape which is closed off just as suddenly as it appears.

Liszt demonstrates not only the musical kinship but also the divergence in approach between himself and Wagner. By drawing more clearly the connection between Wagner's music and his own, Liszt in fact also highlights Herwegh's indebtedness to Schopenhauer. This moves the song away from being a solely personal expression of 'doomed love'. With the addition/insertion of a single bar, Liszt was able to respond to his aesthetic milieu and create an intertextual commentary on the poetic text, as well as highlighting the common mood and philosophy that had informed both his work and those of others – while simultaneously creating a frame within which to interpret his song. It is even more striking to then return to Liszt's first version and see that it functions in an equivalent way musically, that is, preparing for a move into A major. By inserting the Wagner 'quote', Liszt has dramatically increased this section's potency through the listener's perceiving the manifold intertextual links of the song.

'Es rauschen die Winde' and 'Es muß ein Wunderbares sein'

This last section of the chapter is not concerned with the relationship between two versions of the same song, but rather Liszt's possible reuse of material from one version of a song within another song. Set to a poem by Ludwig Rellstab (1799–1860), 'Es rauschen die Winde' was composed in 1845 and then recomposed in 1849, but no version was published until 1860.[44] 'Es muß ein Wunderbares sein' was composed on 13 July 1852. The unusual specificity of the date is drawn from Liszt's correspondence. He relates that Princess Augusta von Preussen selected a short two-verse passage from the epic poem *Amaranth* (1849) by Oskar von Redwitz (1823–91), and he tasked himself with setting it between dinner and the subsequent soirée later the

---

44 Dates of composition in Eckhardt, Mueller, and Walker, 'Liszt, Franz', *Grove Music Online*, 2001 [accessed 10 September 2020].

Table 5.3 'Es rauschen die Winde' (Herbst) (1827) – Ludwig Rellstab (1799–1860).

Es rauschen die Winde	The wind blows
So herbstlich und kalt;	with an autumnal chill;
Verödet die Fluren,	the meadows are bare,
Entblättert der Wald.	the woods leafless.
Ihr blumigen Auen!	Flowering meadows;
Du sonniges Grün!	sunlit green!
So welken die Blüten	Thus, do life's blossoms
Des Lebens dahin.	wilt.
Es ziehen die Wolken	The clouds drift by,
So finster und grau;	so sombre and grey;
Verschwunden die Sterne	the stars have vanished
Am himmlischen Blau!	in the blue heavens.
Ach, wie die Gestirne	Ah, as the stars disappear
Am Himmel entflieh'n,	in the sky,
So sinket die Hoffnung	so does life's hope
Des Lebens dahin!	fade away.
Ihr Tage des Lenzes	You days of spring,
Mit Rosen geschmückt,	adorned with roses,
Wo ich die Geliebte	when I pressed
An's Herze gedrückt!	my beloved to my heart.
Kalt über die Hügel	Winds, blow cold
Rauscht, Winde, dahin!	over the hillside!
So sterben die Rosen	So do the roses
Der Liebe dahin!	of love die.

Ludwig Rellstab, *Gedichte von Ludwig Rellstab* (Berlin: bei Friedrich Laue, 1827), pp. 106–7.

Translation is by Richard Wigmore, *Liszt: The Complete Songs, Vol. 1.*

same evening.[45] 'Es muß ein Wunderbares sein' is one of Liszt's simplest and most popular Lieder. It is my contention that its short composition was in part facilitated by reusing and recomposing a short passage which had originated in the earlier, yet unpublished, second version of 'Es rauschen die Winde'. This song uses well-worn autumnal imagery to depict old age and the coming of death. The beginning of the third stanza offers a brief contrast as memories of spring are evoked. In both versions, Liszt changes the mood through changes in texture and key, creating, in essence, a song within a song. In the first version, which is especially agitated and energetic throughout, Liszt moves from C minor to the parallel major, whereas in the second version the contrasting section has been completely rewritten. There is a change of tempo, key signature, and piano texture and it is this section that may have been further recomposed by Liszt.[46] In bars 44 and 45 Liszt uses a ii7b–V7–I

---

[45] Liszt, *Franz Liszt's Briefe*, vol. 4, pp. 38–9.

[46] First version, Franz Liszt, *Musikalische Werke* (Leipzig: Breitkopf & Härtel, 1921), VII. II, pp. 53–7 (pp. 55–6). Second version, Franz Liszt, *Gesammelte Lieder* (Berlin/Leipzig:

Example 5.6. 'Es rauschen die Winde' (second version) (bars 41–50).

chord progression over a dominant pedal, and the vocal line descends a minor 3rd by step before rising a major 3rd to a chromatically altered appoggiatura. It is this brief harmonic move along with the melodic contour of the section that Liszt seems to have seized upon and elaborated when setting 'Es muß ein Wunderbares sein'.

It is in bars 5 to 7 of 'Es muß ein Wunderbares sein' that the link is most clearly discernible. There are some extra chromatic alterations in the first two beats of bar 7 in the piano chords, but otherwise the similarity between the two passages is striking (the key and texture change apart). If one includes the preceding bars of both sections, the similarity is not as obvious even though both are harmonically and melodically similar. However, with just a small alteration to the opening of the central section in 'Es rauschen die Winde', the link becomes clearer.[47] Allowing for the transposition down a semitone, if the first two notes from the second phrase are substituted into the first phrase, we can see a much great similarity to the opening phrase of 'Es muß ein Wunderbares sein'.

The assertion is not that 'Es muß ein Wunderbares sein' is based on an exact copy of the central section in the second version of 'Es rauschen die Winde', but rather

---

Schlesinger/Kahnt, 1859), V, pp. 3–7 (p. 5).

[47] Liszt, *Gesammelte Lieder*, V, pp. 3–7.

Example 5.7, 'Es muß ein Wunderbares sein' (Schlesinger/Kahnt 1859) (bars 3–7).

Example 5.8, 'Es rauschen die Winde' (modified version) (bars 41–5).

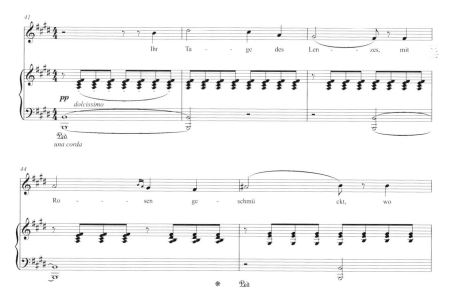

that, given the time frame of just a few hours, Liszt reused material that expressed, however briefly, a similar sentiment as a springboard to compose a new Lied.

I created a modified version to illustrate the relatedness between Examples 5.6 and 5.7 more clearly. That is, that with only minor modification they become extremely similar, excepting changes in texture and key (see Example 5.8).

The difference in mood between the poems can be seen to explain the divergent musical trajectories. Whereas 'Es rauschen die Winde' has only a fleeting moment of repose, 'Es muß ein Wunderbares sein' sustains its mood throughout the song. Thus, when pressed to compose in a short space of time and for a private musical soirée, Liszt created one of his most genre-conforming works, with a simple accompaniment, highly singable vocal part, a sustained mood, subtle harmonic inflections, and no modulation.

Table 5.4. 'Es muß ein Wunderbares sein' from *Amaranth* (1849) –
Oskar von Redwitz (1823–91).

Es muß ein Wunderbares sein	How wondrous it must be
Ums Lieben zweier Seelen,	When two souls love each other,
Sich schliessen ganz einander ein,	Locking each other wholly in,
Sich nie ein Wort verhehlen,	Never concealing a single word,
Und Freud und Leid und Glück und Not	And sharing with each other
So mit einander tragen;	Joy and sorrow, weal and woe;
Vom ersten Kuss bis in den Tod	Talking only of love
Sich nur von Liebe sagen.	From the first kiss unto death.

Oskar von Redwitz, 'Amaranths stille Lieder' / 'Es muß ein Wunderbares sein,' in *Amaranth* (Mainz: Kirchheim und Schott, 1849), p. 117.

Translation is by Richard Stokes, *Liszt: The Complete Songs, Vol.II*, Angela Kirchschlager (mezzo-soprano), Julius Drake (piano), Hyperion CDA67934, 2012.

The connection between 'Es rauschen die Winde' and 'Es muß es wunderbares sein' is considerably more distant than that often found between variants or recompositions of the same song. However, the purpose was to highlight that intertextual connections between songs extend to those with shared similar themes or mood and in which Liszt chooses to employ similar musical solutions. In essence, not only did Liszt choose to return to completed works to revise, refine, and recompose them, but also to small sections of works, motifs, or distinctive harmonic devices in order to reuse and adapt them. To fully explore this mode of inquiry is beyond the scope of this study; nevertheless, it is worth highlighting, since it demonstrates how seemingly unrelated works can share material that has been reused or adapted.

In choosing the three examples above, the purpose was to show the range of ways in which Liszt returned to older compositions and created a variety of different forms of intertextual connections between works. From the parallel versions of 'Am Rhein, im schönen Strome' to its recomposed later version, from the addition of a single bar in 'Ich möchte hingehn', changing the interpretation of the song from a highly personal expression of farewell to a more universal commentary on the themes contained within the poem, to the reusing of a short harmonic pattern to express a similar mood in two different songs, Liszt created a nexus of intertexts that stands in complete opposition to the notion of the autonomous work of art. Indeed, by exploring the textual fluidity and interconnections between versions of specific works, we inevitably perceive the act of composition as a process, and versions of works as results of that process. Set in relief against the composer's circumstances, both societal and personal, and along with other contemporaneous works, we then better understand how a composer interacted with the society of their time.

CHAPTER 6

'Not "Carthage is to be destroyed", but "Weimar is to be constructed"': Textual Fluidity in Liszt's Goethe Lieder

> a song by Liszt is not just the result of grappling with the poet's words but of relationships forged in tone and rhythm with other musicians.
>
> —Susan Youens, 'Heine, Liszt and the Song of the Future'[1]

Susan Youens's insight regarding the perceptible connection between Liszt's songs and those of other composers is perhaps most evident in his settings of six poems by Johann Wolfgang von Goethe (1749–1832). Youens is far from alone in noticing this trend; indeed, both Charles Rosen and George Steiner make similar claims regarding Liszt's music in general. For example, Steiner goes as far as to term Liszt's operatic paraphrases and transcriptions as 'enacted criticism'.[2] In reference to Liszt's Goethe Lieder, the 'other musicians' must refer to Beethoven and Schubert; indeed, especially in their earliest versions, some of Liszt's Goethe Lieder have a clearly discernible relationship to the works of Schubert. As a matter of fact, like Schumann – and in contrast to both Brahms and Hugo Wolf – Liszt had no qualms setting texts that had already been set by Schubert. Indeed, all the Goethe texts Liszt chose had been set before by Schubert; and 'Es war einmal ein König', 'Freudvoll und leidvoll', and 'Kennst du das Land' were also set by Beethoven. These precedents by two of Liszt's most beloved of composers may explain why he was willing to publish two musically unrelated and highly contrasting settings of 'Freudvoll und leidvoll', side by side, within the same volume of Lieder in 1848 for Haslinger of Vienna – this, even though the second version was composed four years after the first.[3] In total, Liszt set six of Goethe's texts as Lieder, all of which exist

1   Susan Youens, 'Heine, Liszt and the Song of the Future', in Christopher Gibbs and Dana Gooley (eds), *Franz Liszt and His World* (Princeton: Princeton University Press, 2006), p. 41.

2   'Liszt's transcriptions for piano from Italian opera, from classical symphonies, from the compositions of his contemporaries, notably Wagner, go a long way to suggest that Liszt's was the foremost critical (if not self-critically) tact in the history of Western music. Together, these transcriptions make up a syllabus of enacted criticism.' George Steiner, *Real Presences* (Chicago: University of Chicago, 1989), p. 20.

3   The first version dates from 1844, the second from 1848. Liszt did not obviously conceive of this second version as overwriting the previous one; however, in the next year he wrote

in at least two versions, bringing the total of separate versions published within Liszt's lifetime to sixteen.[4] He chose to set some the most famous of Goethe's texts, all of which were linked either directly or indirectly to characters with whom he had a strong affinity: Faust, Egmont, the Harper, and the Wanderer. His Goethe Lieder are among his most popular and highly regarded works in any vocal genre.

Goethe in Liszt's Music and Intellectual Life

Before discussing the various versions of Liszt's Goethe Lieder in detail, it is worth examining Liszt's relationship to Goethe. Liszt's connection to Goethe goes back to 1830, in Paris, where he was introduced to *Faust* by Hector Berlioz in Nerval's French translation. Berlioz recounts in his memoirs his first meeting with Liszt which took place on the eve of the premiere of his *Symphonie fantastique*:

> Paris, December 4, 1830
>
> … Liszt came to see me. We did not yet know each other. I spoke to him about Goethe's Faust, which he confessed he had not read, and of which he soon became as passionate an admirer as I was.[5]

Indeed, Ben Arnold places Goethe's works at the centre of Liszt's core reading in German. And in his memoir dating from 1929, pianist and Liszt pupil August Stradal even recounted that 'No work he [Liszt] said had brought about such a revolution in his views as did Goethe's *Faust*'.[6]

During the early 1840s, Liszt made an active effort to create a German-friendly image as he concentrated his concert activities in Germany. By his second visit to Weimar in 1842, he had accepted the title of Court Conductor in Extraordinaire there (*Hofkapellmeister im außerordentlichen Dienst*), which he took up on a part-time basis. Detlef Altenburg suggests that Liszt accepted in part because he saw

---

what is normally referred to as the second version of the first setting, but which from now on I will refer to as the third version. The lag between composition and publication was much longer in this case of a third version, as it did not appear until 1859 in an edition by Schlesinger of Berlin, along with the five other revised Goethe Lieder. This was the first volume of a projected seven that Liszt would seek to 'put his house in order' with regard to his Lieder. The 1848 volume for Haslinger also contained the first versions of two other Goethe settings: 'Wer nie sein Brod mit Thränen ass' and 'Über allen Gipfeln ist Ruh'.

4 The following is the final order which Liszt decided upon when collecting his six Goethe Lieder for publication by Schlesinger in 1859. Where two voice designations are shown, Liszt also prepared a different version for the second voice designation: 1. 'Mignon's Lied' (Mezzo-Soprano)(Alto); 2. 'Es war ein König in Thule'; 3. 'Der du von dem Himmel bist'; 4. 'Freudvoll und leidvoll' (Mezzo Soprano)(Soprano); 5. 'Wer nie sein Brod mit Thränen ass'; 6. 'Über allen Gipfeln ist Ruh'.

5 Hector Berlioz: *Mémoires de Hector Berlioz*, trans. David Cairns (New York: Alfred A. Knopf, 1969), p. 139.

6 Ben Arnold, 'Liszt as Reader, Intellectual, and Musician', in Michael Saffle (ed.), *Franz Liszt and His World* (Stuyvesant, NY: Pendragon Press, 1998), p. 47. Quoting from August Stradal, *Erinnerungen an Franz Liszt* (Berne: P. Haupt, 1929), p. 72.

himself as the heir to Goethe and Schiller.[7] It is no surprise then that Goethe and his works would inspire several of Liszt's most important works. The range of pieces includes three works for orchestra: his large-scale orchestral masterpiece *Eine Faust-Symphonie* (1856) (LW G12);[8] the symphonic poem *Tasso Lamento et Triunfo* (1847) (LW G2), and *Festmarsch zur Goethe Jubiläumsfeier* (1849) (LW G5).[9] In addition, works for solo piano include the *Festmarsch zur Säcularfeier von Goethes Geburtstag* (LW A164), and Eduard Lassen's *Aus der Musik zu Hebbels Nibelungen und Goethes Faust* (1878) (LW A285), along with transcriptions of six Goethe Lieder by Beethoven that were arranged into a concert suite/piano cycle of songs without words.[10] There were also piano four-hands and two-piano transcriptions of the *Festmarsch* and *Faust* symphony respectively. In addition, Liszt's own six Goethe Lieder from the 1840s in their first versions were transcribed for solo piano.

However, since Liszt was to place such a centrality and primacy of importance on Goethe's *Faust* in his intellectual life, it may come as a surprise that he did not compose any pieces directly inspired by Goethe in the 1830s. In fact, for this we must wait

---

7   'Not "Carthage is to be destroyed," but "Weimar is to be constructed." Under the late Grand Duke Karl-August, Weimar was a new Athens. Let's dream today of building a new Weimar. Let us renew openly and boldly the traditions of Karl-August. Let us allow talents to move more freely in their sphere. Let us colonize as much as possible.' Letter to Marie d'Agoult of 23 January 1844. Cited in Detlef Altenburg, 'Liszt and the Spirit of Weimar', *Studia Musicologica*, 54:2 (June 2013), p. 167.

8   Liszt only began work in earnest on his great Faustian masterpiece *Eine Faust-Symphonie* in 1850, when it was conceived as an opera. This idea was discarded, and the work was not completed until 1856, though some themes date back to sketches in the 1840s. It did use some material in its final movement which had appeared in the rarely heard *Malediction* [LW H1] for piano and strings from the 1830s. However, Liszt did not ever explicitly link this work with Faust, and in fact its title *Malédiction*, meaning curse, is not Liszt's own, but comes from the name Liszt put above one of the themes in the score. Alan Walker, *Franz Liszt*, 3 vols, rev. edn (Ithaca, NY: Cornell University Press, 1993), p. 334; Jay Rosenblatt, 'Piano and Orchestra Works', in Ben Arnold (ed.), *The Liszt Companion* (Westport, CT: Greenwood Press, 2002), pp. 281–308, at p. 287. *Malédiction* was first published posthumously in Franz Liszt, *Musikalische Werke 1* (Leipzig: Breitkopf & Härtel, 1915), XIII, pp. 183–214.

9   It should be noted that one of Liszt's most celebrated 'Faust' pieces, *The Dance at the Village Inn*, from *Zwei Episoden aus Lenaus Faust: 1 Der nächtliche Zug, 2 Der Tanz in der Dorfschenke*, usually referred to by its nickname, 'The Mephisto Waltz', does not originate with Goethe but rather the Austro-Hungarian poet, Nikolaus Lenau (1802–50). It could be argued that Liszt created an entire 'Mephisto' genre, with four waltzes all having associations with the Faust myth (the others being *The Mephisto Polka, Bagatelle sans Tonalité*, and *Valse Oubliée no. 1*. Liszt was followed in this by Sergei Prokofiev (1890–1953), who composed his own *Mephisto Waltz* which exists in two versions: one for piano, *3 Pieces for Piano* (1942), op. 96 no. 3, and one for orchestra, *Waltz Suite* (1947), op. 110 no. 3, both taken from his music for the film *Lermontov* (1942).

10   In a similar fashion to his work on Chopin's *Chansons Polonaises* and both Schubert's *Schwanengesang* and *Wintereisse*, Liszt changes the keys as well as the order of songs in the cycles to create his own cycles of 'songs without words' which in effect comment on the works of both these composers (Schubert and Chopin) and those of Ruckert, Rellstab, Heine, and Seidel. For an illuminating discussion on Liszt's process, see Jonathan Kregor, *Liszt as Transcriber* (Cambridge: Cambridge University Press, 2010).

until 1841 and in the most unlikely of genres for the most celebrated pianist of his age: unaccompanied male-voice choir. Also, rather unexpectedly, settings for male-voice choir, both accompanied and unaccompanied, form the largest collection, in terms of number, of pieces directly inspired by or based on settings of Goethe. It is worth noting that Liszt set two texts for male choir which he also set as Lieder, 'Über allen Gipfeln ist Ruh' and 'Es war ein König in Thule'. The choral version pre-dates the former while it post-dates the latter, though neither choral setting bears any significant connection with its respective Lied, apart from sharing the same source text.

However, if Liszt's transcriptions are included among the works with a link to Goethe, it is imperative to look at the Schubert Lieder transcriptions, which appeared with regularity in the 1830s, helping to popularise his Viennese predecessor's works. This close study of Schubert would surely have been highly influential in the forming of Liszt's early Lieder style, and indeed this has been posited by scholars Christopher Gibbs, Michael Abu Hamad, and Rena Charnin Mueller, who declares in her introduction to the Dover edition of the Schubert Lieder transcriptions: 'It is not overstating the case to say that Liszt honed his talent in the song genre while transcribing these Schubert settings.'[11] With Liszt having also transcribed six of Beethoven's Goethe Lieder for solo piano – and it is well documented that he was one of the pre-eminent interpreters of Beethoven in the nineteenth century – Beethoven's songs may likewise have influenced Liszt's development in this genre. However, in terms of songwriting, it seems that Schubert was of greater influence than Beethoven, given the frequency of Liszt's efforts to promote Schubert's Lieder through performance, transcription, and in print. And, as mentioned earlier, Liszt's Lieder often adopt certain procedures and characteristics of Schubert's Lieder.

'Mignon's Lied' ('Kennst du das Land') (LW N8)

In 'Mignon', Liszt engaged with a poem which had already been set by both Beethoven and Schubert. Indeed, in taking on the task of setting one of Goethe's most famous poems, Liszt was well aware of the 'fifty other musicians'[12] who had come before him. Liszt first read *Wilhelm Meisters Lehrjahre* (Wilhelm Meister's Apprenticeship) in 1837, and, by his own reckoning, composed the first setting of 'Mignon' in Berlin in February 1842.[13] Liszt's preoccupation with the poem was such that he would eventually complete four different versions between 1842 and 1860, the last version with both orchestral and piano accompaniments. Furthermore, Liszt transcribed both Beethoven's and his own first setting for solo piano, while also creating an orchestral version of Schubert's.[14] Thus, having published seven separate

---

[11] Rena Charnin Mueller, *The Schubert Song Transcriptions for Solo Piano*, Series I (New York: Dover Publications Inc., 1995), p. x.

[12] Arnold, 'Liszt as Reader, Intellectual and Musician', p. 56.

[13] Franz Liszt, *Franz Liszt's Briefe*, ed. La Mara, 8 vols (Leipzig: Breitkopf & Härtel, 1905), vol. 7, pp. 157–8.

[14] LW A97 *Buch der Lieder für Piano allein: no. 3* 'Mignon' (1843 for solo piano), LW A161 *Beethovens Lieder von Goethe* (1849 for solo piano), LW N63 *Sechs Lieder von Schubert* (1860 for orchestra).

versions of the musical text within his own lifetime, it may be surprising to learn of Liszt's declaration to Princess Carolyne zu Sayn-Wittgenstein on 28 September 1876 that 'to tell the truth, I have never keenly felt for Italy, its lemon trees and oranges, the *Sehnsucht* of Goethe's Mignon'.[15] In any case, many scholars and commentators have esteemed Liszt's setting highly, placing it among his finest Lieder.[16] Indeed, Liszt himself seems to have been more than satisfied with the result:

> When I composed the song 'Kennst du das Land?' in Berlin in February 1842, after 50 other musicians [had already set it] I identified myself somehow or other with the dreamy sentiments of a young girl. Several of Goethe's friends, in particular Chancellor [von] Müller, told me that I had succeeded passably – even that the stress on *dahin! dahin!* would not have displeased the great poet.[17]

In approaching this text, Liszt was happy to plough his own furrow, and his first setting of 'Mignon' is far removed from the precepts and aesthetic of the second Berlin *Liederschule* which heavily informed the criticism received by Liszt's *Buch der Lieder*. And 'Mignon' was not exempt from these criticisms. This might be expected, considering that it approaches in both scale and emotional heft the proportions of a quasi-operatic concert aria. The avoidance of the *Volkston* does not, however, indicate a disregard for the text: Liszt's setting pays close attention to every word, reflected with numerous examples of word-painting and subtle inflections in both the vocal and piano parts that mirror the text throughout. The modified strophic form employed by Liszt allows for the addition of an improvisatory element, while still retaining a link to the structure of Goethe's text.

'Mignon' is drawn from one of the most famous episodes in *Wilhelm Meisters Lehrjahre*, during which Wilhelm hears Mignon singing 'Kennst du das Land' ('Mignon') while accompanying herself on a zither.

The character of Mignon has often been contrasted with that of Goethe's other female characters, Klärchen and Gretchen. Mignon is a child of incest and was kidnapped by a company of acrobats in her youth. Throughout the novel, Mignon displays both female and male characteristics and could be thought of as a representation not only of the many dualities of life (male/female, earthly/spiritual), but also of otherness.[18]

'Kennst du das Land' has been set by numerous composers throughout the nineteenth and twentieth centuries, from Berg to Zelter. Goethe was famously critical of Beethoven's setting, as he considered it closer to an aria and not the simple folk-like

---

[15] Arnold, 'Songs and Melodramas', p. 425.

[16] Martin Cooper, 'Liszt as a Song Writer', *Music & Letters*, 19:2 (April 1938), pp. 171–81 (p. 177); Charles Osborne, *The Concert Song Companion* (New York: Da Capo), p. 59; Alan Walker, *Reflections on Liszt* (Ithaca, NY: Cornell University Press, 2005), p. 156; Arnold, 'Songs and Melodramas', p. 425, to name a few, have all cited 'Mignon' as one of Liszt's finest Lieder.

[17] Arnold, 'Songs and Melodramas', p. 425, citing Liszt, *Franz Liszt's Briefe*, vol. 7, pp. 157–8.

[18] Lorraine Byrne Bodley, *Schubert's Goethe Settings* (Aldershot: Taylor and Francis, 2003), p. 248.

Table 6.1. 'Mignon' – *Wilhelm Meisters Lehrjahre* (1795) – J.W. von Goethe.

Kennst du das Land, wo die Zitronen blühn,	Do you know the land where the lemons blossom,
Im dunkeln Laub die Gold-Orangen glühn,	Where oranges grow golden among dark leaves,
Ein sanfter Wind vom blauen Himmel weht,	A gentle wind drifts from the blue sky,
Die Myrte still und hoch der Lorbeer steht?	The myrtle stands silent, the laurel tall,
Kennst du es wohl?	Do you know it?
Dahin! dahin	It is there, it is there
Möcht' ich mit dir, o mein Geliebter, ziehn.	I long to go with you, my love.
Kennst du das Haus? Auf Säulen ruht sein Dach;	Do you know the house? Columns support its roof;
Es glänzt der Saal, es schimmert das Gemach,	Its great hall gleams, its apartments shimmer,
Und Marmorbilder stehn und sehn mich an:	And marble statues stand and stare at me:
Was hat man dir, du armes Kind, getan?	What have they done to you, poor child?
Kennst du es wohl?	Do you know it?
Dahin! dahin	It is there, it is there
Möcht' ich mit dir, o mein Beschützer, ziehn.	I long to go with you, my protector.
Kennst du den Berg und seinen Wolkensteg?	Do you know the mountain and its cloudy path?
Das Maultier sucht im Nebel seinen Weg;	The mule seeks its way through the mist,
In Höhlen wohnt der Drachen alte Brut;	Caverns house the dragons' ancient brood;
Es stürzt der Fels und über ihn die Flut!	The rock falls sheer, the torrent over it!
Kennst du ihn wohl?	Do you know it?
Dahin! dahin	It is there, it is there
Geht unser Weg! O Vater, laß uns ziehn!	Our pathway lies! O father, let us go!

Johann Wolfgang von Goethe, *Wilhelm Meisters Lehrjahre* (Berlin: J.F. Unger, 1795).

Translation is by Richard Stokes, *Liszt: The Complete Songs Vol. 4*, Sasha Cooke (mezzo-soprano), Julius Drake (piano), Hyperion CDA68117, 2016.

melody that he had envisioned.[19] Schubert's setting also fell foul of similar criticisms, and yet Liszt follows both Schubert and Beethoven in creating a quasi-dramatic setting. Liszt, however, moves further away from his predecessors by eschewing strict strophic form, and instead he creates a modified strophic form that contains recurring elements which are never presented the same way twice. This gives the song a sense of continuous development similar to a through-composed setting while retaining a sense of musical logic and continuity.

'Mignon' first appeared as the third song of Liszt's *Buch der Lieder*, published by Schlesinger of Berlin in 1843. The first three versions are closely related. While extensive revisions are made in some bars to the vocal melody and piano accompaniment between the 1843 and 1856 versions, these versions should be described as variants, since changes are localised, and they are all clearly recognisable as the same setting. The fourth version, however, which dates from 1860 and which also exists in a version

[19] Byrne Bodley, *Schubert's Goethe Settings*, p. 259; Jan Smaczny, 'Goethe and the Czechs', in Lorraine Byrne (ed.), *Goethe: Musical Poet, Musical Catalyst* (Dublin: Carysfort Press, 2004), pp. 159–84 (p. 170); Amanda Glauert, '"Ich denke dein"; Beethoven's Retelling of Goethe's Poetry', in *Goethe: Musical Poet, Musical Catalyst*, pp. 100–158 (p. 101).

with orchestral accompaniment, has more fundamental revisions, such as changes in metre and phrasing. These revisions render it much more of a recomposition.

'Mignon' – Schlesinger 1843 (First Version)

Before discussing in any further detail the various revisions that Liszt undertook over the course of his four separate versions, it is worth addressing a bone of contention that has arisen between many scholars and critics when discussing Liszt's songs, and 'Mignon' in particular. This is that each of the first three versions of Liszt's 'Mignon' contains one of his most 'glaring offences' in songwriting, which Walter Beckett described as 'doing violence to the poems'.[20] Indeed, Liszt's handling of the opening phrase 'Kennst du das Land, wo die Citronen blühn?' has generated pages of criticism and has often been presented as evidence of Liszt's poor grasp of both the German language and text-setting in general.[21] Liszt's offence was to put 'du' (you) and 'die' (the) respectively on the first beats of the two bars that cover the phrase in question, thus placing strong beats on a relatively unimportant words. The criticism over the text-setting seems more than a little overstated. It could be argued that with this emphasis on 'du' Liszt is addressing the audience, while the 'die' looks worse on the page than it sounds in practice; as the setting is in $\frac{4}{4}$ and as both 'Land' and the second syllable of 'Citronen' also fall on strong beats, the perceptive interpreter would naturally shape the phrase towards those beats (see Example 6.1). The later and similar phrase 'Kennst du es wohl?' is rendered more standardly, as in fact is the rest of the poem. The question is then raised: why would Liszt commit such an apparent oversight? Indeed, one would need only the most basic level of German to understand where the normal stresses would lie. It is such a rudimentary error in text-setting that it is my contention that it may well have been deliberate.

To illustrate this hypothesis, we need to consider the poem not as a stand-alone work but rather within the context of the novel. Wilhelm hears music emanating from outside his door. Initially he assumes it is the harper, but soon realises that the instrument is instead a zither and that the voice is Mignon's. Wilhelm opens the door, and Mignon enters and sings 'Kennst du das Land' to him. Wilhelm is captivated by her song; he asks her to repeat it and explain the meaning so that he can translate it into German. However, he is not able to capture it as:

> He could not even approximate the originality of the phrases, and the childlike innocence of the style was lost when the broken language was smoothed over, and the disconnectedness removed. The charm of the melody was also quite unique.[22]

---

[20] Walter Beckett, *Liszt* (London: J.M. Dent, 1963), p. 126.

[21] Ibid.; Peter Raabe, *Franz Liszt: Leben und Schaffen*, vol.2 (Stuttgart: Cotta, 1931), pp. 112–31; Frederick Niecks, 'Modern Songwriters — II. Franz Liszt', *The Musical Times* (1 November 1884), 627; Monika Henneman, 'Liszt's Lieder', in Kenneth Hamilton (ed.), *The Cambridge Companion to Liszt* (Cambridge: Cambridge University Press, 2005), pp. 192–205 (p. 201); Christopher Headington, 'The Songs', in Alan Walker (ed.), *Franz Liszt, The Man and His Music* (New York: Taplinger Publishing Company, 1970), p. 226.

[22] Johann Wolfgang von Goethe, *Goethe: The Collected Works: Wilhelm Meister's Apprenticeship*, ed. Eric A. Blackall and Victor Lange (Princeton: Princeton University Press, 1995), ix, p. 83.

Example 6.1 'Mignon' (first version), Schlesinger 1843 (bars 1–3).

The important aspect here is that in the novel the song is not sung in German and is described as containing 'broken language' and 'disconnectedness'. Thus, by introducing unnatural stresses into a prominent position in the song, Liszt was perhaps merely attempting to recreate the effect of Goethe's description, or rather introduce a foreign accent, without actually altering the text. There follows a description of Mignon's rendition, which acts almost as a set of performance indications that Liszt follows quite closely in his setting:

> She intoned each verse with a certain solemn grandeur, as if she were drawing attention to something unusual and imparting something of importance. When she reached the third line, the melody became more sombre; the words 'You know it, yes?' were given weightiness and mystery, the 'Oh there, oh there!' was suffused with longing, and she modified the phrase 'Let us fare!' each time it was repeated, so that one time it was entreating and urging, the next time pressing and full of promise.[23]

Here, it seems pertinent to note how Mignon is described as varying the repetition of the last phrase of each verse, thereby changing its character. Variation in phrase repetitions is a technique Liszt would utilise not only in this Lied, but also in numerous others, especially in his Lieder of the pre-Weimar era.

As would be expected, the first version (1843) has the most pianistically elaborate accompaniment of the four versions. It is written for a mezzo-soprano voice, although in the first publication the normal mezzo-soprano tessitura is pushed to its limits. The tempo is marked 'Langsam, überspannt' (Slowly, extravagantly, or wild/overstrung), and it is indeed one of Liszt's most emotionally charged settings. Interestingly he chooses the key of F sharp major for his setting. In Liszt's music, F sharp major is often used to connote a higher plane of spiritual, beatific music such as in *Bénédiction de Dieu dans la solitude*. However, in this case we can read it instead as an expression of distance and naiveté: the remoteness of the key mirrors Mignon's longing for her homeland and memories of a lost childhood, while also capturing her otherness.

---

[23] Ibid., p.84.

Liszt's setting divides each verse into three parts, and with each succeeding verse he varies the piano accompaniment and/or vocal line for each respective part, with the third verse being the most varied, creating an AA'A'' form. Each A section is itself divided into three sections. The brief though striking piano introduction contains just two chords, I – vii°7d over an F♯ pedal, with the diminished 7th chord arpeggiated. This is a clear imitation of the zither and instantly establishes an otherworldly mood full of longing and remoteness. This is further heightened by the prepared appoggiatura (A♯) in the top voice. Then Liszt, perhaps betraying the influence of Schubert, moves through a series of 3rd-related harmonies, first to A sharp major, which is then notated as B♭ and finishing on D major. The transition to D major is negotiated by a series of diminished 7th chords over a D♮ inverted pedal in both the voice and piano, bringing the first section of the verse to a close. The inverted pedal is significant as it gives a sense of symmetrical structure to a somewhat rhapsodic opening. The last of the four lines set at this point functions as a transition, and though harmonically similar in each verse the passage is never repeated exactly. This section also shows Liszt's close attention to the meaning of the words as he engages in word-painting in the vocal line in the fourth line of each verse, which is then rendered differently in each analogous section. For example, in the first verse at the line 'die Myrte still und hoch der Lorbeer steht' (see Example 6.2), the first four words are all on D♮, and then on the word 'hoch' (high) the melody rises a perfect 5th to A♮ before descending a 12th in an arpeggio pattern, which adds to the sense of height. 'Hoch' is further emphasised with a *crescendo* leading up to the high A♮ and a fermata placed above it.

The next line 'Kennst du es wohl?' is repeated twice and forms the second section of each verse, the shortest of the three sections. The use of a distinctive leap of a rising diminished 5th has a questioning quality that is mirrored in the harmony, as the whole section prolongs a V7 sound that is left unresolved at the end of the section. These are two ways in which Liszt musically reflects the text's questioning nature, and which allows for a seamless move back to F sharp major and the repeated 'Dahin' of the following section. For the closing section of the verse, Liszt indicates a change of tempo to *Tempo Animato*, and repeats the last two lines in a slightly truncated form. A sense of restlessness in this third section is created through flowing triplet arpeggios and modulation moving back and forth between the keys F sharp major and B major by means of a German augmented 6th chord. The original form of the last two lines and Liszt's repetitions to the end of the first verse, which further link the song to the operatic tradition, are shown in Table 6.2 below. [24]

Each of the following verses proceeds along similar lines, albeit with different tempo markings, along with transformations to the texture that heighten the drama as the song progresses. There are changes in each of the respective sections of each verse, with the third verse being the most extensively transformed. Here, for example, in the opening section of the verse for the question 'Kennst du den Berg und seinen Wolkensteg?' the series of rolled chords in the piano accompaniment is now played with fast-moving triplet arpeggios in both hands, and the tempo – *Quasi*

---

[24] Text repetition was a much more common feature of earlier and contemporary-period operatic arias than it was in Lieder.

Example 6.2. 'Mignon' (first version), Schlesinger 1843 (bars 9–12).

Table 6.2. Comparison of Goethe's text with Liszt's.

Goethe	Liszt (repetitions in italics)
Dahin! Dahin	Dahin! Dahin *Dahin!*
Möcht' ich mit dir, o mein Geliebter, ziehn.	Möcht' ich mit dir, o mein Geliebter, ziehn.
	Dahin! Dahin Dahin!
	Möcht' ich mit dir, mit dir, o mein Geliebter,
	mit dir, o mein Geliebter, ziehn.

Andante in the second verse – is now *Allegro Moderato*. 'Es stürzt der Fels, und über ihn die Flut', which closes the first section of the third verse, is divided into two examples of word-painting, the first half rendered as an octave drop to depict the sheer cliff, whereas the scale passage that follows depicts the torrent over it. This is reflected by widely spaced *ff* chords which also move in quick triplets.

The central section of this verse includes a reprise of the first lines from each of the three verses: 'Kennst du es wohl?' is followed by 'Kennst du das Land?', 'Kennst du das Haus?', and 'Kennst du den Berg?'. The addition of earlier lines before the final climax of the song is a masterstroke, as it forces the listener to recall all three verses and experience their own reminiscence, giving a great sense of immediacy to one of the song's main themes, the act of remembering. There are only some minor melismas, but an operatic quality emerges full-heartedly in this section not only from the many word repetitions and rearrangement of the original text, which now finishes with the word 'Dahin!', but also from the dramatic nature of both vocal and piano parts. The piano accompaniment in this section has fast-moving semiquaver arpeggios in sextuplets divided between the hands, and stretches of a 10th become common, while the voice reaches its highest point during this section, hitting a high A♯ on the word 'Vater' with an almost rhetorical flourish. Example 6.4 is also a good representation of Liszt's early notational style, where there is an abundance of performance indications, more than twenty in just six bars. His intended performers would need to be of a professional calibre, as the demands placed on the performers,

Example 6.3 'Mignon' (first version), Schlesinger 1843 (bars 61–2).

Example 6.4. 'Mignon' (first version), Schlesinger 1843 (bars 98–103).

while not quite at the transcendental level, take the song out of the reach of the occasional player or singer.

'Mignon,' Schlesinger 1854/6 (Second and Third Versions)

Two further editions of 'Mignon' were released close together: the first in 1854, published by Schlesinger; the second in 1856, also by Schlesinger; and then again in another edition by Kahnt in 1860. Normally these editions are considered the same version, and indeed no distinction is made between them in all the standard catalogues, but there are in fact a number of small differences between the Schlesinger and Kahnt editions. Therefore, under the typology I have proposed, these second and third editions would be considered different versions and classified as variants.

The 1854 Schlesinger title page declares this publication to be a 'new and improved edition' (*neue verbesserte Ausgabe*). Indeed, the changes between the first and second versions are significant. The opening tempo marking has been modified from *Langsam, überspannt* to *Sehr langsam überspannt*, and there are also more detailed dynamic markings in the second version. The tempo change in the second section of each verse has been omitted, and the tempo of the third section for 'Dahin!' has been altered from *Tempo Animato* to *Bewegter*. The amendments in this third section are typical of the sort that Liszt made when revising his earlier Lieder during his Weimar period: the piano part has been simplified and the texture made a little thinner, especially in chords and in the bass, while the vocal part has also been made less overtly demanding and its range lowered.

The changes made to the third verse are the most significant of this revision. Liszt alters the time signature to $\frac{6}{4}$ from common time, the tempo from *Allegro Moderato* to *Più mosso*, and he heavily rewrites the piano part and modifies the vocal part (see Example 6.5). In particular the character of the piano part undergoes a transformation; tremolos in both hands situated close together in the piano's middle register give an orchestral sound in contrast with the more pianistic first version. The second section of the verse returns to common time and is almost unaltered, whereas in the final section the difficulty of the piano part has been greatly reduced, and the vocal part has been significantly lowered.

The nature of these changes which create variant versions of the songs seems to imply that during this period Liszt did not fundamentally reject earlier versions but rather was in the process of updating or fine-tuning them. The changes between the second and third versions are only very minor, and the third version should very much be considered a variant of the second version; nevertheless, some differences are worth highlighting here. The tempo is now marked *Sehr langsam, Sehnsuchtsvoll* (Very slowly and longingly), there are even more dynamic markings, and further melismas have been removed from cadential points such as in 'mit dir, o mein Geliebter, ziehn!' from the first verse.

Example 6.5. 'Mignon' (second version), Schlesinger 1854 (bars 62–3).

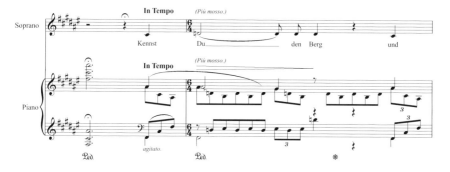

'Mignon,' Kahnt 1863 (Fourth Version)

The revisions between the third and fourth versions of 'Mignon' are the most wholesale and wide-ranging. The nature of the changes is such that this could be considered a recomposition of earlier material. Even though certain aspects have remained unaltered, such as the overall form and the tempo marking *Sehr lang-sam und sehnsuchtsvoll*, both vocal and piano parts have been so thoroughly revised that the work's scale and emotional heft have increased significantly. Among the most prominent changes here are the new time signature of $\frac{6}{4}$ and the addition of a striking piano introduction of a rising diminished 7th harmony with chromatic appoggiaturas (see Example 6.6). Allen Forte suggests that this introduction antici-pates a compositional procedure common to non-tonal music of the early twentieth century, what he calls the 'linearization of the vertical tetrachordal subsets of the thematic sonority', and he points to Webern's *Five Pieces for String Quartet*, op. 5 no. 4, in this regard.[25] Essentially, the process of 'linearization' prepares the listener for the characteristic chord of the opening lines by first playing its constituent notes as an unharmonised motif. The change of time signature also allows Liszt to rectify his previous 'infringement' of faulty declamation. He extends the word 'Kennst' for an extra beat across the bar line, creating a syncopation and moving the offending 'du' onto the second beat of the bar. This change, however, is not universally considered to be an improvement. Alan Walker states that 'The revision may be more respectful of Goethe's verbal rhythms, but it is by no means superior, musically speaking, to the first version'.[26] Walker, however, does concede that this final version 'would make a ravishing adornment to any orchestral concert today'.[27]

---

[25] Allen Forte, 'Liszt's Experimental Idiom and the Music of the Early Twentieth Century', *19tth Century Music*, 10:3 (Spring 1987), p. 217. Forte astutely identifies that the two slurred four-note motifs that begin the piece are in fact derived from the distinctive diminished 7th chord in bar 4.

[26] Alan Walker, 'Liszt and the Lied', in *Reflections on Liszt*, p. 159.

[27] Ibid., p.162.

Example 6.6. 'Mignon' (fourth version) (voice and piano parts), Kahnt 1863 (bars 1–6).

This music first appeared in an edition for voice and orchestra for Kahnt in 1863 and in this respect could be considered a precursor to Mahler's *Rückert Lieder*, which are well-known in both piano and orchestral versions. The 1863 edition contains a piano part printed beneath the orchestral accompaniment. However, this was not intended to be used as a rehearsal part, or as a piano reduction, but rather as a stand-alone version which would be an alternative to the orchestral accompaniment. Liszt makes this clear in a letter to his publisher Kahnt along with his intention to have a piano version published.[28] Unfortunately, it seems that no 'piano accompaniment-only' edition was issued within Liszt's lifetime. The first 'piano accompaniment-only' edition of this version appeared in Band 7, Vol. 2 of the Breitkopf & Härtel edition of 1921.[29] Like most of Liszt's transcriptions of orchestral parts, it does not slavishly follow the original, but creates an accompaniment that captures its spirit if not its letter, deviating to produce more pianistically satisfying passages. Thus, it is worth considering it as independent and not merely a 'study-score' version of the orchestral accompaniment. Interestingly, Liszt refers to this $\frac{6}{4}$ version as the second edition of 'Mignon', even though he would obviously have been well aware that three different versions with not insubstantial changes had already been published. This makes it clear that what Liszt considered to be a separate version of a piece stemmed from quite different criteria from those in this book or indeed in any of the current Liszt catalogues in use today.

---

[28] Michael Short (ed. and trans.), *Liszt Letters in the Library of Congress* (Hillsdale, NY: Pendragon Press, 2003), letter 168, pp. 155–6.

[29] Franz Liszt, *Musikalische Werke* (Leipzig: Breitkopf & Härtel, 1921), VII.II.

Example 6.7. 'Mignon' (fourth version), Kahnt 1863 (bars 99–104).

In contrast with many of Liszt's revisions from this period, here he made the vocal part significantly more demanding and dramatic, and even the piano part is more taxing than that in the third version from 1856. Liszt also increased the number of performance indications written in German. This proliferation of performance indications is different from the myriad of expression marks that can be found in his earlier compositions; instead, Liszt's mature style suggests a preference for description rather than an overloading of the page with numerous articulation and dynamic markings. German indications found in the fourth version include *verhallend* (resigning), *sehr leidenschaftlich betont* (very passionately emphasised or stressed), and *etwas bewegter* (somewhat more agitated).

Another change, which is not in keeping with other revisions, is that the number of text repetitions and melismatic passages has increased. Indeed, Liszt restores some of the additions that had been excised in the 1856 version, the third verse being the most heavily reworked in this fashion. In a sense, then, we have a case of an artist reasserting their initial convictions, now in a more refined and confident way. Liszt seems to have been quite happy with this last version, citing improvements to the prosody and vocal part, and expressing satisfaction with the instrumentation in a letter to Emilie Genast, on 8 November 1860.[30]

---

[30] Klára Hamburger, 'Franz Liszts Briefe an Emilie Merian-Genast aus den Beständen des Goethe und Schiller Archivs, Weimar Teil 1', *Studia Musicologica*, 48:3/4 (Sept. 2007), pp. 350-90, p. 386.

The revisions that take place across the versions cannot be explained solely by changes to the instrument[31] or merely a refining of sonorities. They speak not only to a development of Liszt's view of the poem, but also the genre of the Lied in terms of intended performer and venue. In this case it seems as though Liszt has returned to the concert hall by the fourth version, but with an orchestral sonority that looks forward to the songs of Mahler and Strauss in contrast with the virtuosic character of his first version.

'Der du von dem Himmel bist' (LW N10)

Liszt published three versions of 'Der du von dem Himmel bist' between 1843 and 1860. Though all three are intricately linked, the changes in mood, accompaniment texture, and vocal demands between the second and third versions reflect Liszt's extensive re-conceptualisation of the poem. This even extends to the title; though never published as 'Süsse Friede', Liszt referred to it as such as late as June 1843, just before its publication, in a letter to his publisher Heinrich Schlesinger.[32] The poem was entitled 'Wanderers Nachtlied' by Goethe, and according to the manuscript the poem was composed 'On the Etterberg hillside, 12 February 1776'.[33] The wanderer was commonly employed as a guise for poets,[34] and Goethe recounted that he was called the wanderer in his early years in Frankfurt.[35] By utilising an alter-ego, Goethe's wanderer signifies not only literal journeying, but also a departure from one's own self and a quest for unattainable peace. With themes of self-realisation and the image of restless journeying, it is not difficult to see how Liszt would have identified closely with the figure of the wanderer, especially as he set the poem at the height of his concert-touring years.[36]

---

[31]   This is a reference to there being many developments in the construction of the piano during this period, the 1840s to the 1860s, and – though I do not believe it applies in the case of the fourth version of 'Mignon' – it could be argued that the thinning out of the piano textures in Liszt's Lieder was a response to the increasingly more resonant and powerful instruments of the time.

[32]   Short, *Liszt Letters in the Library of Congress*, p. 25. Incidentally, in this letter Liszt suggested that Theodore Kullak could prepare facilitations of his Lieder, obviously keenly aware of the difficulties of his first essays in the genre.

[33]   Byrne Bodley, *Schubert's Goethe Settings*, p. 121; Letter to Charlotte von Stein, 12 February 1776. *Repertorium der Goethe-Briefe* <https://ores.klassik-stiftung.de/ords/f?p=402:210:29462661323351> [accessed 22 September 2018].

[34]   Deborah Stein and Robert Spillman, *Poetry into Song* (Oxford: Oxford University Press, 1996), p. 7.

[35]   Ibid, p. 121.

[36]   Later in 1847 Liszt would return to these themes in his cycle *Harmonies poétiques et religieuses* for solo piano, most especially in *Bénédiction de Dieu dans la solitude*. In this piece Liszt places the opening verse of the poem of the same name by Alphonse de Lamartine at the head of the music. Lamartine's poem, like Goethe's, also deals with themes of self-realisation and a restless search for peace; however, in this case Larmartine's protagonist has finally achieved peace. Liszt wrote *Bénédiction* while staying on Caroline Sayn-Wittgenstein's estate at Woronice in Polish Ukraine. It was at this time that he made the momentous decision to retire from his concert-touring life to concentrate on

Table 6.3. 'Der du von dem Himmel bist' (1776) – J.W. von Goethe.

Der du von dem Himmel bist,	You who come from heaven,
Alles Leid und Schmerzen stillest,	Soothing all pain and sorrow,
Den, der doppelt elend ist,	Filling the doubly wretched
Doppelt mit Erquickung füllest,	Doubly with delight,
Ach, ich bin des Treibens müde!	Ah, I am weary of this restlessness!
Was soll all der Schmerz und Lust?	What use is all this pain and joy?
Süsser Friede!	Sweet peace!
Komm, ach komm in meine Brust!	Come, ah come into my breast!

Translation by Richard Stokes, *Liszt: The Complete Songs, Vol. 2*, Angelika Kirschlager (mezzo-soprano), Julius Drake (piano), Hyperion CDA67934, 2012.

Liszt's first setting of 'Der du von dem Himmel bist' is full of restless anxiety, and even among modern scholars it has received its fair share of criticism. Monika Henneman's remarks in the *Cambridge Companion to Liszt*, that the first version is 'gifted with a profoundly beautiful main melody – one of Liszt's great Romantic tunes – but otherwise shows the composer at his most rambling and overeffusive', are representative of the criticisms levelled at the song.[37] In line with Alan Walker's assessment of the first version of 'Mignon', Henneman believes that the solo piano transcription of 'Der du von dem Himmel bist' is superior to the original:

> Liszt's transcriptions sometimes score over the original songs: over-repetition of text or clumsy word-accentuation can hardly be a problem in a piano solo, with the result that listening to a transcription like that of the first version of 'Der du

---

composition. And this may go some way to explaining the sense of spiritual calm that pervades that work: 'D'où me vient, ô mon Dieu! cette paix qui m'inonde?/D'où me vient cette foi dont mon cœur surabonde?/A moi qui tout à l'heure incertain, agité,/Et sur les flots du doute à tout vent ballotté,/Cherchais le bien, le vrai, dans les rêves des sages,/Et la paix dans les cœurs retentissants d'orages./A peine sur mon front quelques jours ont glissé,/Il me semble qu'un siècle et qu'un monde ont passé;/Que, séparé d'eux par un abîme immense,/Un nouvel homme en moi renaît et recommence' (Whence comes, Oh God! this peace which floods over me?/Whence comes this faith with which my heart overflows?/To me who, not long ago, uncertain restless,/And tossed on waves of doubt by every wind,/Sought the good, the true, in the dreams of worldly sages/And peace in hearts resounding with tempests?/Scarcely have a few days brushed past my brow,/And it seems that a century and a world have passed away/And that, separated from them by an immense abyss,/A new man is reborn and begins again in me). Translation by Stanley Applebaum, in Franz Liszt, *Sonata in B minor and Other Works for Piano* (New York: Dover, 1989), p. 50; Alphonse de Lamartine, *Harmonies poétiques et religieuses* (Paris: C. Gosselin, Furne et Cie, Pagnerre, 1830), pp. 29–36.

[37] Henneman, 'Liszt's Lieder', p. 201.

von dem Himmel bist' is arguably a more satisfying experience than listening to a singer emote through the often-naïve vocal part. Here a truly memorable melody can be enjoyed purely for itself in an imaginative and apt piano setting that exploits Liszt's unsurpassed mastery of keyboard colour.[38]

'Der du von dem Himmel bist', Schlesinger 1843 (First Version)

The first version of 'Der du von dem Himmel bist' was composed no later than 1842, and the first edition, published for Schlesinger of Berlin in 1843, was dedicated to the Princess Augusta of Prussia.[39] Liszt's setting is in modified ternary form, ABA', giving a through-composed feel which develops alongside Goethe's verse while still maintaining a sense of musical unity. In the A section Liszt set the first four lines of the poem, in the B section lines 5 and 6, and in the A' section the final two lines. Liszt repeats and edits the lines of the final two sections considerably in order for the song not to be musically unbalanced. Both the transcription for solo piano of the first version and the second version (1856) bear the subtitle 'Invocation' in first editions, Liszt obviously wishing to highlight the prayer-like entreating of the poem, as is borne out by his setting being in E major, which Paul Merrick convincingly argues is Liszt's religious key.[40]

The first version begins with an eight-bar solo piano introduction which, although marked *Langsam* and *sotto voce*, and never rising much above *p*, serves to signal the imminent mood of unsettled agitation. Liszt uses a harmonically rich series of chords (Ic, iii°7, vii°7, V7 with a 4-3 suspension before finally arriving at V7) over a B♮ pedal note to prolong a V7 harmony through these initial eight bars. The pedal note, however, is disturbed by chromatic auxiliary motion, which helps to create the sense of agitation. The introduction also contains a short motif of four semiquavers, slurred in pairs, rising from F♯ to G, and then falling from G to F♯, that reappears in the accompaniment in various transpositions throughout the song (see Example 6.8). The vocal writing is mostly syllabic, though with some occasional ornaments to add colour to certain words such as 'Schmerzen' (pain) in bar 12, which Liszt embellishes with a move in auxiliary motion from the tonic to the flat 9th and back. The accompaniment is in right-hand arpeggios, with octaves in the left hand. During the four-bar passage that transitions into the B section, the piano writing changes into a more overtly nocturne-like style.

The B section begins in C minor and moves to G sharp minor before arriving at a five-bar passage marked *Agitato* based on the alternation between the secondary dominant in diminished 7th form (V°7 of V) and the dominant in the home key of E major. The piano accompaniment adds a sighing motif in the right hand, which adds to the sense of restlessness as the singer questions 'What use is all this pain and

[38] Ibid.

[39] Liszt also dedicated his *Élégie sur des motifs du Prince Louis Ferdinand de Prusse* to Princess Augusta. Liszt first met her in Berlin in December 1841.

[40] Paul Merrick, *Revolution and Religion in the Music of Liszt* (Cambridge: Cambridge University Press, 1987), p. 297.

Example 6.8. 'Der du von dem Himmel bist' (first version), Schlesinger 1843 (bars 1–8).

joy?'. A brief cadential flourish in arpeggios based on V9 finishes on a D major chord in preparation for the return of the opening motif. However, it is a false return, as it is set in the key of G major. Liszt uses this to employ some keen harmonic sleight of hand as he moves to the relative minor before coming back to the home key of E major while setting the words 'Süsser Friede! Komm, ach komm in meine Brust!' (Sweet peace! come back to my breast), mirroring the return to more peaceful times for which the poet yearns.

The A' section proper begins at bar 39. The piano accompaniment is fuller at this point and contains the original two-note motif along with a similar counter-motif played in the tenor register. The piano writing thickens to encompass, eventually, a full statement of the opening vocal melody in large four-note chords in the right hand. However, the vocal writing is not based on the opening vocal melody but rather on the two-note motif of the piano introduction. Liszt recalls two earlier lines ('Ach, ich bin des Treibens müde!' and 'Der du im Himmel bist') and places them in between repetitions of 'Süsser Friede!' and 'Komm, ach komm in meine Brust!'. These interpolated lines bring about the climax of the song and display Liszt's operatic tendencies in vocal writing. His change of the line 'Der du von dem Himmel bist' to 'Der du im Himmel bist' is significant, as it adds a sense of narrativity to the song: it implies that the peace the poet seeks is indeed attainable only in death, something present but more veiled in the original.

The heavy editing of the poem by Liszt in the A' section allows him to recall earlier motifs and combine them together in a compositional device like that found at the climaxes of some of his greatest operatic fantasies.[41] Similar in effect to a fugal stretto, it serves to bring the nervous agitation of the song to a satisfying climax.

---

[41] *Réminiscences de Norma* contains probably the most famous example.

Example 6.9. 'Der du von dem Himmel bist' (second version),
Schlesinger 1856 (bars 1–7).

'Der du von dem Himmel bist', Schlesinger 1856 (Second Version)

The second version was composed in July 1856 and published soon after by Schlesinger. It would best be described as a variant that functions as a facilitation of the 1843 version. It retains many of the features of the original, in terms of key, motifs, and form, but Liszt has pared back the difficulties for both pianist and singer while also tempering the climax and removing some repetitions of phrases, most significantly the line 'Der du im Himmel bist'. In this version we can perceive Liszt still viewing the poem as he did in his earlier setting but modifying his vision to fit into a more conventional Lied aesthetic. The result is less demanding for both musicians, and at a level of sonority that would not sound overbearing in the confines of a salon, versus the concert-aria proportions of the earlier setting.

'Der du von dem Himmel bist', Kahnt 1860 (Third Version)

The third version is the most significantly revised. Indeed, the revisions are such that the entire aesthetic of the song could be said to have been recomposed from the salon (in the second version) to the symphonic. And although it is the shortest of the three versions, Liszt created a work that is expansive, looking forward to the music of Mahler, treading ground not unlike the fourth movement of Mahler's Symphony no. 3.

The third version of 'Der du von dem Himmel bist', like the previous two, is marked *Langsam* and is cast in the key of E major, but Liszt has changed the time signature from $\frac{3}{4}$ to $\frac{4}{4}$. The addition of the harmonically striking piano introduction (the opening harmonic gesture is V7–iii–V7, V7–♭III–V7) signals the change in aesthetic. In stark contrast with the earlier versions, the piano accompaniment here consists of large

Table 6.4. Summary of changes between versions of 'Der du von dem Himmel bist'.

Version 1	Version 2	Version 3
N/A	Facilitation of vocal line and accompaniment. Removal of some textual repetitions.	Complete change of form, time signature, texture, and mood. Pianistic difficulties are greatly reduced. Vocal range is narrowed but is now more independent and exposed. New harmonic and melodic material is introduced.

slow-moving chords that are mostly rhythmically independent of the vocal line and devoid of thematic material. Liszt has also altered the form, making the song closer to a through-composed setting, with only the opening piano introduction and coda being related. As the coda draws heavily on the introduction, but in an expanded form, the ensuing form (Introduction–A–B–C–Coda) creates a cyclical feel while following the development of the poem's content (see Example 6.10.

Liszt has also greatly reduced the number of repetitions of phrases even from the second version. The vocal part has been lowered and the range narrowed, but that is not to say that Liszt does not place heavy demands on the singer. Due to the relative independence of both parts, the singer is more exposed and must manage many entries with the utmost control, not to mention the negotiation of numerous chromatic passages along with the need to colour each word appropriately.

Liszt has changed the declamation slightly by shifting the opening phrase back a beat to begin on an anacrusis. By contrast, in this opening section the piano plays only two chords per bar, on the weak beats of 2 and 4. The chords are slurred and function similarly to the sighing motif of the first version, though at a much slower pace and with much less restlessness.

This radical recomposition of the song speaks of several elements coming together: firstly, Liszt's re-reading of Goethe's poem, finding a calmer, almost resigned perspective; secondly, the significant development of his Lieder aesthetic, including but not limited to a refinement of the prosody; and lastly the changing circumstances of his life. At the time of composing the third version (1859) Liszt's tenure as *Hofkapellmeister* in Weimar was coming to an end. Though he would not leave until 1861, his departure was precipitated by, among other setbacks, the calamitous premiere of Cornelius's two-act opera *Der Barbier von Bagdad*, which Liszt had conducted in Weimar in 1858. Liszt and Carolyne were still trying to procure an annulment of her first marriage so that they could wed; by 1859 the couple had been unsuccessfully making efforts for nearly ten years. The task must have seemed impossible at the time, and it would ultimately prove a fruitless endeavour. Liszt would look back at his time in Weimar as a disappointment, and indeed the wanderer of this third version is a much more resigned and world-weary figure.[42]

---

[42] A note of caution should be sounded about linking the revisions in this third version of 'Der du von dem Himmel bist' to Liszt's fortunes too definitively. A perusal of other works

Example 6.10. 'Der du von dem Himmel bist' (third version), Kahnt 1860 (bars 37–54).

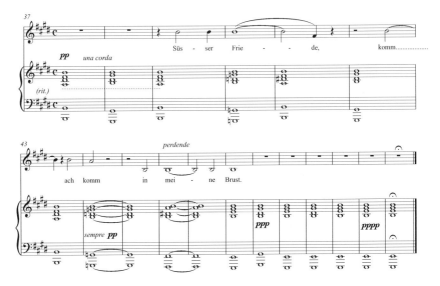

'Freudvoll und leidvoll' (LW N23)

Within his lifetime, Liszt published three different versions of 'Freudvoll und leid-voll' based on 'Klärchen's Song' from Act 3 Scene 2 of Goethe's *Egmont*. This study focuses on the first and last versions.[43] It explores Liszt's evolving responses to the text and proposes that the last version be considered a separate version (a recomposition) rather than a variant of the first setting, even though it clearly retains several key features. The intermediate version, normally known as the second setting, is unrelated to the others, with the key, harmonic changes, melodic contour, and rhythmic patterns all being different. Indeed, it is even highly contrasting in terms of mood and character, and the term resetting would best describe it.

Normally the three versions are described chronologically: first setting, version 1; second setting; and finally, first setting, version 2. However, I will argue that it is more accurate to consider them as three separate versions – with the third reusing some material from the first but recomposing it significantly and introducing new material in such a way as to constitute a separate entity – thus, highlighting a greater disparity between the versions than the current designation of revision implies. I will demonstrate that the form is only seemingly retained between the first and

---

composed at the same time reveals many works that would not fit this interpretation. In drawing attention to Liszt's circumstances, the intention is to highlight parallels rather than present intuitive leaps as concrete assertions.

43 Liszt also published a transposed version in E major of the third version alongside the original in A flat major. There are some differences between these two later versions, but due to space restrictions a detailed comparison of these two later versions has not been included.

Table 6.5. 'Freudvoll and leidvoll' – *Egmont* (1788) – J.W. von Goethe.

Freudvoll	Full of joy,
Und leidvoll,	And full of sorrow,
Gedankenvoll sein;	Full of thoughts;
Langen	Yearning
Und bangen	And trembling
In schwebender Pein;	In uncertain anguish;
Himmelhoch jauchzend,	Exulting to heaven,
Zum Tode betrübt–	Cast down unto death–
Glücklich allein	Happy alone
Ist die Seele, die liebt	Is the soul that loves.

Translation is by Richard Stokes, *Liszt: The Complete Songs, Vol. 2*.

Table 6.6. 'Freudvoll und leidvoll' – comparison of form by lines set in versions 1 and 3.

Section	*Intro*	*A*	*B*	*C*		*Coda*
Version 1						
Length (bars)	16	16	16	21		16
Lines set	N/A	1, 2, 3, 4, 5, 6	7, 8	9 10, 9 10, 10, 10, 9 10		N/A
Version 3						
Length (bars)	4	8	10	10		5
Lines set	N/A	1, 2, 3, 4, 5, 6	7, 8	9 10, 9, 9 10		N/A

third versions, the harmonic and melodic similarities are only present in the opening sections of each version, while there are differing textures and musical gestures, as well as contrasted harmonic schemes. It is enormously interesting to glimpse Liszt's compositional processes and see how he integrates older material here and specifically how his command of texture allows him to mould it to his later aesthetic.

From Table 6.6, which indicates the length of each section in both versions and where each line of the poems appears, including repetitions, it seems that the two versions do indeed share the same form. Between versions the length of each section varies little proportionally in relation to the whole, except in the case of the introduction and coda, each of which has been significantly shortened in the later version. However, when one considers the motivic and harmonic structure, the first version is cast in a symmetrical form while the third version is through-composed, but with a repeat of the introduction acting as a coda.

Both versions are in A flat major and begin with solo piano introductions that state the open melodic theme with the highly recognisable falling 6th and the distinctive harmonic gambit of I–i–♯V7–I. Interestingly, however, in the later version when Liszt uses the same harmonic pattern, he changes the enharmonic 'spelling' to I–i–Ger6–V7–I, changing the raised V7 chord to an augmented Ger6 on F♭. The original spelling may simply have been to facilitate an easier reading of the accompaniment, or perhaps it signals a further development in his compositional or notational style, as the Ger6 in the later version functions as would be expected (that is, used as a pre-dominant chord) in the new spelling. With such similar distinctive features, it is easy to see why this last version is, in general, considered a revision. However, by examining both versions more closely, it is possible to consider it a recomposition. Even though both the introduction and A section share harmonic similarities, it is worth noting the difference in structure of both introductions. In the third version Liszt merely has the piano play the first four bars of the A section. However, in the earlier version he included a motif that does not feature in the later version at all but is further developed in the C section and the Coda of the first version only (see Example 6.11, bars 9–14).

The most obvious changes are to the time signature and tempo marking, from a ⅜ *Quasi Allegretto* to a ¼ *Andantino*. On the face of it there is little difference between the two tempi; however, the alteration in time signature is significant as it creates a more meditative and sombre mood, further heightened due to the modifications in texture and rhythm in the accompaniment. The nocturne-like piano introduction of the first version begins with the characteristic arpeggio accompaniment in the left hand with the motivic falling 6th in the right hand. This is contrasted in the third version with larger-spread arpeggios which also have a motivic function, by trailing the right hand in canon. The rhythmic change to the crotchets in the second half of each bar creates a type of musical punctuation. By breaking the even flow of quavers, matching more closely the prosody of Goethe's text, these longer notes could be read as rhetorical pauses that match the line breaks in the poem. Also, the new rhythm gives a clearer emphasis to the first syllable of the words 'freudvoll' and 'leidvoll', likewise on 'langen' and 'bangen', whereas in the first version both syllables of each word fall on strong beats. (In this first version Liszt counteracts any chance of stressing both syllables by placing an accent above the first syllable of each word.)

The newer texture introduces more variety of register by placing the falling 6th above the range of the singer, whereas in the early version it is simply restated at the same octave (see Example 6.12). The newer texture is reminiscent of the central *lagrimoso* section (bar 56 ff.) of Liszt's gloomy masterpiece, *Funérailles*, no. 7 from the *Harmonies poétiques et religieuses* (LW A158 No.7), a piece that was in response to the execution of Hungarian nationalists in October 1849. The link between it and 'Freudvoll und leidvoll' may seem tenuous at first, but when we remember that Goethe's Egmont also fought for independence, his subsequent fate, and Klärchen's despondent reaction, a strong parallel can be drawn. Not unlike the combination in Liszt's song, the *lagrimoso* section of *Funérailles* is a mix of mournful sighing and nostalgia. *Funérailles* does not feature in the earlier unpublished first version of *Harmonies*, and due to the nature of its inspiration it is unlikely that it was composed earlier than 1850. Therefore, while this section may indeed be a veiled and apt reference to the earlier song, it should be noted that Liszt had not yet published this third version of the song, which contains the texture in question.

The contrasting B and C sections do not share any surface similarities with the earlier version in terms of texture, harmony, or musical gesture. In the B section the motif is based on arpeggio movement in the first version and stepwise melodic

Example 6.11. 'Freudvoll und leidvoll' (first version), Haslinger 1848 (bars 3–18).

Example 6.12. 'Freudvoll und leidvoll' (third version), Schlesinger 1856 (bars 1–8).

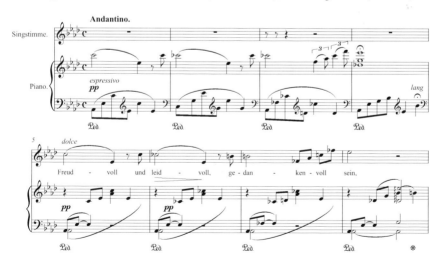

Table 6.7. A comparison of form by motivic material in version 1 and version 3.

Section	Intro	A	B	C	Coda
Version 1	Motif 1: Motif 2	Motif 1	New material	Motif 2	Motif 2: Motif 1
Version 3	Motif 1	Motif 1	New material	New material	Motif 1

movement in the third version. The accompaniment is also quite different, with the arpeggios thickening and the introduction of large emphatic chords with semiquaver anticipations in the right hand. The vocal part reaches its highest, longest, and loudest notes during this section, which is heavily marked with accents and marked *rinforzando.* In the third version we also reach a louder dynamic; however, this is quickly negated by a quaver rest with a fermata, again mirroring a more rhetorical and meditative reading of the poem. The C section in the first version is derived from the second motif of the introduction, while in the third version new material is heard at this point. And indeed, the coda in the first version bears little resemblance to the third version as it is also based on the second motif of the introduction. The version 1 coda is substantially longer and contains passagework that is, again, reminiscent of the nocturne genre, with its appoggiatura embellishment of the distinctive four-against-six arpeggios of the introduction. However, there is further reference to the opening motif by introducing the Ger 6–I progression; thus, the coda reverses the harmonic structure of the introduction. By comparing the equivalent forms and motifs it becomes clear that in the third version Liszt has, in fact, altered the original structure in a considerable way.

By the time Liszt composed the first version of 'Freudvoll und leidvoll' he had already received negative reviews for his two *Bücher der Lieder* and the *Sechs Lieder* from Oswald Lorenz in the *Neue Zeitschrift für Musik.* As already mentioned, Lorenz did not even recognise the songs as Lieder, instead preferring to call them 'glittering vocal pieces' (*glänzende Pracht- und Paradestücke*).[44] Lorenz was extremely scathing of Liszt's failure to follow the conventions of the genre in terms of harmony and the demands placed on both singer and pianist, which may explain the delayed publication of the first version of 'Freudvoll und leidvoll' and why the technical demands are noticeably tempered. However, the first version undoubtedly draws its musical lineage if not as much from the operatic tradition as from Lieder, with its large climaxes, while also being similar in texture to a Field or Chopin nocturne. The third version is one of Liszt's most approachable Lieder, even though he has raised the vocal register into the soprano range.[45] It demonstrates how Liszt was able to mould older material to fit within his developing aesthetic of the Lied, and Alan Walker goes as far as to claim that it invokes the musical language of 'High Romanticism', looking more to the future and inhabiting a world that Mahler and Richard Strauss would make their own.[46]

---

[44] *Neue Zeitschrift für Musik*, 28 December 1843, p. 205.

[45] This is tempered by the fact that, alongside it, Liszt published the lower E major version, which sits comfortably in the mezzo-soprano range.

[46] Walker, 'Liszt and the Lied', p. 152.

'Es war ein König in Thule' (LW N9)

During his lifetime, Liszt composed and published at least three versions of 'Es war ein König in Thule'. The first was composed in 1842 and published by Schlesinger in Berlin in 1843 as part of the *Buch der Lieder*. The second, intermediary version, perhaps better categorised as a variant, was composed no later than 1856 and also published by Schlesinger. A third version was composed no later than 1859 and published by both Schlesinger of Berlin and Kahnt of Leipzig that year. This study examines the evolution between the first and third versions and omits discussion of the second version.

Both the first and third versions are similar in length – 90 and 99 bars respectively – and they have several features in common. Indeed, many bars are the same or nearly identical. This, however, should not be taken as an indication that the third version represents a minor revision. The changes in scale are such that the reading of the poem, while retaining certain features such as a very closely related structure, has been radically altered. The main changes between the first and third versions could best be categorised as ones of proportion. As well as the form, the melodic material and harmony are retained between the versions, with relatively minor changes. The song's technical demands and sonorities, on the other hand, have been significantly pared back in sections, while retaining plenty of the drama present in the original.

Goethe's poem is a miniature ballad of six stanzas written in 1774. It was published separately several times before being included in a revised form in *Faust I* and therefore may be regarded as a work of considerable textual fluidity in and of itself. However, it is unlikely that Liszt was aware of the genesis or earlier versions of the poem, and his familiarity with the ballad was most probably confined to his knowledge of *Faust*, which he re-read throughout his life, and with which he was intimately acquainted.

The main theme of 'Der König in Thule' is of unending fidelity. The ballad is replete with symbolism: the choice of the lover as a mistress, the use of the goblet to represent the consecration of fidelity, and the setting in the mythical kingdom of *Ultima Thule*, which gives the ballad an otherworldly parable-like quality.

In *Faust*, 'Es war ein König in Thule' is sung by Gretchen. Gretchen returns to her room after seeing Faust for the first time; unbeknown to her, Faust and Mephistopheles had just been present in her room. Sensing that something is untoward, Gretchen sings the song of fidelity absent-mindedly. Thus, in a case of dramatic irony, Gretchen is unaware of the source of her unease, creating a sense of impending doom; there is also the irony of Gretchen singing of unending fidelity when she herself will be betrayed by Faust, even though she will remain loyal to him beyond the grave.

Table 6.8. 'Der König in Thule' – (1774) – J.W. von Goethe.

Es war ein König in Thule	There was a king in Thule,
Gar treu bis an das Grab,	Faithful to the grave,
Dem sterbend seine Buhle	To whom his mistress, as she died,
Einen goldnen Becher gab.	Gave a golden beaker.
Es ging ihm nichts darüber,	He valued nothing higher,
Er leert' ihn jeden Schmaus;	He drained it at every feast,
Die Augen gingen ihm über,	And each time he drank from it,
So oft er trank daraus.	His eyes would fill with tears.
Und als er kam zu sterben,	And when he came to die,
Zählt' er seine Städt' im Reich,	He counted the cities of his realm,
Gönnt' alles seinen Erben,	Gave all he had to his heirs,
Den Becher nicht zugleich.	The beaker though excepted.
Er saß beim Königsmahle,	He sat at the royal banquet,
Die Ritter um ihn her,	Surrounded by his knights,
Auf hohem Vätersaale,	There in the lofty ancestral hall,
Dort auf dem Schloß am Meer.	In the castle by the sea.
Dort stand der alte Zecher,	There he stood, that old toper,
Trank letzte Lebensglut,	Drank his life's last glow,
Und warf den heil'gen Becher	And hurled the sacred beaker
Hinunter in die Flut.	Into the waves below.
Er sah ihn stürzen, trinken	He saw it fall and fill
Und sinken tief ins Meer.	And sink deep into the sea.
Die Augen täten ihm sinken;	His eyes closed;
Trank nie einen Tropfen mehr.	He never drank another drop.

Translation is by Richard Stokes, *Liszt: The Complete Songs, Vol. 2.*

'Es war ein König in Thule' (First Version), Schlesinger 1843

Though 'Es war ein König in Thule' does not number among Liszt's many transcriptions of Schubert's Lieder, he was almost certainly familiar with his forerunner's song when he composed his own setting. Just as in the first setting of 'Wer nie sein Brot mit Tränen aß', Liszt's earliest version of 'Es war ein König in Thule' has a clear link to Schubert's setting, especially in the melodic contour and rhythm of the vocal line, to the extent that it could almost be viewed as a commentary on the earlier composition.[47] However, it should not therefore be assumed that Liszt's setting is uninspired or redundant; on the contrary, the indebtedness to Schubert serves in this case to draw attention to Liszt's original approach to text-setting, form, and harmony.

47 Franz Schubert, 'Der König in Thule', D. 367 (op. 5 no. 5) (Vienna: Diabelli, 1821), p. 11.

Liszt's setting, like Schubert's, avoids a strictly strophic approach such as those of Tomášek or Zelter.[48] However, unlike Schubert, who groups the six stanzas into three, two-verse strophes, Liszt creates a modified ternary form, ABA', with a highly transformed A' section. Indeed, due to the level of transformation through modulation, changes of tempo, and piano texture in the A' section, a designation of through-composed would not be unmerited. The use of thematic transformation in this setting is so pronounced that Edwin Hughes highlighted it as an example of the technique in Liszt's Lieder.[49] Most of the melodic material in the A section, in both vocal line and piano accompaniment, is formed from a descending minor 3rd motif. The piano texture is changed for the arrival of each new section in order to allow the music to follow the thematic developments within the poem closely. This choice of modified ternary is an interesting one, as it allows Liszt to reflect both the thematic development of the poem and its actual structure (as each stanza is clearly delineated), while also creating an independently satisfying musical design. The problem of how to set a strophic text to music successfully is twofold: firstly, if the text is narrative in nature the same music may not serve to best accompany each verse; and secondly, a strictly strophic setting runs the risk of excessive musical repetition if there are many verses to set.

'Es war ein König in Thule' is in the key of F minor in a $\frac{3}{4}$ time signature. Marked *Allegretto*, it begins with a six-bar solo piano introduction, where a descending minor 3rd motif is introduced. The motif is repeated a 4th lower with alternating diminished 7th chords which create an uneasy atmosphere. This uneasiness is heightened by the rhythmic displacement, with the second beat of each bar being stressed. This could be seen to represent Gretchen's growing unease on re-entering her room, at the same time foreshadowing her fate. The initial accompaniment texture is one of simple arpeggios in the right hand with single notes in the left hand. This is maintained consistently for the first two verses which comprise the A section. When the singer enters, the accent is placed firmly on the first beat of the bar. The minor 3rd motif is used to construct a simple folksong-like melody, and Liszt places it above an advanced harmonic underlay. Each strophe is then developed using thematic transformation so that the melody is recognisable from verse to verse, but each transformation follows the content of the verse. So, for example, as we will see in verse 4, the horn-like gestures and heroic-sounding chords can be understood to reflect the knights, the royal hall, and the banquet mentioned in that verse.

The descending minor 3rd motif returns for the first half of the third verse, but now with the emphasis firmly placed on the first beat of the bar. The second half of the third verse is set to a new texture of unaccompanied voice in dialogue with chordal piano writing, the change in texture seeming to symbolise the King giving his final proclamation. The harmony proceeds through a series of Ic–V7–Ib progressions in the keys of A major and B flat minor, before moving chromatically to

[48] Václav Tomášek, 'Der König in Thule', *Gedichte von Goethe*: VII, op. 59 no. 2 (1815); Carl Friedrich Zelter, 'Der König von Thule', no. 3 in *Zelter's Sämtliche Lieder, Balladen, und Romanzen,* 4 vols (Berlin: 1812), III, p. 137.

[49] Edwin Hughes, 'Liszt as Lieder Composer', *The Musical Quarterly*, 3:3 (July 1917), pp. 390–409.

Example 6.13. 'Es war ein König in Thule' (first version), Schlesinger 1843 (bars 72–5).

V7 in the key of D flat major which leads directly into the central B section, also in D flat major.

The central section has one of the most clear-cut examples of word-painting in the song. The call-and-response texture is transformed into trumpet or horn-like writing which is clearly meant to imitate the festive atmosphere of the King's banquet hall. Liszt's setting is sensitive to the structural significance of the ballad's fourth verse, the only one that does not contain an explicit reference to death. He uses this opportunity to change key and texture, with a heroic dotted rhythm and chordal density – of orchestral proportions in the first version – that evokes the regal splendour of a banquet hall with knights in attendance.

The A' section sees the return of the descending minor 3rd motif, but this time much more animated and agitated with a fuller accompaniment. It is followed by the most technically demanding section of the song for both singer and pianist. The climax is as pianistically demanding as a concert étude: both hands have fast chromatic semiquaver scales while simultaneously the left hand is in 3rds and the right has chords which punctuate all four beats of each bar Add in at the end of this sentence: (see Example 6.13). This texture resembles that of Liszt's own concert étude *Mazeppa* and Chopin's op. 10 no. 2 Étude in A minor. That Liszt was aware from the start of the need for facilitation is evident from the inclusion of an extended *ossia* passage (it is this passage that Lorenz labelled an 'aesthetic sin' in his review, in reference to the more chromatic textures). Liszt's propensity to include passages such as this in his Lieder is just one of the elements that took his early vocal compositions far beyond his critics' horizons of expectations.

Es war ein König in Thule,' Schlesinger 1856 (Second Version)

As was normal in Liszt's revisions of his earlier Lieder, pianistic and vocal demands have been reduced in the second version, with the dramatic scale passages of the song's final four pages significantly tempered. As Liszt's first version was quite true to the prosody of the ballad – a syllabic setting with idiomatically correct declamation – it was already closer to Liszt's more mature Lieder style and did not need much revision from this perspective. Indeed, the much more pianistically elaborate 1843 version contains only very mild ornamentation in the vocal part, with limited melismata or textual repetition. One major change is the addition of a new piano texture in the A section. In the first version Liszt sets each line of each verse in the same texture, while in the second version he changes the texture for the second couplet of each verse. In the first two verses the piano part introduces a shift to the treble register for the second half of each verse, an effect which adds to the musical variety.

With the revision of 'Es war ein König in Thule' we see not so much the re-thinking of the concept of his original setting, but rather a re-thinking of its performance. By reducing both the vocal and pianistic demands markedly, Liszt removed the technical barriers which impeded the song's wider adoption. The thinning out of piano textures, especially the chromatic scale passage, would also make the song more feasible in smaller performance spaces.

Liszt's setting is sensitive to the layers of dramatic irony present in Goethe's ballad when seen as part of the whole play. The introduction, with its syncopations and diminished 7th harmony, is in sharp contrast to the almost antique style of the vocal melody. The juxtaposition of the harmony, which is full of tension, with the more straightforward melody mirrors Gretchen's situation as she absent-mindedly sings this ballad, unaware of the impending tragedy of her fate.

Liszt's setting initially may seem overblown, especially in the earlier version, but it belies a deep understanding of Goethe's work. Its power is enhanced when considered within the context of the play, and thus the sense of foreboding and agitation, along with the foreshadowing of dramatic and tragic elements, is amply justified. Liszt's reading attempts to encapsulate every turn in the text, and brings to mind his own words describing Schubert's songs:

> Even his shortest Lieder become a fully tragic and dramatically passionate miniature opera. Instinctively, he takes refuge in recitative, and he does it often. And, like Gluck, he accentuates every nuance of the poetic idea with every emerging word and its corresponding musical expression.[50]

---

[50] Franz Liszt, *The Collected Writings of Franz Liszt*, vol. 3, part 1: *Dramaturgical Leaves*, ed. and trans. Janita R. Hall-Swadley (Lanham, MD: Rowman & Littlefield, 2014), p. 44.

Example 6.14. 'Es war ein König in Thule' (second version),
Schlesinger 1856 (bars 77–83).

'Wer nie sein Brot mit Tränen aß' (LW N34)

Liszt published three versions of 'Wer nie sein Brot mit Tränen aß', a song taken from Goethe's *Wilhelm Meisters Lehrjahre*, his *Bildungsroman* from 1795. Two of the versions are closely related variants, while the third is a highly contrasted resetting. This study will look at the publication history of the first and third versions, and show how the resetting, though showing a more developed, intimate, and personal reading of the poem, may not have been intended to supersede the first version.

'Wer nie sein Brot mit Tränen aß' is the second of three songs performed by the harper in the novel, and it appears in Book II, Chapter 13. The harper is overheard by Wilhelm singing 'Wer nie sein' behind a closed door. Wilhelm was searching for the harper 'in the hope that his music might dispel the evil spirits', and was directed to 'a shabby inn in a remote part of the town; and then up a flight of stairs to an attic room from which came the sweet sounds of the harp. The sombre, deeply moving music was accompanied by anguished melancholy singing.'[51]

Lorraine Byrne has noted that Goethe's harper was inspired by the classical myth of Orpheus, and indeed there are many parallels between the two characters, in

---

[51] J.W. von Goethe, *Goethe: The Collected Works: Wilhelm Meister's Apprenticeship*, ed. Eric A. Blackall and Victor Lange (New Jersey: Princeton University Press, 1995), vol. 9, p. 77.

Table 6.9. 'Wer nie sein Brot mit Tränen aß' – *Wilhelm Meisters Lehrjahre* (1795).

Wer nie sein Brot mit Tränen aß,	Who has never eaten his bread with tears,
Wer nie die kummervollen Nächte	who, through nights of grief,
Auf seinem Bette weinend sass,	has never sat weeping on his bed,
Der kennt euch nicht, ihr himmlischen Mächte!	knows you not, heavenly powers.
Ihr führt ins Leben uns hinein,	You bring us into life;
Ihr lasst den Armen schuldig werden,	you let the poor wretch fall into guilt,
Dann überlasst ihr ihn der Pein:	then you abandon him to his agony:
Denn alle Schuld rächt sich auf Erden.	for all guilt is avenged on earth.

Translation is by Richard Wigmore. *Liszt: The Complete Songs, Vol. 3*, Gerald Finley (baritone), Julius Drake (piano), Hyperion, CDA67956, 2015.

particular the Orpheus of Virgil.[52] The harper has beauty and power in his voice, and is able to charm his listeners; he gains the attention of his object of desire, Sperata, through song, but by a combination of his uncontrolled passion and the whim of the gods he is destined never to achieve love. Whereas (in Act 3 in Monteverdi's *Orfeo*) Orpheus is guided from the underworld by Speranza, hope personified, Goethe's harper laments giving up the expectation of love with Sperata. He is presented as an isolated, itinerant musician removed from society, one who has mystical priest-like qualities and can impart wisdom through his art, but who is ultimately a pitiful figure, who rails against fate and his situation.

The poem has been likened to an Orphic lament and the genre of *planctus*.[53] It is a profound expression of guilt and remorse, the deep guilt of having fathered Mignon unknowingly through an incestuous union with his sister. Mignon is unaware of the harper's true identity, and her parentage is gradually revealed throughout the novel. The harper is seen as an outsider by virtue of not only being among a troupe of travelling performers but also physically residing in a remote corner of the small village inn that is likewise removed from the centre of that village. The harper's grief and guilt are depicted as all-consuming, and he sees himself as a victim of fate and 'heavenly powers', with no possible end to his plight. Through the combination of the poem's lamenting style, defiance of the divine, and use of the harper as the performer of the poem, Goethe connects it to the ancient bardic performing traditions of Virgil's Orpheus. Liszt was well acquainted with this tradition as well as with various other interpretations of the Orpheus myth, including his conducting of Gluck's *Orfeo ed Euridice* and Pierre-Simon Ballanche's *Orphée*, which he got to know during the 1830s when the latter was a much-discussed and praised work in Parisian salons. Liszt also composed his own symphonic poem based on the myth, *Orpheus* (LW G9); this was premiered in Weimar before a performance of Gluck's *Orfeo ed Euridice* with Liszt himself conducting.

Liszt's first setting of 'Wer nie sein' was written in 1845 and published in 1848 by Haslinger of Vienna along with three other settings of Goethe poems: 'Über

---

[52] Byrne Bodley, *Schubert's Goethe Settings*, pp. 286–94.

[53] Ibid. A *planctus* is a song of lament or a dirge expressing mourning or grief.

allen Gipfeln ist Ruh' and two settings of the *Lied aus Egmont*, 'Freudvoll und leidvoll'. They were dedicated to Liszt's friend, the portrait artist Ary Scheffer, as were the Schiller Lieder of the previous year. A second edition of this first setting appeared in the first volume of Liszt's *Gesammelte Lieder* for both Schlesinger and Kahnt in 1859 with only some minor revisions. The second setting (third version), according to the *Grove* catalogue compiled by Maria Eckhardt and Rena Charnin Mueller, was written in 1849 but remained unpublished until 1861 and appeared in the seventh volume of the *Gesammelte Lieder*. The two settings, while having some basic features in common, are entirely unrelated compositions, poetic text excepted. Indeed, Liszt seems to have self-consciously avoided creating any similarities between the settings.

'Wer nie sein Brot mit Tränen aß' (First Version), Haslinger 1848

It is unclear whether Liszt knew all three of Schubert's settings of 'Wer nie sein Brot mit Tränen aß', as the first two were published in 1895, after his death; the third setting, however, was published in 1822 as the second of three songs of his op. 12, *Gesänge des Harfners aus 'Wilhelm Meister'*. Liszt never transcribed any of these three songs for solo piano or orchestrated them as he did over fifty of Schubert's other Lieder. He did not refer to them in his letters, and also did not choose the same key (A minor) as Schubert. Notwithstanding these differences, there are several similarities, both motivic and in terms of character and piano texture, which indicate that Liszt not only knew Schubert's third setting, but also wished to comment on it in his own way. By the time he composed his second version of 'Wer nie', Liszt may also have known Robert Schumann's setting as it was published contemporaneously (Liszt would go on, in 1874, to transcribe two of Schumann's songs from his cycle *Songs from Wilhelm Meister*).

Liszt's first version is marked *Andante Mesto*, and he uses a chromatic descending four-note motif to evoke the character of a lamentation. The piano plays arpeggios marked *p* and *un poco pesante*, a standard musical means of evoking the harp; Liszt even marks these *quasi Arpa*. The setting is in E minor and follows Goethe's poetic form loosely by dividing the song into two sections of similar length matching up with the two stanzas of the poem. Each section is itself divided into a binary form, again both similar in length, creating an [AB] [AB]' form, with the first three lines of each stanza set in the A and final line set in the B. Liszt's choice of form allows his setting to reflect both the form and content of Goethe's poem, the two quatrains of which – though of equal length and sharing the same rhyming scheme – have quite different content. The first three lines of the first stanza serve to isolate the harper and express his grief, despair, and sorrow. The last line of the stanza, which is a challenge to the heavenly forces and a damning of fate that has condemned the harper, is a change of tack that links smoothly to the second stanza. This change of tone is reflected by the form of each [AB] section. In the novel, Wilhelm is described as overhearing the harper behind a closed door, performing many phrases repeatedly; Liszt uses this opportunity to balance the song by repeating the last line of each verse and thus making each A and B section similar in length. He uses a short instrumental passage to prepare for the second stanza, which is in the parallel major key

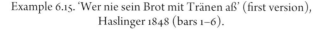

Example 6.15. 'Wer nie sein Brot mit Tränen aß' (first version),
Haslinger 1848 (bars 1–6).

(E major), reflecting the change of tone in the second stanza; interestingly, in his setting Schubert also moves to the parallel major (A minor to A major). The fermata at this point in Liszt's setting links it to the novel, as the harper is also described as starting and stopping passages. By closely following Goethe's verse while also being true to the *Bildungsroman*'s descriptions, Liszt's setting creates a song that evokes the atmosphere described in the novel.

'Wer nie sein Brot mit Tränen aß'
(Third Version/Second Setting), Kahnt 1860

The second setting is one of Liszt's most remarkable and, if the 1849 date in the *Grove* catalogue is correct, most forward-looking settings, having some of the earliest examples of the sparse and austere idiom found in the late piano works.[54] It is nominally in the key of A minor, but the constant modulation and heavy chromaticism are such that it borders on atonality and may be described as having no fixed key.[55] The formal design, length, melodic motifs, piano textures, and harmonic outline for this setting are

---

[54] Maria Eckhardt, Rena Charnin Mueller, and Alan Walker, 'Liszt, Franz', *Grove Music Online*, 2001, -0000048265> [accessed 29 August 2018]. Works that exemplify this style include *Nuages gris*, *La Lugubre Gondola I & II*, and *Am Grabe Richard Wagners*, which all date from the 1880s and are widely considered to presage many of the innovations found in early twentieth-century music.

[55] This is not to state that there is no tonality implied, but rather that the song never settles on a particular tonality.

Example 6.16. 'Wer nie sein Brot mit Tränen aß' (third version),
Kahnt 1860 (bars 1–13).

all different (see Example 6.16). The only similarity is the choice of vocal range – mez-zo-soprano. This may seem odd, since the text would suggest a male voice; however, it was not uncommon at the time for singers to perform Lieder normally associated with the opposite gender. Indeed, by placing the setting in the mezzo-soprano range, Liszt was opening the song up to the widest circle of performers. The length is vastly reduced from 82 to 29 bars. It is now in ABA' form. Each A section is built around chro-matic appoggiatura ornamentation of the ii7c chord. With no repetition in text-setting and A' being a variation on the initial section, we get a sense of constant development bringing to mind a through-composed setting such as Schubert's, while also maintain-ing musical unity with which to better absorb this unusual idiom. The harp imitation is confined to the central B section, in which Liszt uses sequential modulation that rises by step to set lines invoking the divine.

In this setting Liszt seems to alter the focus of the song, adding a sense of inte-riority which evokes the harpist's innermost feelings and pangs of guilt. This move to a more inward-looking form of expression is one of the most pronounced differ-ences between the early Lieder and his more mature style. Rather than 'describing' the scene through word-painting, the constantly wandering unresolved tonality of Liszt's third version mirrors the harpist's itinerant life, as well as the never-ending

quality of his guilt. This is further highlighted by the end, as there is no tonal reso-
lution; the song merely stops on a second-inversion chord. Thus, the ending exem-
plifies the Romantic fragment, which, paradoxically, as Richard Kramer has noted,
must be complete to appear fragmentary.[56]

'Über allen Gipfeln ist Ruh' (LW N46)

Liszt published five versions of 'Über allen Gipfeln ist Ruh' within his lifetime:
three for male-voice choir, and two Lieder. The choral versions only resemble the
Lieder in the choice of key and time signatures. And though they do not form a
part of this study, the choral versions should be considered further proof of Liszt's
ability to conceive of setting a text in a variety of ways, in which one version does
not necessarily replace another. Regarding the Lieder, some major changes take
place between the two versions; however, I believe they would still be best categorised as variants, as significant portions go almost unchanged, and the fundamental
character of the setting is not altered from one version to the next. Once criticised
by Alfred Einstein as an example of Liszt's lack of ability in songwriting, 'Über allen
Gipfeln ist Ruh' upon close inspection reveals – especially in the second version – a
thorough command of both form and the development of motivic material, where
Liszt creates a rigorous construction down to the intervallic level.[57]

Goethe signalled that this poem was connected to 'Der du von dem Himmel
bist' by designating it 'Ein Gleiches' (Another one), that is, another 'Wanderers
Nachtlied'. 'Über allen Gipfeln ist Ruh' conjures the serene calm of an evening which
Goethe experienced while staying at a hunting cabin on the Kickelhahn mountain
in Ilmenau on 6 September 1780.[58] Goethe's masterpiece (a mere eight short lines)
has an ingenious construction, including palistrophic structures, and is often cited
as a pinnacle of German lyric poetry. The language is so highly charged that it raises
several profound concepts in its brief span: of man as an integral part of nature, of
death as an aspect of life, the notion of 'nothingness', and death as a release from
conflict or pain.

'Über allen Gipfeln ist Ruh,' Haslinger 1848 (First Version)

'Über allen Gipfeln ist Ruh' was first published in a volume of Goethe Lieder by
Haslinger of Vienna in 1848. The other Lieder were 'Wer nie sein Brot' and the first
two versions of 'Freudvoll und leidvoll'. The volume was dedicated to Liszt's friend,
the painter Ary Scheffer, who was also the dedicatee of the three Schiller Lieder,
another Haslinger publication, but in the previous year, 1847.[59] Like 'Der du von

---

[56] Richard Kramer, *Unfinished Music* (Oxford: Oxford University Press, 2008), p. 358.

[57] 'With Liszt, song lost its form.' Alfred Einstein, *Music in the Romantic Era* (New York:
W.W. Norton, 1947), p. 195.

[58] Byrne Bodley, *Schubert's Goethe Settings*, pp. 123–4.

[59] The dates supplied here are from the Oxford music online catalogue compiled by Rena
Charnin Mueller and Maria Eckhardt. The Goethe-Schiller Archive in Weimar date both

Table 6.10. 'Über allen Gipfeln ist Ruh' (1780).

Über allen Gipfeln	Over every mountain-top
Ist Ruh,	Lies peace,
In allen Wipfeln	In every tree-top
Spürest Du	You scarcely feel
Kaum einen Hauch;	A breath of wind;
Die Vögelein schweigen im Walde.	The little birds are hushed in the wood.
Warte nur, balde	Wait, soon you too
Ruhest du auch.	Will be at peace.

Translation is by Richard Stokes, *Liszt: The Complete Songs Vol.2.*

Table 6.11. Lines and corresponding sections of Liszt's setting 'Über allen Gipfeln'.

Über allen Gipfeln	A (bars 1–10)
Ist Ruh,	
In allen Wipfeln	
Spürest du	
Kaum einen Hauch;	
Die Vögelein schweigen im Walde.	B (bars 11–17)
Warte nur, balde	C (bars 18–31)
Ruhest du auch	D (bars 32–47)

dem Himmel bist' (the first 'Wanderers Nachtlied'), 'Über allen Gipfeln ist Ruh' is set in Liszt's religious key of E major. The setting is divided into four sections ABCD, with the first six lines, which form the poem's first complete sentence, set in sections A and B.

The opening tempo is marked *Langsam* with a time signature of $\frac{4}{4}$. A short two-bar piano introduction evokes the serene calm depicted in Goethe's poem, through slow-moving minim chords in contrary motion. In E major, the first section is based on two phrases moving in descending 3rd harmonies before finishing on a G sharp major chord. The bass moves down in 3rds from E–C–A –F♯–D–B–E, keeping the chords in root position: I–vi–IV–ii–♭VII–V7–I. By keeping the chords moving steadily with the left and right hands in contrary motion, a sense of space and peace is created during this opening (see Example 6.17). Liszt marked the piano part *piano* and *una corda*. The voice enters in bar 2 with the expression marking *ruhig, begeistert* (quiet, rapturously) before the completion of the chord change. As can be seen from Table 6.11 above, Liszt joins together lines one and two, then lines three, four, and five of the poem to form two longer, more natural-sounding phrases ('Über allen Gipfeln ist Ruh' and 'In allen Wipfeln spürest du kaum einen Hauch'), as Schubert

---

the Schiller and Goethe Lieder Haslinger editions as 1847. Maria Eckhardt, Rena Charnin Mueller, and Alan Walker, 'Liszt, Franz', *Grove Music Online*, 2001

Example 6.17. 'Über allen Gipfeln ist Ruh' (first version), Haslinger 1848 (bars 1–10).

does in his setting. Line 3 moves to C sharp minor and finishes on a chord of V, which through some enharmonic moves brings the song into the key of F minor.

At this point (bar 11), section B begins, and Liszt changes the time signature to ¾. The piano introduces a new chromatic motif, and the voice echoes this motif in a call-and-answer fashion. By leaving the first beat of the bar empty in the piano part, Liszt adds a slightly breathless quality to this brief section. The music is built upon a chromatic motif over a V7–I chord progression, and it transitions into the next section with a iv7–i chord change, a D flat major descending arpeggio providing the transition into section C (see Example 6.18).

Section C is a modulatory passage in repeated quaver chords. There are a series of V7d–Ib chord progressions in the keys of F sharp minor, D minor, B flat major, and E major, highlighting the structural importance of the above-mentioned 3rd-related harmonies.[60] The section is a build-up towards the climax of the song, Liszt adding the indication *nach und nach bewegter* to emphasise this function. The repeated chords, though initially quite manageable, become more difficult to control as the left hand's span stretches to a 10th while also requiring the holding of internal notes (although this difficulty is mitigated by the gradual increase in dynamic and the *rf assai* indication). Liszt also provides an *ossia* for the voice at this point, and unlike many of Liszt's vocal *ossias*, it is an actual facilitation. As the passage progresses, the singer is given the choice to continue at a lower octave. The concluding section begins with a brief transition passage, which also brings the Lied back to ¼ and into the return of the opening harmonic passage in descending 3rds. The extended

---

[60] This was foreshadowed in the opening chordal sequence as the bassline moved in descending 3rds.

Example 6.18. 'Über allen Gipfeln ist Ruh' (first version), Haslinger 1848 (bars 11–19).

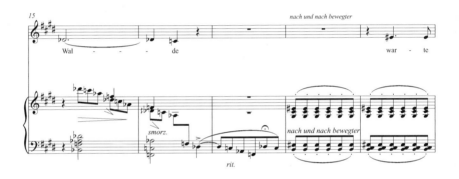

cadential passage (V7, I–iv–I) ends the song in the most tranquil fashion, the borrowed iv adding its own dark colour.

'Über allen Gipfeln ist Ruh' (Second Version), Kahnt 1860

Liszt's second version, published by both Schlesinger and Kahnt in 1860, was part of Volume 1 of his *Gesammelte Lieder*. Liszt retained several fundamental features, such as the key and time signatures. The form remained the same, with almost identical music in the first version in the A and D sections, the most extensive modifications occurring in the central B and C sections. The first A section has only minor changes such as the re-voicing of certain chords, but a noteworthy alteration is the addition of spread chords at significant junctures and the thinning out of chords in the bass register that refine the sonority and add more clarity.

The B section has more significant changes. In contrast with the first version, the voice presents the motivic material first, and when the piano answers it is not a straight repeat, but rather a foreshortened response. The C section also has been greatly revised; even though the original harmonic structure remains the same, the repeated chords have been altered to create its own three-part texture, which is in keeping with the general trend among Liszt's Lieder to have greater independence between the voice and the piano. Paradoxically, it is the changes in the transition passage back to the D section (bars 29–34) and the D section itself that are the most significant, even though they are quite subtle. In the transition passage the underlying harmony (ii–vi–IV7–V7–I) supports the modified vocal line in a much more effective way, the rise of a fourth to C♯ above the IV7 chord being particularly expressive. In the final cadence the downward progression in 3rds is now continued a step further to ♭III, then further downwards to I. The effect is threefold: firstly, by completing the harmonic sequence only implied at the very start of the song (I–vi–IV–ii–♭vii–V7–♭III–I) Liszt avoids the more conventional V7–I while still providing finality and unity to the composition; secondly, by descending a full two octaves in an unbroken progression in the bass, a great sense of expansive calm is created; and lastly, the distinctive V7–♭III change serves to link this song to the third version of 'Der du von dem Himmel bist' written contemporaneously.[61] The link seems more than circumstantial, as both songs present the progression prominently, with large slow-moving chords at triple or double *piano* dynamic. Indeed, the two songs in their later incarnations would work well as a pair, with 'Der du von dem Himmel bist' proceeding naturally into 'Über allen Gipfeln ist Ruh'. In this second version of 'Über allen Gipfeln ist Ruh' Liszt was able to achieve a remarkable fusion of music and text, not only expressing the philosophical and emotional content of Goethe's verse, but also creating a structural unity that successfully complements that of the poem (see Examples 6.19 and 6.20).

Liszt valued Goethe's works so highly that when he came to begin anthologising his songs in the 1850s, the Goethe Lieder would form Volume 1 of the collection.[62] By comparing the early and later versions of the Goethe Lieder, we can see how Liszt engaged with a genre that was arguably as far removed as was possible from the virtuoso idiom that he was so closely associated with.

His first essays in the genre can be viewed as a miscalculation on his part as to how far he could expand his audiences' and critics' horizon of expectations by grafting his own virtuosic persona onto a genre in which some quarters seemed to value, above all, simplicity of expression. Liszt was well versed in much of the Lied repertoire of the day, being aware that the Goethe texts he chose had been set many times previously, and was intimately acquainted with the settings of the same texts by Schubert and Beethoven. However, as he had not lived in a German-speaking land since his youth, when he composed his first Lieder he had not been part of a society where Lied performance formed an integral part of the cultural identity.

---

[61] It is unclear which setting was written first, for the ending of the third version of 'Der du von dem Himmel bist' also contains the distinctive V7–♭III progression. Moreover, both songs present the progression in a similar structural position with an almost identical texture. Indeed, Liszt seems to have taken Goethe's designation of 'another one' to heart when crafting the later versions of these two songs.

[62] 'Wer nie sein Brot mit Tränen aß' (third version) appeared in Volume 7 but would have undoubtedly been included in the first volume had Liszt revised/collected his Lieder for a third time. Rena Charnin Mueller maintains that this was something that Liszt seriously contemplated doing in the late 1870s. Rena Charnin Mueller, 'The Lieder of Liszt', in James Parsons (ed.), *The Cambridge Companion to the Lied* (Cambridge: Cambridge University Press, 2004), pp. 168–84 (p. 173).

Example 6.19. 'Über allen Gipfeln ist Ruh' (second version), Kahnt 1860 (bars 1–17).

Example 6.20. 'Über allen Gipfeln ist Ruh' (second version), Kahnt 1860 (bars 37–43).

Liszt's Goethe Lieder are truly eclectic in style. Several distinct influences are palpable, most notably that of Schubert, but the individuality and originality of Liszt's vision remain intact and are not overshadowed by those influences, especially in the later versions. However, Liszt was also wont to include many elements that would have been perceived as contrary to the very nature of the genre. Among these were having French or Italianate elements in the melodic line; writing of a virtuosic and instrumental nature such as the imitation of orchestral sonorities; the inclusion of operatic gestures; readings of the texts that were, on the whole, dramatic instead of lyrical; and a harmonic language that was far from simple and unadorned. The lack of adoption of his Lieder, therefore, can be readily understood.

The revisions, on the other hand, can be seen as forming part of a process of negotiation between Liszt and his intended audiences. Through experimentation in his salon in Weimar along with a greater direct connection to German musical life, he was able to curb those elements in his early Lieder which would have constructed barriers to adoption by a wider audience. Not only that, but Liszt's longer and closer engagement with German culture affected his readings of Goethe's poems, resulting often in more subtle later versions which display a refined sense of texture and sonority. Looking at the development of his Lieder through their multiple versions makes clear the remarkable variety of ways in which Liszt chose to revise his songs, taking each one on its own terms and finding a multitude of creative solutions to update them to his more mature Lied aesthetic.

Chapter 7 examines two versions of Liszt's only true song cycle, 'Drei Lieder aus Schillers *Wilhelm Tell*', and explores how the changes made between them can be seen to reflect a sea-change in Liszt's view of the Lied as a genre, especially in terms of intended performer and venue. The first version was completed in 1845, the second no later than 1859. As we have seen, during his Weimar period Liszt reacquainted himself with the German language and placed himself at the centre of a nexus of musical activity for thirteen years, as he set out to create an 'Athens of the north'. The major revisions had the effect of removing the transcendental difficulties present in the earlier version for both performers and making the work accessible to the amateur. While still technically demanding, the result was more restrained, with the focus now more firmly placed on tonal shading, and nuance.

CHAPTER 7

From the Concert Hall to the Drawing Room ... and Back: *Drei Lieder aus Schillers 'Wilhelm Tell'*

'There must, in particular, be some simplifications in the accompaniment,' Liszt claimed in a letter in 1853 to his friend and fellow composer, Louis Köhler, with reference to his early songs. In this letter Liszt made his intentions clear: that he was to collect and revise his 'earlier songs', among which 'Die Loreley' and 'Mignon' had been quoted in Köhler's own recently published book, *Die Melodie der Sprache*.[1] As was discussed in Chapter 4, Liszt's experiences on the concert stage and in Parisian salons, with their focus on virtuosity, undoubtedly influenced his first forays in song composition.[2] His songs dating from the 1840s are often highly demanding from a technical point of view, and the Schiller Lieder are no exception.

This chapter focuses on two published versions of *Drei Lieder aus Schillers 'Wilhelm Tell'* for voice and piano, one by Haslinger in 1848 and the other by Schlesinger in 1859.[3] It explores how the differences between the two versions can be seen to reflect a sea change in Liszt's perception of the Lied, especially in terms of intended performer and venue.[4] I will first highlight the main differences between the two versions and then explore the rationale and development in aesthetic principles that informed Liszt's revisions, including cuts and reuse of older material.

---

[1]   Franz Liszt, *Letters of Franz Liszt*, vol. 1: *From Paris to Rome*, ed. La Mara, trans. Constance Bache (New York: Haskell House Publishers Ltd, 1968; orig. 1898), letter 103, p. 172; Louis Köhler, *Die Melodie der Sprache* (Leipzig: J.J. Weber, 1853), p. 46.

[2]   Liszt's experiences ranged from competing in the epochal piano duel with Sigismond Thalberg in Princess Cristina Trivulzio di Belgiojoso's Parisian salon, to playing piano four-hand duets with Chopin and, more pertinently, accompanying the celebrated opera tenor Adolphe Nourrit in performances of Schubert Lieder.

[3]   For reasons of space the third orchestral version will be mentioned later, but not discussed in detail.

[4]   LW numbers are used by the *Grove* catalogue prepared by Rena Charin Mueller and Maria Eckhardt. These gradually replaced the older and incomplete R (Raabe) numbers. A revised and updated S(Searle) numbers catalogue is currently being prepared by Leslie Howard and Michael Short. The dates given are taken from the *Grove* online catalogue. Maria Eckhardt, Rena Charnin Mueller, and Alan Walker, 'Liszt, Franz', *Grove Music Online*, 2001 [accessed 29 September 2022].

Drei Lieder aus Schillers 'Wilhelm Tell' (LW N32)

Liszt composed the two versions of *Drei Lieder aus Schillers 'Wilhelm Tell'* either side of his pivotal decision in 1847 to give up the life of a travelling virtuoso and settle in Weimar to concentrate his efforts on composition. When the first versions of the Schiller Lieder cycle were composed in 1845, he was at the height of his concert-touring years and had no regular base.[5] The *Drei Lieder aus Schillers 'Wilhelm Tell'* composition is Liszt's only true song cycle, and although individual songs are occasionally performed as stand-alone numbers, Liszt undoubtedly intended them to be performed as a set. This can be borne out by contrasting the Schiller Lieder with two of Liszt's most famous song collections: the *Liebesträume* (LW N18) and the *Tre sonetti di Petrarca* (LW N14). While these two other collections are themed and can be performed as sets, they lack the interconnecting features such as the *attacca* indications and the cross-referencing of songs that make the Schiller songs a true song cycle. This is especially clear in the 1848 edition, where each song leads directly into the next and there is a reprise of music from both 'Der Fischerknabe' and 'Der Hirt' in the closing pages of 'Der Alpenjäger'.

The title of each song derives not from the poem's incipit or subject matter, but from the character that performs it in *Wilhelm Tell*. The three songs open Schiller's most famous play and are sung by the minor characters: 'fisher boy', 'herdsman', and 'alpine hunter' respectively. Schiller's instructions are that the first song should be sung to a *Ranz des Vaches* or *Kuhreihen* melody, a traditional alpine herding call, while the following two songs are to be based on variations of the initial *Ranz des Vaches*. These seem to indicate his intention that the poems be set in a simple folk-song-like manner. Liszt's settings are anything but simple, and yet even in the more elaborate 1848 version the Schiller songs evoke a suitable sense of landscape and atmosphere.

It is worth noting that the Schiller settings were not Liszt's first works inspired by *Wilhelm Tell*, Schiller, or Switzerland, or even based on *Ranz des Vaches*-style melodies. In 1841 Liszt completed his *Album d'un voyageur* which comprised three books of piano pieces.[6] The first book, entitled *Impressions et Poesies*,[7] contained five pieces that would eventually make it into the first book of the *Années de pèler-inage*[8] – all of which are inspired by Switzerland and two of which bear inscriptions

---

[5]   The *Grove* catalogue gives the date of 1845 as the year of composition. *Grove Music Online*, 2001 [accessed 29 September 2022].

[6]   Franz Liszt, *Album d'un voyageur*, 3 vols (Vienna: Haslinger, 1842). The Haslinger edition was the first to collect the three separately published books. This collection was undoubtedly influenced by Liszt's travels throughout Switzerland and informed by his time living in Geneva where he taught piano at the conservatory during the first year of its existence, 1835–6.

[7]   Franz Liszt, *Album d'un voyageur, compositions pour le piano, 1re année, Suisse*, 3 books [LW A40], 1, Impressions et poésies (Paris: Richault, 1841).

[8]   Franz Liszt, *Années de pèlerinage, suite de compositions, 1re année, Suisse* [LW A159] (Mainz: Schott, 1858).

by Schiller.[9] The second book, entitled *Fleurs mélodiques des Alpes*, is a collection of arranged folk material.[10] Two pieces from this book would also appear in the *Première année*, though now revised and with new titles: *Mal du pays* (which is based on the *Appenzeller Kuhreihen*) and *Pastorale*.[11] Finally, a collection of three virtuoso concert paraphrases on melodies composed by popular song composers, Ferdinand Huber and Ernest Knop, makes up the last book.[12] *Montée aux Alpes: Improvisata*, the first of these paraphrases, bears the subtitle *Ranz des Vaches*. Liszt had also transcribed the overture to Rossini's *Guillaume Tell*,[13] which regularly featured in his concerts of the 1840s. His transcription of Berlioz's *Symphonie fantastique* contains yet another example of *Ranz des Vaches* writing in the third movement. Later, in 1856, Liszt would return to Schiller, taking the poet's *Die Ideale* as the basis for his symphonic poem of the same name and also composing three versions of *An die Künstler* (LW L 9) for male chorus between 1853 and 1857.[14]

'Der Fischerknabe'

The subject of the first song, 'Der Fischerknabe', is a German variation on the water myths common to many cultures: a boy has fallen asleep on the shore of a lake, and as he awakens, he hears beautiful music, the tide rises, and drags him down below.

The first version of 'Der Fischerknabe' opens with a long 24-bar solo piano introduction. The horn-like motif in bars 3–5, which traces a D flat major chord, forms the basis of most of the song's thematic material. The atmospheric introduction to this Lied is striking. It is in a highly pianistic key with unyielding arpeggios in demisemiquavers forming the basis of the opening texture. Initially these can be split between the hands, in a manner reminiscent of the third of Liszt's *Trois études de concert* (LW A118), nicknamed 'Un sospiro' (also in the same key and composed contemporaneously between 1845 and 1849); however, it becomes necessary to play them with the left hand alone. As the tempo is marked *Allegretto, senza slentare*, these arpeggios present a significant technical obstacle to overcome, especially as the right hand must simultaneously negotiate large spread chords and numerous changes of position (see Example

---

9   The pieces from *Impressions et Poesies* that would also later appear in the *Années de pèlerinage, première année, Suisse* are: 2a *Le lac de Wallenstadt*, 2b *Au bord d'une source*, 3 *Les cloches de G******, 4 *Vallée d'Obermann*, and 5 *La chapelle de Guillaume Tell. La chapelle de Guillaume Tell* and *Au bord d'une source* have inscriptions by Schiller. It was around the time that Liszt was completing the Swiss *Année* (1853) that he had a number of heated exchanges with Bettina von Arnim, in which he professed a preference for Schiller's works over Goethe's. Adrian Williams, *Portrait of Liszt* (Oxford: Clarendon Press, 1990), p. 301.

10 Franz Liszt, *Album d'un voyageur, compositions pour le piano, 1re année, Suisse*, 3 books, II, *Fleurs mélodiques des Alpes* (Paris: Latte, 1840).

11 These two pieces appeared originally as *Fleurs mélodiques des Alpes*, no. 2 Lento and no. 3 Allegro pastorale respectively.

12 Franz Liszt, *Album d'un voyageur, compositions pour le piano, 1re année, Suisse*, 3 books, III, *Paraphrases* (Basle: Knop, 1836). This book was originally published as *Trois airs suisses*.

13 Franz Liszt, *Ouverture de l'opéra Guillaume Tell* [LW A54] (Mainz: Schott, 1842).

14 Franz Liszt, *Die Ideale, sym. poem after Schiller* [LW G15] (Leipzig: Breitkopf & Härtel, 1858); Franz Liszt, *An die Künstler* [LW L9] (Berlin: Schlesinger, 1854).

Example 7.1. 'Der Fischerknabe' (first version), Haslinger 1848 (bars 1–6).

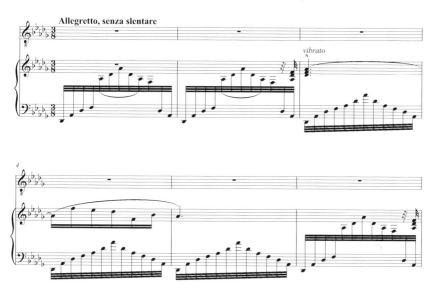

7.1). The arpeggios reach their widest spread, over five octaves, with the arrival of the V7 chord in bar 18. In bar 24, as the voice enters, the first dynamic markings appear: a decrescendo hairpin followed by *p* which is also marked *dolce*. This implies that the introduction should be played at a robust volume, and the performance indications of *vibrato*, *rinforz.*, and *marcato* confirm this. Arpeggios are often used by Liszt (and many other composers) as a tone-painting device/trope to depict flowing water, but in this case the rapidity, dynamic level, and size of the arpeggios create a more monumental atmosphere. The intention, it seems, may not have been to depict the calm, clear waters of an Alpine lake, but rather the Alps themselves, including lake and green pastures. Moreover, there is the visual aspect to consider: on the page the arpeggios have a mountain-like triangular shape evocative of the landscape that the song depicts.

In contrast, the second version from 1859 depicts a much more placid scene. The piece is still in D flat major, though now in ⅜ and marked *Allegretto tranquillo*, creating a barcarole-like effect as the arpeggiated accompaniment is now in semiquavers. This version is closer to Schiller's stage directions, as the fisher boy sings the song from his boat on the lake. Here the *una corda* pedal is deployed throughout the introduction, and the dynamic never rises above *piano*. The texture is more limpid, with fewer notes in the arpeggios and an avoidance of extended passages in a lower register of the piano. The introduction of the second version features a brief episode in A major with a *tremolando* right-hand texture which adds a shimmering quality.

The main harmonic outline is the same for both versions. In the second version, however, some transitional chords that smoothed out the harmonic movement in the first version have been removed, creating more abrupt and surprising turns. For example, Liszt moves from V7 in G flat major directly to ii in A major (bars 29–30), while in the first version in the corresponding section (bars 33–36) he repeats the V7 chord but now in its enharmonic equivalent in the key of F sharp minor, before using

Example 7.2. 'Der Fischerknabe' (second version), Schlesinger 1859 (bars 1–14).

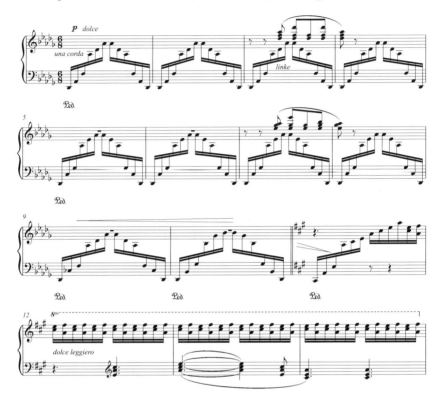

ivb in F sharp minor as the pivot chord into A major, a move somewhat reminiscent of Schubert.[15] Most of the thematic material is still clearly derived from the same horn motif that traces out the D flat major chord, but the passing notes have been removed, and the motif has also been rhythmically shortened with its range reduced, making the result much easier to sing. Indeed, the first version of 'Der Fischerknabe' places some extreme demands on the singer. The relationship between the first and second versions of 'Der Fisherknabe' is that of a recomposition.

Though Liszt retains the main harmonic progressions and melodic outline, the changes in piano texture, metre, vocal range, and expression markings transform the effect of the music markedly. At this point it is pertinent to remind ourselves to attempt to listen to these revisions in a 'sonoristic' manner. Indeed, in *The Romantic Generation*, Charles Rosen, while not citing Chomiński, expresses similar ideas and credits Liszt's command of piano texture and sonority, in reference to the *Grandes Études*, as the reason for his being able to turn 'an uninteresting student's effort into a radical work of great originality' without changing the elements more normally

---

[15] The use of enharmonic spellings to facilitate modulations to mediants is common in Schubert's music.

considered fundamental, that is, the melodic line, harmonic background, and rhythmic structure. Rosen declares that 'Liszt was the first composer in history to understand *fully* [my italics] the musical significance – dramatic and emotional as well as aural – of new techniques of execution'.[16] Therefore, though it is beyond the scope of this chapter to explore fully Liszt's multifarious use of texture, it is worthwhile highlighting the differences in texture that Liszt introduces in his second version, as these are much more than simply 'surface' changes.

Between first and second versions significant changes in texture are introduced. Whereas in the first version the texture is generally one of consistent demisemiquaver arpeggios, the second version moves between $\frac{6}{8}$ semiquaver arpeggios, *tremolando* right-hand chords in the treble with a left-hand counter-melody, also in the treble, and a third texture of repeated chords, also with both hands in the treble. This allows the structure of the poem to be more easily discerned: the textural continuity in the first version gave the Lied an étude-like quality, with many melismata and repetitions of the text, which blurred the structure of the poem; in contrast, in the second version each quatrain is punctuated by a change in texture which keeps the structure clearly intelligible. The textures also serve as text-painting devices; for example, in the second version, to highlight the lines 'Da hört er ein Klingen, Wie Flöten so süss' Liszt uses the right-hand *tremolando* texture and a counter-motif high in the treble clef for the left hand, giving a lighter quality and clarity to the 'flutes so sweet'.

The final four lines of the song also highlight the difference in approach to text-setting:

Und es ruft aus den Tiefen:	And a voice calls from the depths:
Lieb' Knabe, bist mein!	Dear boy, you are mine!
Ich locke den Schläfer,	I lure the slumberer
Ich zieh ihn herein.	And drag him down.[17]

In the first version this quatrain is preceded by a cadenza based on the alternation of the V7 chord and French augmented 6th in C sharp minor. The piano texture thickens with a bass motif in octaves and low *tremolando* chords in the right hand (see Example 7.3). As we reach the dominant 7th chord to allow for a return to D flat major both hands play *tremolando*, heightening the intensity. The vocal codetta articulates many repetitions of the text and virtuosic melismata, including brief forays into keys of G flat major and E major, as if the singer is imitating the siren-like being that has lured the fisher-boy (see Example 7.4). The song ends with a reprise of the opening material in the piano.

In the second version, the music comes almost to a halt. The piano texture is reduced to a single note while the voice is rendered declamatory in style, introducing a new motif based on the interval of a tritone. This motif is mirrored in the piano,

---

[16] Charles Rosen, *The Romantic Generation* (Cambridge, MA: Harvard University Press, 1998), pp. 491–6. Jim Samson also highlights the importance of piano texture in his chapter, 'Making and Remaking', in *Virtuosity and the Musical Work* (Cambridge: Cambridge University Press, 2004), pp. 103–33 (pp. 108–9).

[17] Translation is by Richard Stokes. *Liszt: The Complete Songs, Vol. 1*, Matthew Polenzani (tenor), Julius Drake (piano), Hyperion CDA 67782, 2010.

Example 7.3. 'Der Fischerknabe' (first version), Haslinger 1848 (bars 72–80).

heightening the sinister nature of the text. The effect of this complete change of texture is dramatic and is akin to preparing listeners for the final revelations of a ghost story. The vocal part becomes more independent of the piano, and there is no longer any ostinato; instead, the piano gently supports the vocal line with soft harp-like rolled chords, acting more as a musical commentary. Liszt's surprising harmonic turn at this point – alternating between the V7 and IIIc chords in C sharp minor – gives the closing lines an ethereal and otherworldly quality. The coda, in D flat major, ends with a faint reminiscence of the original opening motif, and the barcarole-like arpeggios are now played in quavers but combined with the repeated-chord texture (see Examples 7.5 and 7.6.

Example 7.4. 'Der Fischerknabe' (first version), Haslinger 1848 (bars 105–14).

Example 7.5. 'Der Fischerknabe' (second version), Schlesinger 1859 (bars 58–68).

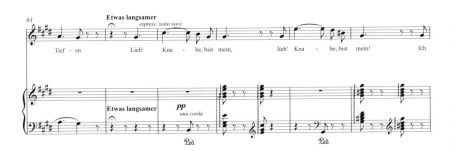

Example 7.6. 'Der Fischerknabe' (second version), Schlesinger 1859 (bars 73–82).

'Der Hirt'

The second song, 'Der Hirt', captures the wistful farewell of a herder as he leaves the mountains for the winter; it is the emotional centre of the cycle. The song's opening bars contain a similar gesture to the opening of *Mal du pays* (homesickness) (LW A159 No.8), namely a rapid oscillation between tonic and dominant chords in a broken-chord figuration.[18] As both pieces are expressions of the 'Swiss disease', Liszt seems to be using this figuration as a musical signifier (see Examples 7.7 to 7.10).

Liszt alters the form of Schiller's poem by repeating the first stanza to create a modified strophic ABA' form, one often explored in Brahms's Lieder. The differences between his two versions of 'Der Hirt', however, are less dramatic. There are no changes in tempo marking, key, or time signature. The main vocal melody of Liszt's second version is almost identical to that in the first version, though there are some occasional deviations, such as the piquant B♮ in bar 18, and the addition of a fermata in bar 22 to observe the poetic prosody. The B section in the second version has more alterations; there are fewer melismata, the supporting chords have been thinned out, as has the 'homesickness' figuration, and the *quasi corno* sections, which resemble the 'alphorn' theme from *La chapelle de Guillaume Tell*, have been omitted.[19] There are further simplifications in the solo piano section that brings the song back to A', and in the second version the A' section itself no longer has the ostinato from the first version, which had added a sense of movement to the return. *Tremolo* textures play a key role in the first version of 'Der Hirt' as Liszt uses them in both hands to create a sense of unease and foreshadowing of the stormy music of 'Der Alpenjäger'. There is a much longer transitional passage between 'Der Hirt' and 'Der Alpenjäger' (26 bars plus a further 18 bars in 'Der Alpenjäger' in the first version, versus only 10 bars in the second). They are used as a counterpoint to the voice on the repeated line 'Der Senn muss scheiden'; interestingly, in this first version Liszt omits the last line of the stanza 'der Sommer is hin', but reinstates it in the second version.

---

[18] This figuration first appears in the earlier version of *Mal du pays* entitled *Fleurs mélodiques des Alpes* no. 2 [LW A40b 7b] from the *Album d'un voyageur*.

[19] This 'alphorn' theme only appears in the earlier version of *La chapelle de Guillaume Tell* found in the *Album d'un voyageur*. Liszt also removed it from the revised version in *Années de pèlerinage, 1re année, Suisse* (1855), indicative, perhaps, of a conscious move away from such obvious musical symbols and topoi.

Example 7.7. 'Der Hirt' (first version), Haslinger 1848 (bars 21–6).

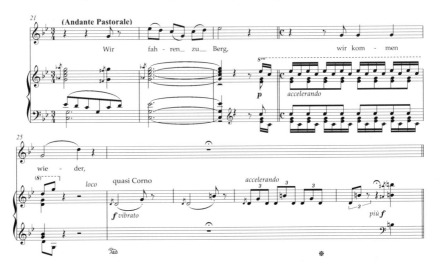

Example 7.8. *Fleurs mélodiques des Alpes* no. 2, Latte 1840 (bars 6–8).

Example 7.9. *Mal du pays*, Schott 1855 (bars 6–7).

Example 7.10. *La chapelle de Guillaume Tell* (first version), Richault 1841 (bars 7–11).

'Der Alpenjäger'

In 'Der Alpenjäger' the revisions are wholesale, with the song's overall length dramatically reduced from 117 bars to 49. The reprise of material from 'Der Hirt' and 'Der Fischerknabe' has also been excised. The time signature has changed, moving from a galloping $\frac{6}{8}$ to a more measured *Alla breve*. One of the most striking features of the first version – the virtuosity of one of Liszt's most challenging accompaniments – is completely removed (see Examples 7.11 and 7.12). Pianistic effects in the first version reminiscent of *Orage* from the Swiss *Années des pèlerinage* – such as double octaves, fast arpeggios, changes of position, and *tremolando* effects – are replaced in the second version with a simple octave *tremolo* in the right hand where the left hand doubles the vocal melody in octaves. The texture occasionally becomes a little thicker, but it also lightens to non-thematic *tremolos* which focus the attention more squarely on the singer and the text. There are some significant harmonic alterations in the later version. Liszt changes the more standard i–II7–V–i found in bars 21–2 to the less conventional i–II–iv–I of bars 12–14 in the analogous section in the second version. This helps to convey a more continued sense of foreboding and tension, and almost completely removes any heroic allusions present in the earlier version. In both versions the singing is more syllabic than in the previous two songs. However, in the first version there are many repetitions of the text to allow each musical idea to be more fully explored, while in the second version only one word is repeated, thus better preserving the original poetic development.

Removing the recall of material from the previous songs has a profound effect on the structure of the cycle and its overall impression. The first version has a sense of cyclical unity and ends on an ultimately positive tone. The second has a more fragmentary finish, suggestive of belonging to a larger unheard structure or even leading into the action of the play itself. Liszt composed several of his symphonic poems as overtures to productions of plays in Weimar. While I have come across no record of Liszt's intention to do so with the Schiller songs, it is far from implausible.

Example 7.11. 'Der Alpenjäger' (first version), Haslinger 1848 (bars 19–27).

Example 7.12. 'Der Alpenjäger' (second version), Schlesinger 1859 (bars 10–17).

Orchestral Versions

A third version of the Schiller Lieder was published by Kahnt in 1872 for tenor with orchestral accompaniment, composed shortly after the versions for piano and voice. This third version is really an orchestral transcription of the second version; however, as with all his transcriptions, Liszt did not transcribe the piano part from the second version in an overly literal manner, but instead adapted it idiomatically for orchestra, occasionally adding new counter-melodies such as the flute motif in the opening bars to 'Der Fischerknabe'. The third version has a colourful and imaginative orchestration that realises the instrumental sonorities that were only hinted at or implied in the piano version. Some scholars, including Susan Youens, have voiced a preference for the first versions of the Schiller Lieder, due to the excessive pruning in the second version by Liszt, especially in 'Der Alpenjäger'. However, on considering the orchestral transcriptions we can see that Liszt, in trimming down the thickness of the original accompaniment, had been intending to create orchestral effects on the piano that were intended not for the concert hall, but rather for the salon.

The significant technical demands placed on both performers in the first version of the Schiller Lieder take these works out of reach for the amateur performer and indicate that Liszt had two professional performers in mind. This cycle demands a highly accomplished level of technical proficiency and would necessitate rehearsal and preparation time for even seasoned professionals. These are not works designed to be performed at informal gatherings on a small instrument with little preparation. However, even though these works are indeed challenging, the piano parts fall far short of requiring the out-and-out virtuosity of Liszt's most demanding works for solo piano, such the *Réminiscences de Don Juan* (1841) or the *Grandes Études* (1839), where the technical difficulties approach the limits of the humanly possible. Indeed, even the more contemporaneous *Variations de bravoure pour piano sur des thèmes de Paganini* or the *Trois grandes études de concert*, both from 1845, are significantly more demanding in terms of the piano writing.

The same cannot be said for the vocal writing, which does require a voice of the first rank. The treatment of the voice is quite different in both versions. The first version requires a much larger vocal range and higher degree of flexibility, breath control, and mastery of tone in the high register. The writing is more operatic with numerous melismata, long high notes, as well as repetitions of and small additions to the text. The closing pages of the first version of 'Der Fischerknabe' illustrate this: here, Liszt provides an equally challenging *ossia* in the voice; the second option, in this case, is one of choice rather than a facilitation. Given that Liszt, as early as 1843, knew that his Lieder would need some form of facilitation to be accessible to the amateur market, the first version of the Schiller Lieder demonstrates that as late as 1848 he still envisaged his intended performers, especially the singers, as being of a professional standard.

In the second version of the *Drei Lieder aus Schillers 'Wilhelm Tell'*, the difficulties have been very much reduced, allowing the works to be successfully performed by amateurs, and there are textural details which are arguably more effective and subtle. My assertion is that Liszt's changing view of both the intended performer and venue for his Lieder informed his revisions. The nature of the revisions implies a much smaller venue, and does not demand so agile a voice, or one with so large and high a range, so that the emphasis can be refocused on the text and not on the performers' virtuosity. Liszt orchestrated the second version, indicating that he intended the songs to be performed as part of an orchestral concert, moving the intended venue back to the concert hall. Indeed, the second version has less overtly pianistic textures, allowing the process of orchestration to be more straightforward, although there are still differences between the piano and orchestral second versions. This fine-tuning of textural detail is characteristic of his revisions, and also – typical of the revisions in general – there are far fewer performance indications. For example, the *sotto voce*, *tristamente*, and *slargamendo* in the first version of 'Der Hirt' find no equivalent in the second version. The second versions of *Drei Lieder aus Schillers 'Wilhelm Tell'* are much more than simply facilitations. They are fully reworked and reimagined interpretations of the source material, utilising the same basic musical material but informed by a different aesthetic. Interestingly, each of the individual songs shows a different level of recomposition, with 'Der Hirt' being the most closely related to the first version, while 'Der Alpenjäger' in its second version is not only a complete recomposition, and a re-conceptualisation, but the material is so transformed that it could be mistaken as a resetting, which speaks to Liszt's rereading of the poem and perhaps the play. These revisions were undoubtedly informed by his position as court composer in Weimar, the home of Schiller studies.

Liszt presided over one of the most prestigious salons in Europe during his tenure in Weimar. When he took to revising his collected Lieder in the late 1850s, he had been in Weimar for ten years and had engaged with German musical life, language, and culture. Thus, even though he had the best possible resources at his disposal, he came to see a simpler ideal in an almost domestic genre. This is borne out by his championing of 'Es muß ein Wunderbares sein', one of his simplest Lieder, as a model of songwriting to his pupil Felix Mottl in 1879.[20] In his letter to Heinrich Schlesinger dated 18 December 1855 (see also Chapter 4), Liszt sets out how his approach to the Lied had developed – his Lieder becoming accessible to most singers and pianists – presuming they would now reach more of an audience. He also indicates how through witnessing their performances he could gauge their effect:

> ['Die Loreley'] … has now become more human in its accompaniment, without losing any of its effect, if I can partly judge from the good reception given to it when this Lied was excellently sung in its present form in local circles by Fräulein Genast. Nowadays the mezzo-soprano voice is the order of the day and Lieder composers especially should scarcely allow themselves to use the upper register without exposing themselves to the silent protest of singers on all sides. Just as it is necessary for the piano accompaniment to be easily playable, and to keep the singer, now supported, now free, as I have attempted in this new edition.[21]

---

[20] Williams, *Portrait of Liszt*, p. 568.

[21] Short, *Liszt Letters in the Library of Congress*, p. 118.

Liszt was clearly keen for as many singers as possible to take up his Lieder, because he was looking for a wider subscription. He was aware of, and was now willing to follow more closely, the conventions of the day, having been obviously disappointed by the silent and not-so-silent protests that greeted his early Lieder. This is evidenced by the preponderance of mezzo-soprano voice designations, easily playable accompaniments, and the variety of textures, 'now supported, now free',[22] present in the second versions. In contrast, in the earlier versions we find a flouting of convention, with nearly all aspects pushed past their then-acceptable limits, demonstrating that Liszt envisaged these first versions to be performed by singers of the highest calibre. Even though he did disavow his earlier versions, it is difficult to say if this was for commercial reasons – that is, to reach a wider audience by offering less technically demanding music, as well as the likelihood of the second versions selling better if they were seen as the only authentic version – or whether they in fact no longer conformed to his current aesthetic. Also worth noting in the above extract is Liszt's concern that a revision be completed without 'losing any of its *effect*' [my italics]. However, this statement seems at odds with the reality of the revisions in the case of the Schiller songs, as these do have a profound change on the effect of the music, both aurally and from a psychological dimension.

In hindsight, it may seem obvious that Liszt should have known that making his early Lieder extremely challenging would naturally limit their attractiveness to performers. However, the inclusion of near-insurmountable difficulties had not hindered the sale of his piano works, such as the operatic paraphrases and the *Grand Galop chromatique*.[23] James Deaville posits, via the ideas of Walter Benjamin, that 'Lisztomaniacs' were purchasing music beyond their technical capabilities in substantial numbers to 'possess an artefact of transcendent power and to participate vicariously in the Lisztomania of the time'.[24] It is my contention that Liszt may have been thinking along these lines when composing the first versions of the Schiller Lieder; in other words, he wished to create a transcendental musical object that the public would prefer to *own* rather than perform. By this, I do not mean that he was fixated on the commercial dimension, but rather that, in a similar fashion to his solo piano works, he felt a favourable reception depended upon virtuosos championing them in *performance* – something that was not forthcoming at the time.

The Schiller Songs as Part of Liszt's German Identity

As already mentioned, Liszt's move into Lied composition can be seen as part of a larger effort to create a more German or at least German-friendly image. In *The Virtuoso Liszt* Dana Gooley makes the convincing case that it was in fact a very self-conscious and definite strategy by Liszt, which began in earnest around

---

[22] Ibid.

[23] James Deaville, 'Publishing Paraphrases and Creating Collectors', in Christopher Gibbs and Dana Gooley (eds), *Franz Liszt and His World* (Princeton: Princeton University Press, 2006), pp. 255–88. Deaville states that within six years the *Grand Galop chromatique* sold more for Hofmeister than the entire oeuvre of Chopin within the same timeframe.

[24] Ibid., p. 271.

1840.[25] It is illuminating that by 1842, after a short intensive period of concertising and engaging with German cultural life, Liszt had managed to win enough support that he was appointed *Kapellmeister* in Weimar, a position he accepted only on a part-time basis. Over the period 1840–45, he would become involved in several artistic projects, including raising money for the Beethoven Bonn festival of 1845 and for the completion of Cologne Cathedral through a series of charity concerts, further winning favour.[26] Peter Bozó suggests that it was also during this time that Liszt made abortive plans to compose a German *Année de pèlerinage*. Interestingly, this would be based, in the main, on vocal genres, including Lieder and works for male chorus, including the pro-German and nationalistic 'Rheinweinleid'. Bozó asserts that 'Die Loreley', 'Am Rhein im schönen Strome', and 'Die Zelle en Nonnenworth' originate in these plans.[27] What is not clear is if this German *Année de pèlerinage* would have been composed for solo piano or conceived of as a collection of vocal works.

When Liszt completed the first version of the Schiller Lieder in 1845, he had only recently taken up his part-time position in Weimar. It would be natural for him to compose a work inspired by, and commemorating, one of Germany's national writers. This would also fit very well into the longer-term project of an integration into German culture and the creation of a German-friendly identity. Indeed, the first version was published just a year before the 1849 Goethe and Schiller festival in Weimar, which Liszt had organised, and which featured several of his own works commemorating the writers.

Therefore, we can see that by the time Liszt came to write the Schiller Lieder he was well acquainted with Swiss life, landscape, and popular songs, and that he was also an experienced performer and composer of Lieder with over twenty works already published in the genre. Although he had performed in many of the most prestigious salons throughout Europe during his years as a touring virtuoso, it was not until he took up residence in Weimar and presided over his own salon, trying out and experimenting with new compositions, that he began to temper the demands placed on singers and pianists in his Lieder. The later versions were part of the larger project to bring his youthful works 'up to date'; the revisions contained therein were informed by his time in Weimar, as well as by the reception and by the sales of the earlier versions.[28]

[25] Dana Gooley, *The Virtuoso Liszt* (Cambridge: Cambridge University Press, 2004), pp. 156–7.

[26] Ibid., pp.168–9, and Michael Saffle, *Liszt in Germany, 1840–1845: A Study in Sources, Documents, and the History of Reception* (Stuyvesant, NY: Pendragon Press, 1994), p. 105.

[27] Péter Bozó, 'Liszt's Plan for a German *Année de pèlerinage*: "Was ist des Deutschen Vaterland?"', *Studia Musicologica Academiae Scientiarum Hungaricae*, T. 47, Fasc. 1 (March 2006), pp. 19–38.

[28] Liszt's comments from his essay on Schubert's *Alfonso and Estrella* are illuminating with regard to his own views on the function or nature of revision. 'He did not reflect upon the plan of this latter work very long, nor did he take care to improve the work after it was completed or offer any proportional accountability regarding where it stands in comparison with the art of the past or future.' Franz Liszt, *The Collected Writings of Franz Liszt*, vol. 3, part 1: *Dramaturgical Leaves*, ed. and trans. Janita R. Hall-Swadley (Lanham, MD: Rowman & Littlefield, 2014), p. 135.

Epilogue

It is my hope that the reader is convinced that textual fluidity is not something to be avoided but rather welcomed. It forces us, in the broadest sense, to contextualise works or, rather, their texts; furthermore, it asks us to reconsider what works are or could be. Moreover, encountering textual fluidity reminds us that divergences and contradictions are to be expected as a natural consequence of most compositional practices. A chain of conflicting or varying scores may simply reflect the natural fluidity of human thought. When we consider all the other actors (for example editors and copyists) that may also interact with a score before, or indeed after, it reaches publication, it is not surprising that the composer that notates their work directly into a score, never to revise or correct, is the exception not the norm. And in terms of performance, textual fluidity does not excuse us from our interpretive responsibilities. That is, when confronted with numerous textual possibilities we must decide which one(s) to actually perform, while recognising that there may be numerous choices that are equally valid. Abandoning the teleological approach is key. As we cross this Rubicon we stop being passive servants to the composer and, instead, use our own agency to become co-creators.

Once the concept of the fluid text is accepted the question must be answered: how do we present the textual fluidity of a composer's work? The most obvious answer is in a digital critical edition or an online fluid-text edition. So what does an online fluid-text edition look like? One thing seems clear: any fluid-text edition must draw our attention to points of textual fluidity, rather than solely preserving them. Most online digitisation projects function more as digital repositories than editions. While not to the same degree as a physical inspection would allow, they do, in general, preserve the materiality of their objects to an excellent standard, allowing for close and detailed inspection of manuscripts and early editions.[1] If there are some common issues that could see improvement, they would be in the area of search functionality and the tendency for these projects to be siloed. Nevertheless, even if these were resolved, a large searchable database is a different proposition to a digital edition. An interesting digital repository is the Josquin Research Project. Its researchers have transcribed/re-notated original early music scores by numerous composers into several digital formats. Firstly, they are transcribed using Finale and then converted into MusicXML and Humdrum syntax. The online scores are

---

[1]   There are, of course, numerous drawbacks to physical inspections, leaving aside travel expenses, such as the short amount of contact time and the possibility of damaging the materials.

searchable by rhythm, keys, and intervals. The data can be used to generate analyses of the music and graphic scores. One negative accepted by the director of the project, Jesse Rodin, is that they have lamentably not been able to transcribe multiple versions of works. This, however, stems from the original research goals of the project, which were to clarify issues of attribution in the Josquin repertoire. As Rodin explains, in response to the question of why they did not encode variants:

> In an ideal world we would. Unfortunately doing so would take so much time that new works would be added at a snail's pace. This points up an important aspect of the project: the JRP is above all a powerful finding aid and analytical tool. It is not intended to replace published critical editions.[2]

The Online Chopin Variorum Edition (OCVE) is likewise another excellent resource with very intuitive functionality. One feature that is particularly useful is the ability to compare a selection of up to four bars instantly across all the editions in the collection. Where this feature could be improved would be an ability to highlight all the bars in a document/edition where issues of textual fluidity exist. That way we would be guided quickly to the bars most in need of inspection from a textual perspective. While the compared editions in the OCVE are presented in chronological order, it is not always clear that this is the case. The issue is not that the OCVE has not preserved the pertinent information, but that it could be presented more clearly or have a more streamlined navigation. As no music has been re-notated into a new digital score, I am not convinced that it is correct to call the OCVE an edition. Rather, it is a collection of historical ones. There is no value judgement in this as a resource, just a recognition that its description as an edition does not seem accurate.

I would argue that a fluid-text edition of Liszt's music should not only preserve the materials as OCVE does, but also create re-notated digital scores that have a more intuitive and interactive functionality, and that can also refer to the digitised historical editions when necessary. Preserving and referring to the historical sources frees up the new edition to incorporate a range of visualisation techniques that may differ from any one edition from Liszt's time but may yet help us gain a greater understanding of the work across all its iterations. In advocating for visualisations that look quite different from a traditional score I am reminded of Ingarden's conception of the musical work as being separate from its means of preservation/presentation. The recently announced *Franz Liszt Digital* project is addressing some of these concerns, but as the project is very much in its initial stages it is too early to say how this will turn out. Nevertheless, the outlook is promising:

> The composer's works and their *versions* are to be made visible and available to research. The researchers also plan to create a visualisation of the frequently complex connections between the works. ... there is no complete catalogue of sources and works. The reason may also be that Liszt's output is especially resistant to a clear-cut definition of pieces. [There is] hardly a catalogue of a Romantic composer as elusive, colourful, and *fluid* [my italics] as that of Liszt ... The digital Liszt portal is designed to map this complexity and to highlight Liszt's multi-fac-

---

[2] *Josquin Research Project*, 'About' section. <https://josquin.stanford.edu/about/>.

etted [*sic*] inspiration from many different angles. This will also enable users to gain a new understanding of composing in the 19th century.[3]

Interestingly, current research trends in early music have moved away from trying to establish authoritative single fixed texts and instead the goal seems to be to recreate the more fluid relationships with musical texts that the original users of them would have had.

> What all of this means is that we can now look for specific, improvisable contrapuntal structures in a whole stratum of secular polyphony that many of us have always believed is close to the so-called unwritten tradition. Indeed, it raises a question of genuine historiographic significance: is the work before you a composition or just a transcription of a common practice? Motets and masses are implicated here as well, for it only takes a perspectival shift to see how compositional commonplaces, such as stretto fugues, standard imitative techniques, and canons, related to the improvisatory abilities composers would have brought to their imagining of relationships among voices. ... we should probably all be studying how to improvise, for which I recommend Peter Schubert's wonderful short courses on extemporizing canons in two and three voices, and Barnabe Janin's instructions for learning to 'sing on the book.'[4]

In turn this has led to a reexamination of what the function of a critical edition is, and what the underlying precepts are. From the following excerpt, especially when attempting to capture the music of a tradition that does adhere to a single fixed-text model, we can see that notions such as the work concept and *Urtext* are not part of the right conceptual framework.

> But this led to a new questioning of the assumptions underlying a critical edition and underlying the notion that there was just one correct solution to most editorial questions. Inevitably the new developments of the internet offered attractive, multiple solutions. So, the next development was online editions in which the user could choose between various possibilities.[5]

The solution advocated for by musicologists working in that repertoire is likewise a digital critical edition.

> Good critical editions have always aimed to assist smart performers; most editors hope performers will make use of the options presented in the commentaries appended to the edited scores. But for those short on time or the stamina to trawl through the cryptographic tables of variants and decode alternative inter-

---

[3] *Franz Liszt Digital* press release, 17 January 2022 < https://www.uni-heidelberg.de/en/newsroom/franz-liszt-digital> [accessed May 2023].

[4] Elizabeth Eva Leach, David Fallows, and Kate Van Orden, 'Recent Trends in the Study of Music of the Fourteenth, Fifteenth, and Sixteenth Centuries', *Renaissance Quarterly*, 68:1 (Spring 2015), 187–227 (p. 212). Since then, there has been an explosion of interest in improvisation as evidenced by the resurgence of *partimento* practice and the publications of John Mortensen, Giorgio Sanguinetti, Robert O. Gjerdingen, Thomas Christensen, Job IJzerman, and Peter van Tour.

[5] Ibid., p. 202.

pretations, paper editions have always been cumbersome to use to full advantage. In cases like the New Josquin Edition discussed by David Fallows, editors are replacing the old-style critical notes that read like raw HTML with user-friendly prose. Digital critical editions, by contrast, can present alternate readings via visualization tools that allow users to view the variant passages in question simply by clicking on the score.[6]

Taking a cue from Jerome McGann's *A New Republic of Letters* (2014), I would also argue that there is an onus on scholars to create and be involved in digitisation projects. McGann issues a stark warning that it is of the utmost urgency for scholars to take an active interest in these matters as there are numerous large-scale and for-profit endeavours already in place. The crux of his argument is that for digitisation projects to be successful, that is, for those projects to accurately reflect the textual history and materiality of the documents they are digitising, they need to be steered by scholars that are well versed in textual criticism. It is only then that they can engage in the work of enhancing our methods of explicating aesthetic works by expanding our interpretational procedures.

It is my contention that our relationship to the music of the common practice era, and of Liszt in particular, would be enriched if it moved more in the direction of early music practitioners. Destabilising 'the text' helps us to reconceptualise what performance can be. We can expand on the interpretive possibilities and procedures of current performance practice – not only allowing for the redevelopment of older traditions, such as the improvised prelude, but expanding the current practice into new territory.[7] This is not a prescriptive diktat; rather, it is an appeal to performers, listeners, teachers, critics, booking agents, and other gatekeepers to be more pluralistic and, with luck, avoid moralising pronouncements. Both Daniel Leech-Wilkinson and Paulo de Assis have advocated similar shifts in perspective to our relationship with musical works and texts. Leech-Wilkinson advocates a move towards an orientation with musical texts that has a greater similarity to theatre practice.

> I don't suppose we think that Shakespeare is a lesser artist than Beethoven. But relatively few, I imagine, think that Shakespeare still minds how we perform his plays; or that we owe him a duty of faithfulness to perform them in full and in the manner he expected; or that actors must be trained in the correct way of speaking his words; or that if they speak them in a novel way they are being unfaithful or disrespectful; or that they should read a text just as their teacher recommends; or that creativity must be limited to small details of intonation; or that performance norms need be so strictly drawn that a play can be staged on one rehearsal, or as traditionally as a religious ritual. Looked at from the perspective of theatre, and its high public profile and widespread appeal, these beliefs seem quite mad. ... If it works for Shakespeare, bringing fresh insights that help the play to live, then

---

6   Ibid., p. 218.

7   Some recent performances that have ventured into this arena and demonstrated the validity of a freer relationship with musical texts of canonical works include the reimagined opera *Dido and Belinda*, and Paulo de Assis's *Rasch* and *Deleuzabelli Variations*.

why not for Beethoven? Is this why a theatre production can sell enough tickets to sustain a run of repeat performances while few concerts sell out once?[8]

Paulo de Assis, like Leech-Wilkinson, while allowing for normative performances, advocates expanding interpretative boundaries. De Assis, however, conducts this reorientation by reconceptualising the ontology of musical works:

> Works appear then as multiplicities, as highly complex, historically constructed assemblages defined by virtual structures and actual things. While traditional musical ontologies remain attached to hermeneutic, analytical, and interpretative approaches, the new image of work enhances the emergence of creative, per-formative, and experimental events. Beyond transcendental typologies, beyond extreme or qualified versions of Platonism, beyond functional theories of opera-tive concepts, and beyond aesthetic considerations coming from the ivory towers of academia, this new image of work offers a redefinition of musical works as highly flexible, mobile multiplicities with potentially infinite constitutive parts that can be exposed in different modes, to different audiences, and at different times. The shift from a work-centred perspective to a vision of an exploded con-tinuum made of innumerable objects and things, in steady intensive interaction with one another, creates fields of discourse, practice, and perception based on pure difference, leading to processes of differential repetition. ... When looking at those exploded things, a musician or a scholar has two options: one is analyti-cal, remaining at a certain distance from the materials of musical practice, ques-tioning things in terms of what they are, how they appear, which properties they have, and what relations they entertain with each other; the other option is one that decidedly dives into the materialities of music-making, focusing on what to do with these things, how to reactivate them, searching for the yet unseen virtual components that they possess, asking which potentialities they have, and how to express them anew.[9]

Resistance to this sort of reimagining of musical practice and ontology is to be expected. It is destabilising to current practices and power structures. The status quo makes exerting intellectual property rights easier, making aesthetic judgements easier, and likewise the teaching, examining, and adjudicating of music easier. And so, we are left with the question, should we reexamine our own practices and their most fundamental precepts or merely continue to do what is convenient? It seems to me that, despite the obvious challenges, the process of reimagining what musical practice and musical objects can be that de Assis and Leech-Wilkinson are arguing for is precisely the type of action needed to create, preserve, and celebrate the music that we value.

---

[8] Daniel Leech-Wilkinson, 'Comparison with Theatre', <https://challengingperformance.com/the-book-18-2> [accessed 5 May 2023].

[9] Paulo de Assis, 'Virtual Works – Actual Things', in *Logic of Experimentation* (Leuven: Leuven University Press, 2018), pp. 41–68 (p. 67).

Appendix: Transcriptions and Translations of Contemporaneous Reviews of Liszt's Lieder (1843–9)

Review 1: Oswald Lorenz, *Neue Zeitschrift für Musik*, 19:52 (28 December 1843), 205-6.

Original

Lieder
F. Liszt, Buch der Lieder für eine Singstimme m. Begl. des Pfte. – Berlin, Schlesinger –

Der Titel kündigt uns 3 Bände an, von denen hier der 1ste vorliegt. Er enthält sechs Lieder – neun Gesangstücke, glänzende Pracht- und Paradestücke, ausgestattet mit allen Würzen und Reizen einer virtuosenmätzigen Begleitung und einer schwelgerischen, alle Gebiete durchschweifenden Harmonik. Ein recht unstätes, heimatloses Leben führt sie, diese Harmonik, ein wahres Vagabondenleben: überall zu Hause und nirgends daheim! Was die guten Altvordern Tonart nannten, das klingt uns hier nur in träumerischen Andeutungen wie ein halbvergessenes Märchen aus der Kindheit an. Wie es Menschen giebt, die es da am kürzesten leidet, wo es ihnen am wohlsten geht, so hier; wenn es am schönsten klingt, ist es ein sichres Zeichen, das sogleich etwas Unheimliches, Ungeheureliches hereinbricht, ein beißender Accord, der wie ein Kobold in den Elfentanz, der kommt, ein Gesicht schneidet und verschwindet, oder das wir plötzlich Grund und Boden verlieren und in unberechenbaren Kometenbahnen durch schrankenlose Räume in wildfremde Gegenden entführt, das Verwunderlichste um uns erblicken werden, als märe nichts passirt.

Translation

Lieder
F. Liszt, Buch der Lieder for Voice with Pianoforte Accompaniment – Berlin, Schlesinger –

This publication announces three volumes, the first of which is presented here. It contains six Lieder – nine vocal pieces, show-pieces of glittering splendour, furnished with all the trimmings and embellishments of a virtuoso accompaniment, with an ever-wandering luxuriant harmony, which rambles here, there, and everywhere. This harmony leads a rather restless, homeless life, a truly vagabond existence: at home everywhere, and yet with no home anywhere. What the good old-timers used to call 'the key' emerges in dreamy hints like a half-forgotten fairytale from childhood. Just as there are men who can only briefly tolerate being at ease, so is it here; when the song sounds at its most beautiful, it is a sure sign that immediately something eerie and monstrous will interrupt it, a biting chord that intrudes like a goblin into an elf dance, a cutting vision which then bolts, or that we suddenly lose our footing and are abducted in an unpredictable comet orbit through boundless space in savage foreign regions, to see the most amazing things around us, and then return as if nothing had happened.

Das Verwunderlichste von Allem aber ist das Verhältnis dieser Musik zu den Gedichten. Sollte ein der Sprache unkundiger rathen, welcher Art die letztern sein, er wird hier auf eine Mord- und Blutballade, dort aus Geistesspuk und Hexentänze schließen, oder er hält das Ganze für einen guten Spaß. Die Gedichte sind indeß folgende: 'Loreley' und 'Am Rhein' (von Heine), 'Kennst du das Land', 'König von Thule', und 'Der du vom Himmel bist' (von Göthe), und eine zarte Romanze von Bocella ('Englein du mit blondem Haar'). Bei dem letzteren Gedichte, dem einzigen, ist übrigens der Liedcharakter im Ganzen in Form und Auffassung respectirt. Es hat eine einfache, liebliche Melodie, und gleich klare, allmälig etwas gesteigerte Harmonifirung. Durch charakteristische Eigenthümlichkeit der Motive macht sich der 'König von Thule' geltend, so wie auch die formelle Ausführung der ersten Hälfte in ihrer mannhaften, wübigen Einfachheit dem Wesen des Gedichtes zusagt. Die chromatische Malerei aber am schlusse (das sinken des Bechers, das Meeresbrausen) ist eine ästhetische Sünde, bie durch bie beigefügte 'leichter', nach unserm Gefühl richtigere Begleitung allerdings grosentheils neutralisirt wird. Wie die Gesänge nun sind, stellt sich dieser jedenfalls als der charaktervollste und frischeste dar. Ihm zunächst stellt sich, in reiner liedermäßigen Auffassung und Einheit ihm vor-, an Frische der Erfindung etwas nachstehend, das Heine'sche 'Am Rhein'. Auch hier ist gewiß die leichtere Begleitung die schönere. Den meisten sinnlichen Reiz hat die 'Loreley'. Die theatralische Auffassung mag, wo nicht zu rechtfertigen, doch zu vertheidigen sein.

But the most surprising of all is the relationship between this music and the poems. Should one be ignorant of the language, then one would guess here there is a murder or blood ballad, and there a ghost wail or witch's dance, or they will believe that the whole thing is simply in good jest. The poems set are the following: 'Loreley' and 'Am Rhein' (by Heine), 'Kennst du das Land', 'König von Thule', and 'Der du vom Himmel bist' (by Goethe), and a tender romance by Bocella ('Englein du mit blondem Haar'). Incidentally, the last poem is the only one in which the character of the Lied on the whole is respected in form and conception. It has a simple, sweet melody, and an equally clear harmonization, which is elaborated little by little. Distinctively peculiar motifs begin the 'König von Thule' in a convincing fashion, just as the formal execution of the first half has a robust, dignified simplicity that is in sympathy with the essence of the poem. But the chromatic tone-painting at the end (the sinking of the cup, the showering of the sea) is an aesthetic sin, which, however, is for the most part neutralized by the added 'lighter' accompaniment, which, in our opinion, is the more appropriate one. In any case, as the songs now stand, this turns out to be the best and most striking one. He provides at first, in terms of pure Lieder-like conception and unity, a freshness of invention that somewhat follows in Heine's 'Am Rhein'. Here, too, the easier accompaniment is certainly the more beautiful. The most sensuous item is 'Loreley'. The theatrical conception may be, if not justified, defended.

Ganz abzulehnen aber vom rein poetischen standpunct aus erachten wir die Behandlung des Göteschen 'Der du von dem Himmel bist' und des Mignonliedes. In dem weder Frieden hat noch sucht. Nimmt man das lestere aber auch nur als ein schönes selbstständiges Gedicht, so mus diese musikalische Behandlung mindestens als unlyrisch und auf die spitze gestellt erscheinen; denkt man aber an die Individualität der Mignon, und die situation, in der sie das Liedsingt, so wird sie zur parodirenden Uebertreibung. – Dies meine individuelle Meïnung über das Liederbuch, die sich Niemanden als unfehlbar aufdringen foll. Ist sie nicht nach Jedermanns Sinne, so kann ich nur ausrufen: Hier steh', ich, ich kann nicht anders.

O.L.

When we consider the treatment of Goethe's 'Der du von dem Himmel bist' and 'Mignon's Lied', we reject them completely from a purely poetic point of view. In the former profound prayer for peace drifts a spirit which has neither peace nor seeks it. If one takes the latter one only as a beautiful independent poem, then this musical treatment must at least appear un-lyrical and taken to the extreme; but if one thinks of the individuality of Mignon, and the situation in which she sings the song, then she becomes a parodying exaggeration. – This is my own opinion of the songbook, which nobody should consider as infallible. If it is not to everyone's tastes, I can only exclaim: Here I stand, I cannot help it.

O.L.

Review 2: Oswald Lorenz, *Neue Zeitschrift für Musik*, 20:42 (23 May 1844), 165.

Original

Translation

Liederschau.
(Fortsetzung.)

Liederschau.
(Continued.)

Fr. Liszt, Buch der Lieder für eine Singstimme mit Begleitung des Pianoforte. 2ter Band. – Berlin, bei Schlesinger.

Fr. Liszt, Buch der Lieder for Voice with Pianoforte Accompaniment, 2nd Volume – Berlin, Schlesinger.

Dem ersten Bande dieses Werkes, welcher bereits in Nr. 52. des vorigen Bandes besprochen worden, schließt sich vorliegender zweiter Band genau an. Die sechs Lieder (? –), die er enthält, sind ebenfalls glänzende Pracht- und Paradestücke, ausgestattet mit allen Würzen und Reizen einer virtuosenmäsigen Begleitung und einer schwelgerischen, alle Gebiete durchschweifenden Harmonik.

The first volume of this work, which has already been discussed in no. 52 of the previous issue, is followed closely by the present second volume. The six Lieder (?!) – which are contained herein are as before show-pieces of glittering splendour, furnished with all the trimmings and embellishments of a virtuoso accompaniment, with an ever-wandering luxuriant harmony, which rambles here, there, and everywhere.

Wie kleinmüthig und niedergeschmettert stehst du einem solchen dir imponiren-den Werke gegenüber, der du bis jetzt meintest, es gehöre zu den Vorzügen eines Liedes, wenn der Ausdruck der Melodie genau dem Inhalte der Worte entspreche, wenn die Begleitung nur die Trägerin jener sei, obwohl ihr zur stei-gerung des Ausdrucks dann und wann gestattet sei, charakteristisch hervorzutre-ten, und wenn mit einem Worte im Liede neben schöner Einfachheit Bestimmtheit der Empfindung und Wahrheit des Ausdrucks herrsche! Dies Buch der Lieder raubt dir Armen den schönen Wahn! Buch der Lieder? – Aber wir wissen in der That nicht, vor welchem Richterstuhle Liszt die Wahl des Taufnamens für sein Musenkind verantworten kann. Wer wird das Buch 'Geheimnisse von Paris' ein Familiengemälde nennen? – Hat Jemand schon ein Lied componirt gese-hen, worin der Fingersatz zeilenweise den begleitenden Noten beigesetzt ist? Hier ist's zu finden. Bei der unbändi-gen Masse der 𝄪 und ♭♭, der enhar-monischen Verwechselungen, der vollgepfropften Accorde, kurz bei dieser Virtuosenbegleitung gewinnt es manch-mal den Anschein, als habe Liszt ver-suchen wollen, wie es sich ausnehme, wenn der Melodie eines Liedes erlaubt wird, eine solche Claviercomposition zu begleiten. Es gereicht zum Troste, das vorliegende Gesangsstücke ursprüng-lich französischem Terte zugemut-het worden sind, überschwenglichen Victor Hugo'schen Poesieen. Hierdurch werden die vielen Ungereimtheiten, ja das Widersinnige in etwas entschuldigt, denen unser Auge begegnet, wenn es die untergelegten deutschen Worte mit der Melodie zusammenhält. So heißt z. B. das Schlußwort des 8ten Liedes 'ah!' und hat einen Triller und eine Cadenz ad libitum bekommen; im 9ten Liede ist das Wort 'König' als Iambus scandirt :

How humble and downcast to come across such imposing works, you who until now believed it was to the advantage of the song if the expres-sion of the melody corresponded exactly with the content of the words, if the accompaniment was only the vessel for the song, now and again permitted through distinctive inflections to increase the expres-sion with one of the words adding to the beautiful simplicity, then the certainty of feeling and truth of expression would prevail! This book of Lieder robs you of that beautiful delusion! Book of Lieder? In fact, we do not know before which seat of judgement Liszt could justify the choice of baptising the children of his muse like so. He who would call The Mysteries of Paris a family portrait perhaps? Has anybody ever before composed a song in which the fingering is interleaved line by line with the accompaniment? Here you can find such a thing. With the unrestrained mass of double sharps and double flats, the enharmonic confusions, the gnawing chords; in short, with this virtuoso accom-paniment it sometimes seems as if Liszt wished to see if the melody of a Lied would accompany a virtuoso keyboard composition. It is com-forting to note that these singing pieces were originally set to French texts, the excessive poems of Victor Hugo. This excuses the many incon-sistencies, absurdities, that our eyes encounter when they behold together the underlying German words with the melody, e.g. the final word of the eighth song 'ah!', and gets a trill and a cadenza ad libitum; in the ninth song the word 'König' is scanned as an iambus:

Mein Kind, wär ich Kö - nig

Mein Kind, wär ich Kö - nig

Der Angriff der schweren Reiterei und des Kartätschen feuers, dem wir bei der Durchsicht des neunten Liedes ausgesetzt gewesen, worin ein feuriger Liebhaber 'des tiefen Chaos Grund, von Geburten durchzogen', für einen Kuss wegschenken will, hat uns, an solche strapazen nicht gewöhnt, ermattet, weshalb man uns vergönnen wird, die Feder wegzulegen.

The charge of heavy cavalry and the grapeshot to which we were exposed in reviewing the ninth song, in which a fiery lover wants to give away the 'fertile womb of deep chaos' for a kiss, has left us, not accustomed to such exertions, exhausted, for which reason we are given leave to lay down our pen.

Review 3: [O.L.?], *Neue Zeitschrift für Musik*, 20:26 (26 Sept. 1844), 102–3.

Original

Compositionen für mehrstimmigen Gesang. (Schluß.)

F. Liszt, Vierstimmige Männergesänge. –

Cöln, Eck u. Comp. – Part. u. St. 1 1/4 Thlr. stimmen allein 2/3 Thlr. –

Mit dem kräftigen männlichen Trotz des ersten Gedichts ('Wir sind nicht Mumien') und dem düstern murrenden Charakter des zweiten ('Das düstre Meer umrauscht mich schauerlich'), stimmt die kecke Art der Musik mit ihren verwegnen Harmoniewürfen wohl überein. Indeß hat alles Gute sein Mass. Dass das Streben nach Wahrheit der Auffassung harmonische Folgen, wie sie in diesen Liedern zu finden, rechtfertige, will uns nicht einleuchten. Man nehme das erste: Es fängt in c-Moll an, mit dem 7ten Tacte sind wir in E-Dur, der 10te bringt eine Cadenz in G-Dur; nach 7 Tacten fällt ein 6/4 Accord auf G und darauf ein schluß in Des-Dur hinein, dem der Hauptschluß in C-Dur auf dem Fuße folgt.

Translation

Compositions for Polyphonic Singing. (Concluding)

F. Liszt, Four Voice Male Choir Songs –

Cöln, Eck u. Comp. – Score and Parts. 1 1/4 thr. Parts alone 2/3 thlr. –

The invigorating manful defiance of the first poem ('Wir sind nicht Mumien') and the gloomy grumbling character of the second ('Das düstre Meer umrauscht mich schauerlich') agrees well with the cheeky nature of the music and with the bold harmony. However, everything good has its limits. The pursuit of truth does not justify the harmonic sequences as found in these songs; it does not make sense to us. Take the first one: it starts in C minor, by the 7th bar we are in E major, the 10th brings a cadenza in G major; after 7 bars a 6/4 chord falls on G and then a final note in D flat major, followed by the main key in C major.

Wenig anders geht es im 2ten Gesange. Das aber ist nicht das Wirken einer wuchernden Phantasie; im Gegentheil, es ist nur ein surrogat dafür, das in Uebertteibung fällt, wie Geberdensprache ohne innere Wahrheit zur Grimasse wird. Einen einfachern Anstrich haben die beiden letzten Lieder, zumal das dritte ('Ueber' – oder wie es hier heißt: 'Unter allen Gipfeln ist Ruh'). Indes ist in dem letzten der eigenthümliche Ton des Gedichtes ('Gottes ist der Orient') auf eine etwas zu burschikose, sonst wenig eigenthümliche Weise aufgefaßt, das dritte aber ist matt und die harmonische Wendung bei: 'schlafen im Walde' verunglückt zu nennen. – Einzelne technische Besonderheiten herauszuheben, ist unnöthig; nur dass die Lieder, namentlich das Erste, ihre Wirkung, auf Deutsch: Effect machen, sei noch versichert.

The second song is little different. But this is not the work of a fecund imagination; on the contrary, it is only a substitute for one, with too much self-regard, as the language of the speaker becomes a grimace without inner truth. The last two songs have a simpler finish, especially as the third one ('Ueber' – or how it is called here: 'Unter allen Gipfeln ist Ruh'). Meanwhile, in the last one, the peculiar tone of the poem ('Gottes ist der Orient') is caught in a somewhat too bourgeois, otherwise unremarkable, manner; the third, however, is dull and the harmonic turn at 'sleeping in the forest' we would term unsuccessful. It is unnecessary to single out individual technical features, only that the songs, especially the first one, make their impact in German assuredly.

Review 4: Oswald Lorenz, *Neue Zeitschrift für Musik*, 30:26 (10 Oct. 1844), 117–18.

Original

Liederschau

F. Liszt, Sechs Lieder für eine Singstimme mit Pfte. – Cöln, Eck u. Comp.

Gegen das Buch der Lieder, namentlich dessen 1stes Heft (vgl. Bd. 19 Nr. 52. u. Bd. 20. Nr. 42. d. Bl.) gehalten, haben diese Lieder ein recht gemüthliches und friedliches Ansehen. Indeß aber erscheint ihr wahrer Kern nach genauerer Prüfung keineswegs so einfach und friedlich, vielmehr zum Theil als dem Wesen des Liedes geradezu feindselig. Gleichwohl find die Gedichte rechte und wahre Lieder.

Translation

Liederschau

F. Liszt, Six Lieder for Voice with Pianoforte – Cöln, Eck u. Comp.

In comparison with the Buch der Lieder, especially its first volume (see vol. 19 no. 52 and vol. 20 no. 42 [of this publication]) these songs at first seem to be quite relaxed and peaceful. However, on closer inspection their true nature reveals itself to be not quite so simple and tranquil, but instead, rather antagonistic to the essence of the Lied. Nevertheless, the poetry does find some right and true Lieder.

Bei dem Heine'schen 'Du bist wie eine Blume' wird gegen die allgemeine Auffassung, Form, Harmonik wenig eingewandt, höchstens der oft sonderbar gespreizte Rhythmus der Declamation gerügt und vielleicht an der Folgerichtigkeit der Accordforschreitung am Schlusse, bei den Worten 'Gott erhalte so rein zc.' gezweifelt werden können. Auch im folgenden im Ganzen angemessen gehaltenen 'Dichter, was Liebe sei' treten ähnliche Züge in der Declamation hervor, die kokette, künstliche Naivetät des Tertes fast parodirend. Folgender Rhythmus zu den Worten: Dichter, was ein Kuß sei mir nicht verhehle:

ist gewiß nicht der richtige. Im dritten Liede ist weniger die gewaltsame Ausweichung in eine sehr entlegene Tonart an fich verlessend, als vielmehr der garstige Bass, auf den fie gebaut ist: Dis Cis F zc. Auch due Rückkehr nach der Haupttonart, Cis=Moll, ist nicht eben geschickt gemacht. Die milde Trauer des folgenden Gedichtes 'Morgens steh' ich aus und frage' ist in der erften Strophe so einfach schön ausgefaßt und namentlich die stille Entsagung in dem weichem Schlusse nach Cis=Moll so wahr und sprechend, dass man wenig Tacte später durch den Uebergang durch F=Moll noch A=Moll die den Worten: 'Träumend wie im halbern Schlummer wandle ich noch heut' [*sic*] ordentlich erbittert wird. Was hilft es, dass die Begleitung das erste gefühlvolle Motiv wieder aufgreift und das Ganze beruhigend abschließt – der Totaleindruck ist hin, das Lied als Solches – verhunzt. Schade! Das Lied wäre ohne diese Geschmackswidrigkeit nicht blos eines der besten der sechs, sondern überhaupt ein gutes.

In the case of Heine's 'Du bist wie eine Blume', there are no objections to the general conception of the form and harmony, the most we can be is sceptical of the strangely affected rhythm of the declamation and perhaps the harmonic progression at the end during the words 'Gott erhalte so rein'. Also in the following 'Dichter, was Liebe sei', on the whole, similar features emerge in the declamation, almost parodying the coquettish, artificial naiveté of the tale. The following rhythm to the words: 'Dichter, was ein Kuß sei mir nicht verhehle':

is certainly not the right one. In the third song, it is less the forceful modulation into a very remote key than the nasty bass on which it is built: $D\sharp7$–$C\sharp b7$–$Fb4$. The return to the main key, C sharp minor, is not exactly skilful. The mild mourning of the subsequent poem 'Morgens steh' ich aus und frage' is so simple and nicely laid out in the first verse, especially the silent renunciation during the tender conclusion in C sharp minor, is so truthful and eloquent, that a few bars later, a passage through F minor and A minor for the words: 'Dreaming, in a half-slumber if I wander through the day', sours it. What does it help that the accompaniment takes up the first sentimental motif again and the whole thing concludes in an anodyne fashion – the total impression is out, the song as such – is ruined. What a pity! Without this lack of taste the song would not only be one of the best of the six, but a good one in its own right.

Das folgende Lied 'Die tote Nachtigall' ist als Tonstück überhaupt, als Instrumentalstück etwa, dem man das Gedicht als leitende Idee zugesellt sich denken mag, charakterisrisch aufgefasst und auch formell wohlgerundet zu nennen. Als wirklich gesungenes Lied (ein solches ist das Gedicht) ist es zu prentintiös gehalten, die Singstimme zum Theil zu declamatorisch, aphoriftisch, der Triller mit dem anspruchvollen Schluss dem Liede widerstrebend. Das letzte der Lieder kann als das abgerundetfte, wohlgebauteste gelten; zwar wird uns die Feuerprobe des Durchgangs durch starke Harmoniewechsel nicht ganz erspart, allein theils ist die durch das Ganze bindend und einend sich ziehende figur auch hier ein leitender Faden, theils ist dem Ganzen so viel mahrer Gesang un Wohlklang eigen, daß dieses Lied auch von den Sängern wohl den Preis erhalten dürfte. – Die Zelle von Nonnenwerth ist ein ausgeführter Gesang, der Text offenbar ein Gelegenheitsgedicht. Das strophenartig wiederkehrende Hauptmotiv ist nichts weniger als originell und charakteristisch, und erst die harmonische Durchführung giebt dem Stücke Bedeutsamkeit. Auch ist dasselbe bereits vom Componisten für das Pianoforte allein übertragen (F. Nr. 27. b. Bl.), und bedeutsam genug liegt uns mit dem Original schon die zweite Auflage der Bearbeitung vor. Oder hat hier '2te Auflage' eine besondre Bedeutung?

**

*

The next Lied 'Die tote Nachtigall' as a piece of music is distinctively conceived and formally well proportioned, but it is more akin to an instrumental piece to which one may think of the poem as a guiding idea. As an authentically vocal Lied (such as this poem) it is considered too pretentious and aphoristic, [for example] the demanding concluding trill works more against the song. The last of the songs can be considered the most well-proportioned and well-crafted, although we are not spared the ordeal of enduring strong changes in harmony, but in part the ever-present motif has a unifying and guiding effect, and on the whole, there is so much melodiousness and song-like characteristics that singers may get their money's worth. 'Die Zelle von Nonnenwerth' is a well-executed song, the text apparently an occasional poem. The strophe-like main motif is nothing less than original and distinctive, but it is through the harmony that the meaning is conveyed. This piece has already been transcribed for solo pianoforte by the composer (F. No. 27. b. Bl.), and significantly, this second edition is already available to us along with the original. Therefore, one asks: does this 'second edition' have some special significance?

**

*

Review 5: Julius Schladebach (Wise), *Allgemeine Musikalische Zeitung* (1 January 1845), 5.

Original

Gesänge für eine Stimme mit Pianoforte.

1. Franz Liszt: Sechs Lieder. Cöln, Eck und Comp. Preis 11/12 Thlr.

2. Aler. Fesca: Drei Gedichte von R. Burns, für Alt oder Bass. op. 21. Braunschweig, Meyer jun. Pr. 2/3 Thlr.

3. —: Das Zigeunermädchen. Op. 37. Ebendaselbst. Preis 1/2 Thlr.

4. Walther v. Goethe: Sechs Lieder. Op. 14. Wien, Haslinger. Preis 1 Thlr.

5. Taubert: Klänge aus der Kinderwelt. 12 Lieder. Op. 58. Berlin, T. Trautwein. Preis 5/6 Thlr.

6. Louis Köhler: Sechs Gesänge. Op. 2. 2 Hefte. Braunschweig, Meyer jun. Preis à 2/3 Thlr.

Was wir bei Gelegenheit der von Liszt componirten Männergesänge über den Character seiner Gesangs compositionen im Allgemeinen bemerkt haben, findet auch hier, fast noch im erhöhtern Maasse, seine Anwendung; die sechs hier gebotenen Lieder (1) 'Du bist wie eine Blume', von Heine; 2) 'Dichter, was Liebe sei'; 3) 'Vergiftet sind meine Lieder', von Heine; 4) 'Morgens steh' ich auf und frage', von demselben; 5) 'Die todte Nachtigall', von Kaufmann; 6) 'Mild wie ein Lufthauch im Mai' haben ihren Namen, wie der *lucus a non lucendo;*

Translation

Songs for Voice with Pianoforte

1. Franz Liszt: Sechs Lieder. Cöln, Eck und Comp. Price 11/12 Thlr.

2. Aler. Fesca: Drei Gedichte von R. Burns, for Alto or Bass. Op. 21. Braunschweig, Meyer jun. Pr. 2/3 Thlr.

3. —: Das Zigeunermädchen. Op. 37. Ebendaselbst. Price 1/2 Thlr.

4. Walther v. Goethe: Sechs Lieder. Op. 14. Vienna, Haslinger. Price 1 Thlr.

5. Taubert: Klänge aus der Kinderwelt. 12 Lieder. Op. 58. Berlin, T. Trautwein. Price 5/6 Thlr.

6. Louis Köhler: Sechs Gesänge. Op. 2. 2 Books. Braunschweig, Meyer jun. Price 2/3 Thlr.

What we have remarked in general about Liszt compositions for male-voice choir on the character of his song-compositions also applies here, but to an even greater extent. The six songs presented: 1) 'Du bist wie eine Blume' by Heine; 2) 'Dichter, was Liebe sei'; 3) 'Vergiftet sind meine Lieder', by Heine; 4) 'Morgens steh' ich auf und frage', from the same; 5) 'Die todte Nachtigall', by Kaufmann; 6) 'Mild wie ein Lufthauch im Mai' are named like a *lucus a non lucendo;*

der Begriff des deutschen Liedes ist schwerich dem Componisten jemals klar geworden, weder nach Form noch Wesen – es in seiner wesentlichen Eigenthümlichkeit zu produciren, ist ihm unmöglich; er gibt statt dessen Phantasieen, oder besser: phantastische Rhapsodieen, die allerdings einer gewissen poetischen Innerlichkeit nicht entbehren, die den Drang nach dem Aussprechen eines unheilbaren inneren Wehes, vielleicht dem Tonsetzer selbst unbewusst, an den Tag legen, aber an der Unzulänglichkeit der schöpferischen Kraft untergehen, während sie sich unablässig, aber fruchtlos mühen, das geheimnissvolle Zauberwort, die Beschwörungsformel zu finden, welche den Bann zu lösen im Stande ist, der mit unzerreissbaren Banden das Innere ihres Meisters gefesselt hält. Es beschleicht uns allezeit ein wehmüthiges Gefühl, wenn wir dies Ringen und Kämpfen wahrnehmen, wenn uns als die Frucht desselben der Mangel aller Einheit, die Zerfahrenheit und Abgerissenheit der Gedanken, dieses gesuchte und gespreizte Wesen, diese Melodieenarmuth und Harmonieenüberladung, dieses Greifen nach äusseren Mitteln und Effecten vor Augen tritt, das doch nun einmal zum Ausdrucke innerlicher Zustände, zum Ausdrucke von Empfindungen und Gefühlen so gar nicht ausreicht. – Die Behandlung der Singstimme ist hier merkwürdig ungeschickt – wollen das die Anbeter des Virtuosen etwa genial nennen? – auf einer Clarinette vorgetragen, mag sich das leidlicher ausnehmen; die Pianofortebegleitung ist nicht so schwierig, als wir erwartet hatten – aber überall in Erfindung und Durchführung groteske Decorationsmalerei, ja häufig Verzerrung und Unnatur;

the concept of the German Lied has hardly ever become clear to the composer, neither in form nor in essence, it is impossible for him to produce its distinguishing characterics; he gives instead phantasies, or better, fantastic rhapsodies, which, while not lacking a certain poetic inwardness, and which display the urge to utter an incurable inner woe – perhaps unconscious of the composer himself – but which founder due to the inadequacy of creative power. They labour incessantly but fruitlessly, to find the mysterious magic word, the mantra, which is capable of breaking the spell, which holds with unbreakable bonds the interior of their master. It always gives us a sad feeling, when we perceive this wrestling and struggling, when the result of it is the lack of all unity, the frailty and fissure of thoughts, this laboured and affected nature, this lack of melodiousness and overloaded harmony, this grasping for external means and effects which, in the end, are not sufficient for the expression of internal states, for the expression of feelings and emotions. The treatment of the vocal part is strangely awkward here – do the worshippers of the virtuoso want to call it ingenious? – recited on a clarinet, it may be more tolerable; the pianoforte accompaniment is not as difficult as we had expected – but everywhere in invention and execution there is grotesque decorating and painting, indeed often distortion and unnaturalness;

Ebenmaass, Beherrschung des poetischen Stoffes wie der Form sucht man vergebens – wahre Schönheit, die selbst in der auf die Spitze getriebenen Romantik noch immer möglich, ist nirgend zu finden; doch zeichnet sich No. 6 durch seine grössere Haltung vortheilhaft vor den übrigen aus. Wir empfehlen diese Lieder zum Studium Denen, die gern an eclatanten Beispielen lernen wollen, wie man es nicht machen müsse. ...

one searches in vain for balance, mastery of poetic material, and form – true beauty, which is still possible even in Romanticism that has been driven to extremes, is nowhere to be found; yet no. 6, by virtue of its greater style, is superior compared to the rest. We recommend these songs for study to those who like to learn from some striking examples how not to do it. ...

Review 6: Karl Emanuel Klitzsch, *Neue Zeitschrift für Musik*, 30:40 (17 May 1849), 217–18.

Original

Franz Liszt, Lieder aus Schiller's 'Wilhelm Tell':

1. 'Der Fischerknabe'; 2.- 'Der Hirt'; 3. 'Der Alpen jäger'. für eine Singst. mit Begl. des Pfte. – Wien, Tob. Haslinger's Wittwe u. Sohn. Preis: 2 Ml. 30–, fär. G. ft.

– – –, Drei Gedichte von Göthe:

1. 'Wer nie sein Brod mit Thränen aß'; 2. 'Ueber allen Gipfeln ist Ruh'; 3. Lied aus Egmont: 'Freudvoll und leidvoll'. – Ebendas Pr. 1 Fl. 15ßr. C. R.

Spreche ich zunächst von den ersteren. Unstreitig geistreiche Gebilde, mit derjenigen Eigenthümlichkeit behandelt, wie wir ihr bei diesem Künstler stets begegnen. Tritt auch in der Behandlung des Pianoforte der Virtuos mehr hervor als vielleicht Mancher wünschen möchte, so sei dies nicht in der Form eines Vorwurfs ausgesprochen. Der Componist will nicht Compositionen im gebräuchlichen Wortsinne geben, sondern freie Phantasieergüsse mit möglichst genauer, charakteristischer Erfassung.

Translation

Franz Liszt, Lieder aus Schiller's 'Wilhelm Tell':

1. 'Der Fischerknabe'; 2.- 'Der Hirt'; 3. 'Der Alpen jäger'. for voice with pianoforte accompaniment. – Vienna, Tob. Haslinger's widow and son. Price: 2 Ml. 30–, fär. G. st.

– – –, Drei Gedichte von Göthe:

1. 'Wer nie sein Brod mit Thränen aß'; 2. 'Ueber allen Gipfeln ist Ruh'; 3. Lied aus Egmont: 'Freudvoll und leidvoll'. – Ebendas Pr. 1 Fl. 15ßr. C.R.

I will first discuss the former. They are unquestionably brilliant creations, imbued with the singular distinctiveness that we have grown accustomed to with this artist. If there are more virtuoso elements present in the piano writing than some would wish, this should not be cause for reproach. The composer does not want to offer compositions in the usual sense of the word, but free fantasies of the imagination with the most accurate and characteristic notation possible.

Das Gedicht dient ihm als Substrat, er schafft ein neues daraus und reproducirt es in solcher Weise, daß es nur die großen Umrisse liefert zu dem Gemälde, das er nach seiner Anschauung in den kleinsten Details ausführt. In Nr. 1 ist, S. 9, letztes Syst. u. f. eine schöne, charakteristische Stelle und von großer Wirkung. Nr. 2 hat viel Alpenthümliches; der Gesang tritt hier mehr hervor. Durch besondere harmonische Wendungen sind mehrere Stellen hervorstechend. Schön ist die Stelle S. 13, Syst. 4, Tact 2–5; so auch S. 17, Syst. 2, Tact 2–6, und Syst. 3, Tact 1–3. Nr. 3 bietet großartige Malerei; die Worte des Dichters sind bis aufs Kleinste durch die Begleitung zur Anschauung gebracht: wir hören den rollenden Donner und empfinden die schwindelnde Höhe, die der Schütze verwegen wandelt. Nach allen Grauen, durch die der Componist uns geführt, bringt er uns endlich (Schluß) wieder auf die sichere, grünende Erde, es wird uns wieder wohl, es erklingen wieder die alten Klänge (S. 24, Allegretto), die wir früher vernommen. Diese Anspielung auf Nr. 1 ist ein schöner Zug und zeugt von ächt künstlerischer Conception. – Das zweite Heft, die Göthe'schen Gedichte enthaltend, ist nicht minder trefflich. Hier macht sich das vocale Element überwiegend geltend. Der Componist zeigt auch da wieder seine Eigenthümlichkeit. Diese Gesänge sind gleichfalls höchst charakteristisch ausgefaßt, man sieht, wie es dem Componisten darum zu thun ist, Dichterisches zu geben und dem großen Dichter in seinen Intentionen zu folgen. Nr. 2 u. 3 müssen als höchst gelungen bezeichnet werden.

The poem serves him as a substratum, upon which he creates a new one and reproduces it in such a way that it only provides the great outlines of the painting which, in accordance with his view he fills in with the smallest details. In no. 1, p. 9, from the last system onwards is a beautiful and distinctive section of great effect. No. 2 contains lots of alpine evocations; the singing is more prominent, and several passages are highlighted by means of exceptional harmonic twists. The passage at p. 13, system 4, bars 2–5 is beautiful; see also p. 17, system 2, bars 2–6, and system 3, bars 1–3. No. 3 contains great tone-painting; the words of the poet are recreated in the finest detail by the accompaniment: we hear the rolling thunder and feel the dizzying heights, which the archer daringly traverses. After all the trepidation through which the composer has guided us, he finally brings us (at the conclusion) back to the safe, green earth, with an optimistic outlook to play again the old sounds, which we heard earlier (p. 24, Allegretto). This Allusion to no. 1 is a beautiful move and testifies to genuine artistic conception. The second volume, containing the poems of Goethe, is no less excellent. Here the vocal element asserts itself more prominently. The composer again shows his individuality. These songs are likewise highly distinctive; one sees how the composer is concerned with presenting poetic offerings and following the great poet in his intentions. No. 2 must be described as highly successful.

In Nr. 2 (im ¾ Tact, Syst. 3) klingt der Gesang etwas an italienische Weise, so auch in Nr. 3 (erste Version) S. 34, Syst. 2, Tact 4 u. f., und dem Schluß von Nr. 2 und an einigen anderen Stellen, was bei der übrigen Vortrefflichkeit etwas störend wirkt. Außerdem dürfte noch zu erwähnen sein, daß in Nr. 2 der Schluß wirksamer und schöner nach dem ¾ Tacte mit den Noten in der hohen Lage ist; was darauf folgt, ist gegen das Frühere, mit aller Stärke der Empfindung Gegebene, zu matt. Borzüglich schön ist namentlich der Anfang (G-Dur) mit seinen ruhigen Accorden und der Ausweichung nach D-Dur. Nr. 3. 'Freudvoll und leidvoll' hat zwei Versionen, von denen die zweite wegen Stärke der Empfindung wohl den Preis davon trägt. Beide find im Charakter wesentlich verschienden. Die erste giebtuns das Bild einer träumerisch nachfinnnenden Seele, deren Jubel milder erschient freundlicher, mehr nach innen gekehrt. Die zweite Version führt uns einen leidenschaftlicheren Charakter vor, der mehr nach außen hin strebt. Daher die Unruhe gleich im Anfange sehr bezeichnend ist, die unstäte Wendung zum Halbton. Mächtig wirkend ist die Stelle 'Himmelhoch jauchzend', so auch der Schluß vom ritenuto an, S. 39, Syst. 1, Tact 3 u. f., aus As-Dur durch F- Moll nach E- Dur zurück. – Mögen diese wenigen Andeutungen dazu beitragen, Freunde des Höherem für diese Gesänge zu gewinnen.

Em. Klitzsch.

In no. 2 (in ¾ bar, system 3) the vocals sound somewhat Italian, likewise in no. 3 (first version) p. 34, system 2, bar 4 onwards, and the conclusion of no. 2, and also in some other passages, which somewhat disturbs the other excellent qualities. In addition, it should be mentioned that in no. 2 the conclusion is more effective and more beautiful after the ¾ bars with the notes in the high position; what follows is too weak for the former, given all the strength of sensation. Particularly beautiful is especially the beginning (G major), with its quiet chords and the dodge to D major. No. 3 'Freudvoll und leidvoll' has two versions, of which the second, because of the strength of the feeling, probably takes the honours. They are significantly different in character from each other. The first gives us the image of a dreaming soul, whose rejoicings appear milder and more inward. The second version introduces us to a more passionate outgoing character. The restlessness right at the beginning is very characteristic, hence the unsteady twists around the semitone. The passage 'Himmelhoch jauchzend' is powerfully rendered, as well as the conclusion of the ritenuto, on p. 39, system 1, from bar 3 onwards, A flat major through F minor to E major. – May these few comments help these songs win some esteemed friends.

Em. Klitzsch

Bibliography

Primary sources

Berlioz, Hector, *Berlioz on Music: Selected Criticism, 1824–1837*, ed. Katherine Klob, trans. Samuel N. Rosenberg (Oxford: Oxford University Press 2015).

—, *Mémoires de Hector Berlioz*, trans. David Cairns (New York: Alfred A. Knopf, 1969).

Brendel, Franz, 'Zur Anbahnung einer Verständigung', *Neue Zeitschrift für Musik*, 50:24 (10 June 1859), 265–73.

Burger, Ernst, *Franz Liszt: A Chronicle of His Life in Pictures and Documents*, trans. Stewart Spencer (Princeton: Princeton University Press, 1989).

Goethe, Johann Wolfgang, *Goethe, The Collected Works in 12 Volumes*, vol. 9: *Wilhelm Meister's Apprenticeship*, ed. Eric A. Blackall and Victor Lange (Princeton: Princeton University Press, 1995).

Hamburger, Klára, 'Franz Liszts Briefe an Emilie Merian-Genast aus den Beständen des Goethe-und SchillerArchivs, Weimar Teil 1', *Studia Musicologica*, 48:3/4 (Sept. 2007), 350–90.

—, 'Franz Liszts Briefe an Emilie Merian-Genast aus den Beständen des Goethe-und SchillerArchivs, Weimar Teil 2', *Studia Musicologica*, 49:1/2 (March 2008), 143–92.

—, 'Liszt et Pauline Viardot-Garcia (dans l'optique de sept lettres inedites)', *Studia Musicologica Academiae Scientiarum Hungaricae*, T. 34, Fasc. 1/2 (1992).

Hanslick, Eduard, *Aus meinem Leben*, 2 vols, 4th edn (Berlin: Allgemeiner Verein für Deutsche Literatur, 1911).

—, *Geschichte des Concertwesens in Wien* (Vienna: W. Braumüller, 1869).

—, 'Theater und Kunstnachrichten', *Neue Freie Press* (16 January 1900).

Heine, Heinrich, *Buch der Lieder* (Hamburg: Hoffman und Campe, 1827, 1837, 1839, 1841, 1844).

Hirschbach, Hermann, review, *Franz Liszt, Buch der Lieder, Musikalisch-kritisches Repertorium* (1 January 1844), 231.

Hueffer, Francis (ed. and trans.), *Correspondence of Wagner and Liszt*, 2 vols (New York: Charles Scribner's Sons, 1897)

Klitzsch, Karl Emanuel, review, Liszt, *Lieder aus Schillers Wilhelm Tell*, and *Drei Gedichte von Göthe*, in *Neue Zeitschrift für Musik* 30:40 (17 May 1849), pp. 217–18.

Köhler, Louis, *Die Melodie der Sprache* (Leipzig: J.J. Weber, 1853).

La Mara (Ida Marie Lipsius), *Liszt und die Frauen* (Leipzig: Breitkopf & Härtel, 1911).

Lamartine, Alphonse de, *Harmonies poétiques et religieuses* (Paris: C. Gosselin, Furne et Cie, Pagnerre, 1830).

Lange, Otto, review, Julius Schladebach, *Sieben Gesänge Dichtungen*, in *Neue Musikalische Zeitung für Berlin* (27 April 1847).

Liszt, Franz, *An Artist's Journey: Lettres d'un bachelier ès musique, 1835–1841*, trans. and annotated Charles Suttoni (Chicago: Chicago University Press, 1989).

—, 'Bénédiction de Dieu dans la solitude', trans. Stanley Applebaum, in *Sonata in B minor and Other Works for Piano* (New York: Dover, 1989).

—, *Buch der Lieder für Piano allein*, 2 vols (Berlin: Schlesinger, 1844).

—, *Buch der Lieder: Gedichte von Goethe, Heine, Victor Hugo etc. mit Begleitung des Pianoforte/componirt von F. Liszt* (Berlin: Schlesinger, 1843). Vol. 1: Lore Ley, Am Rhein, Mignon, Der König von Thule, Der du von dem Himmel bist Angiolin. Vol. 2: Sechs franzoes/Poesien von V. Hugo mit deutschem Text von Ph. Kaufmann.

—, *The Collected Writings of Franz Liszt*, vol. 2: *Essays and Letters of a Traveling Bachelor of Music*, ed. and trans. Janita R. Hall-Swadley (Lanham, MD: Scarecrow Press, 2012).

—, *The Collected Writings of Franz Liszt*, vol. 3, part 1: *Dramaturgical Leaves*, ed. and trans. Janita R. Hall-Swadley (Lanham, MD: Rowman & Littlefield, 2014).

—, *Drei Gedichte von Göthe/In Musik gesetzt für eine Singstimme mit Begleitung des Piano-Forte* (Vienna: Haslinger, 1847).

—, *Drei Lieder von Franz Schubert*, S. 558 No.4/ LW A42 No.4 (Vienna and Paris: Diabelli and Richault, 1838).

—, *Franz Liszt Musikalische Werke*, VII: *Lieder und Gesänge*, Band II, ed. Peter Raabe (Leipzig: Breitkopf & Härtel, 1921).

—, *Franz Liszt's Briefe*, 8 vols, ed. La Mara (Ida Marie Lipsius) (Leipzig: Breitkopf & Härtel, 1893–1905).

—, *Franz Liszt: Selected Letters*, ed. Adrian Williams (Oxford: Clarendon Press, 1998).

—, *Gesammelte Lieder*, 8 vols (Berlin and Leipzig: Schlesinger and Kahnt, 1859–77). Vols 1–6 (Schlesinger and Kahnt, 1859); Vol. 7 (Kahnt, 1861); Vol. 8 (Kahnt, 1877).

—, *Letters of Franz Liszt*, vol. 1, 'From Paris to Rome: Years of Travel as a Virtuoso', ed. La Mara (Ida Maria Lispius) and trans. Constance Bache (London: H. Grevel, 1893).

—, *Letters of Franz Liszt*, vol. 1: *From Paris to Rome*, ed. La Mara, trans. Constance Bache (New York: Haskell House Publishers Ltd, 1968; orig. 1898).

—, *Letters of Franz Liszt*, ed. La Mara, 2 vols (New York: Greenwood Press, 1969, orig. 1894).

—, *Lieder aus Schillers 'Wilhelm Tell'/In Musik gesetzt für eine Singstimme mit Begleitung des Piano-Forte von Franz Liszt* (Vienna: Haslinger, 1847).

—, 'Pauline Viardot-Garcia', *Neue Zeitschrift für Musik* (28 Jan 1859).

—, preface to *Album d'un Voyageur* (Vienna: Haslinger, 1842).

—, *Sechs Lieder für eine Singstimme mit Pianoforte-Begleitung* (Cologne: Eck, 1844).

—, *Tre sonetti del Petrarca*, S. 270/ LW N. 14.1 (Vienna: Haslinger, 1846).

Lobe, Johann Christian, 'Ein deutscher Gesangsmeister', *Die Gartenlaube*, 20 (1880), 324–7.

Lorenz, Oswald, review, *Franz Liszt, Buch der Lieder für eine Singstimme m. Begl. des Pfte*, in *Neue Zeitschrift für Musik*, 19:52 (28 December 1843), 205–6.

—, review, *Franz Liszt, Buch der Lieder für eine Singstimme mit Begleitung des Pianoforte. 2ter Band*, in *Neue Zeitschrift für Musik*, 20:42 (23 May 1844), 165.

—, review, *Franz Liszt, Sechs Lieder für eine Singstimme mit Pfte*, in *Neue Zeitschrift für Musik*, 30 (10 October 1844), 117–18.

—, review, *Franz Liszt, Vierstimmige Männergesänge*, in *Neue Zeitschrift für Musik*, 20:26 (26 September 1844), 102–3.

Mason, William, *Memories of a Musical Life* (New York: The Devine Press, 1901).

Pocknell, Pauline, Malou Haine, and Nicolas Dufetel (eds), *Lettres de Franz Liszt à Princess Marie de Hohenlohe-Schillingsfürst née de Sayn-Wittgenstein* (Belgium: Librarie Philosophique J. Vrin, 2011).

Quicherat, Louis Marie, *Adolphe Nourrit: Sa vie, son talent, son caractère, sa correspondance* (Paris: L. Hachette et Cie, 1867).

Raff, Helene (ed.), *Franz Liszt und Joachim Raff im Spiegel ihrer Briefe*, in *Die Musik* (Berlin, 1901), vol. 1.

Redwitz, Oskar von, 'Amaranths stille Lieder' / 'Es muß ein Wunderbares sein', in *Amaranth* (Mainz : Kirchheim und Schott, 1849), p. 117.

Rellstab, Ludwig, *Gedichte von Ludwig Rellstab* (Berlin: bei Friedrich Laue, 1827).

Schladebach, Julius, review, *Franz Liszt, Sechs Lieder*, in *Allgemeine Musikalische Zeitung* (1 January 1845), 5–6.

—, review, *Franz Liszt, Vierstimmige Männergesänge*, in *Allgemeine Musikalische Zeitung* (1 January 1845), 3–4.

—, review, *Louis Köhler, Sechs Gesänge op. 2*, in *Allgemeine Musikalische Zeitung* (1 January 1845), 8–9.

Schlesinger, Maurice (ed.), 'Nouvelles – Chronique étrangère', *Gazette Musicale de Paris*, 5 (4 February 1844), 39.

Schubert, Franz, 'Der König in Thule', D. 367 (op. 5 no. 5) (Vienna: Diabelli, 1821).

Schumann, Robert, *Dichterliebe*, op. 48 (Leipzig: C.F. Peters, 1844).

—, *On Music and Musicians*, ed. Konrad Wolff, trans. Paul Rosenfeld (New York: Pantheon, 1946; repr. Norton, 1969).

—, 6 Concert Etudes after Paganini Caprices, op.10 (Leipzig: Hofmeister, 1835).

Short, Michael (ed. and trans.), *Liszt Letters in the Library of Congress*, Franz Liszt Studies Series, 10 (Hillsdale, NY: Pendragon Press, 2003).

(ed. and trans.), *Correspondence of Franz Liszt and the Countess Marie d'Agoult*, Franz Liszt Studies Series, 8 (Hillsdale, NY: Pendragon Press, 2013).

Stradal, August, *Erinnerungen au Franz Liszt* (Berne: Verlag Paul Haupt, 1929).

Tausig, Carl, *Sechs Sätze aus Streichquartetten von L. van Beethoven für Klavier übertragen* (Leipzig: C.F. Peters, 1916).

Tomášek, Václav, 'Der König in Thule', *Gedichte von Goethe: VII*, op. 59 no. 2 (1815).

Wagner, Richard, *My Life*, ed. Mary Whittall, trans. Andrew Gray (New York: Da Capo Press, 1992); originally *Mein Leben* (Munich: Paul List Verlag, 1963).

Weißheimer, Wendelin, *Erlebnisse mit Richard Wagner, Franz Liszt und vielen anderen Zeitgenossen nebst deren Briefen* (Stuttgart and Leipzig: Deutsche Verlags-Anstalt, 1898).

Weitzmann, Carl Friedrich, *Der übermäßige Dreiklang* (Berlin: J. Guttentag, 1853).

Zelter, Carl Friedrich, 'Der König von Thule', no. 3 in *Sämmlichte Lieder, Balladen, und Romzanzen*, 4 vols (Berlin: 1812), vol. 3.

Secondary sources

Allsobrook, David, *Liszt: My Travelling Circus Life* (London and Basingstoke: The Macmillan Press, 1991).

Altenburg, Detlef, 'Liszt and the Spirit of Weimar', *Studia Musicologica*, 54:2 (June 2013), 165–76.

Apel, Willi, *Harvard Dictionary of Music*, 2nd edn (Cambridge, MA: The Belknap Press of Harvard University Press, 1969).

Arnold, Ben, 'Liszt as Reader, Intellectual, and Musician', in Michael Saffle (ed.), *Liszt and His World* (Stuyvesant, NY: Pendragon Press, 1998), pp. 37–60.

—, 'Songs and Melodramas', in Ben Arnold (ed.), *The Liszt Companion* (London and Westport, CT: Greenwood Press, 2002), pp. 403–38.

—, 'Visions and Revisions, Looking in Liszt's Lieder', in Michael Saffle and Rossana Dalmonte (eds), *Liszt and the Birth of Modern Europe: Music as a Mirror of Religious, Political, Cultural, and Aesthetic Transformations*, Proceedings of the International Conference Held at the Villa Serbelloni, Bellagio (Como), 14–18 December 1998, Franz Liszt Studies Series, 9 (Hillsdale, NY: Pendragon Press, 2003), pp. 253–80.

Beckett, Walter, *Liszt* (London: J.M. Dent, 1963).

Blix, Göran, 'Charting the "Transitional Period": The Emergence of Modern Time in the Nineteenth Century', *History and Theory*, 45:1 (Feb 2006), 51–71.

Bloom, Harold, 'Walt Whitman as Center of the American Canon', in *The Western Canon* (New York: Harcourt Brace & Company, 1994), pp. 264–90.

Boorman, Stanley, 'Early Music Printing: Working for a Specialized Market', in Erald P. Tyson and Sylvia Wagonheim (eds), *Print and Culture in the Renaisance* (Newark: University of Delaware Press, 1986), pp. 222–45.

Bozó, Péter, 'A Buch der Liedertől a Gesammelte Liederig: Liszt Összegyűjtött Dalainak Első Négy Füzete és Négy Füzete és Előtárai' (From *Buch der Lieder* to *Gesammelte Lieder*: The First Four Volumes of Liszt's Collected Songs and Their Predecessors) (PhD diss., Liszt Academy of Music, 2009).

—, *A dalszerző Liszt* (The Songwriter Liszt) (Budapest: Rozsavolgyi and Company, 2018).

—, 'Liszt's Plan for a German *Année de pèlerinage*, "Was ist des Deutschen Vaterland?"', *Musicologica Academiae Scientiarum Hungaricae*, T. 47, Fasc. 1 (March 2006), 19–38.

Brendel, Alfred, *On Music: Collected Essays* (London: JR Books, 2007).

Bryant, John, *The Fluid Text* (Ann Arbor: University of Michigan Press, 2002).

Burkholder, J. Peter, 'Museum Pieces: The Historicist Mainstream in Music of the Last Hundred Years', *The Journal of Musicology*, 2:2 (Spring 1983), 115–34.

Busoni, Ferrucio, *The Essence of Music and Other Papers*, trans. Rosamond Ley (London: Rockliff Publishing Corporation, 1957; repr. New York: Dover Publications, 1987).

Byrne, Lorraine, ed., *Goethe: Musical Poet, Musical Catalyst* (Dublin: Carysfort Press, 2004).

Byrne Bodley, Lorraine, *Schubert: A Musical Wayfarer* (London and New Haven: Yale University Press, 2023).

—, *Schubert's Goethe Settings* (Aldershot: Taylor and Francis, 2003).

Celletti, Rodolfo, *A History of Bel Canto* (Oxford: Clarendon Press, 1991).

Charnin Mueller, Rena, 'The Lieder of Liszt', in James Parsons (ed.), *The Cambridge Companion to the Lied* (Cambridge: Cambridge University Press, 2004), pp. 164–84.

—, 'Liszt's Schubert Lieder Transcriptions', in *Franz Liszt, The Schubert Song Transcriptions for Solo Piano*, Series I (New York: Dover Publications Inc., 1995)

—, 'Liszt's Tasso Sketchbook: Studies in Sources and Revisions' (PhD diss., New York University, 1986).

—, 'Reevaluating the Liszt Chronology: The Case of "Anfangs wollt ich fast verzagen"', *19th Century Music*, 12:2 (Autumn 1988), 132–47 [special Liszt issue].

—, 'Sketches, Drafts, and Revisions: Liszt at Work', in Detlef Altenburg and Gerhard J. Winkler (eds), *Die Projekte der Liszt-Forschung: Bericht Über Das Internationale Symposion Eisenstadt*, 19–21 October 1989, Wissenschaftliche Arbeiten aus dem Burgenland, 87(Eisenstadt: Burgenland Landesmuseum, 1991).

Chomiński, Józef, 'Ze studiow nad impresjonizmem Szymanowskiego' (1956) (Studies on Szymanowski's Impressionism), *Studia nad twórczością Karola Szymanowskiego* (Kraków: Polskie Widawnictwo Muzyczne, 1969).

—, 'Z zagadnień techniki kompozytorskiej XX wieku' (Problems of the Compositional Technique in the Twentieth Century), *Muzyka* 20:3 (1956), 23–48.

Cinnamon, Howard, 'Chromaticism and Tonal Coherence in Liszt's "Sonetto 104 Del Petrarca"', *In Theory Only*, 7:3 (August 1983), 3–19.

Cook, Nicholas, 'Beyond Reproduction: Semiotic Perspectives on Musical Performance', *Journal of Musicology* [Serbian Academy of Sciences and Arts], 16 (2014), 15–30.

—, *Beyond the Score: Music as Performance* (Oxford: Oxford University Press, 2013).

Cooper, Martin, 'Liszt as a Song Writer', *Music and Letters*, 19:2 (April 1938), 171–81.

Cormac, Joanne, *Liszt and the Symphonic Poem* (Cambridge: Cambridge University Press, 2017).

—, 'Liszt as Kapellmeister: The Development of the Symphonic Poems on the Weimar Stage' (PhD diss., University of Birmingham, 2012).

—, 'Liszt Language and Identity: A Multinational Chameleon', *19th Century Music*, 36:3 (Spring 2013), 231–47.

Crumbley, Stefanie, 'Liszt's Developing Style: A Comparison Study of Two Settings of "Wer nie sein Brot mit Tränen aß"', in Klára Hamburger (ed.), *Liszt 2000: Selected Lectures Given at the International Liszt Conference in Budapest, May 18–20, 1999* (Budapest: Hungarian Liszt Society, 2000), pp. 157–69.

Dalhaus, Carl, *Foundations of Music History* (Cambridge: Cambridge University Press, 1983).

—, *Nineteenth-Century Music*, trans. J. Bradford Robinson (Berkeley, Los Angeles: University of California Press, 1989).

Dalmonte, Rossana, 'Liszt's 'Lieder: An Essay in Formalization', in Michael Saffle (ed.), *Liszt and His World* (Stuyvesant, NY: Pendragon Press, 1998), pp. 271–94.

Dart, William J., 'Revisions and Reworkings in the Lieder of Franz Liszt', *Studies in Music* [Australia], 9 (1975), 41–53.

Davies, J.Q., *Romantic Anatomies of Voice* (Berkeley, Los Angeles, London: University of California Press, 2014).

Deaville, James, 'Liszt in the German-Language Press', in Ben Arnold (ed.), *The Liszt Companion* (Westport, CT: Greenwood, 2002), pp. 41–54.

—, 'Publishing Paraphrases and Creating Collectors', in Christopher Gibbs and Dana Gooley (eds), *Liszt and His World* (Princeton: Princeton University Press, 2006), pp. 255–88.

Dyck, John, 'Perfect Compliance in Musical History and Musical Ontology', *The British Journal of Aesthetics*, 54:1 (1 January 2014), 31–47.

Einstein, Alfred, *Music in the Romantic Era* (New York: W.W. Norton, 1947).

Embry, Jessica L., 'The Role of Organicism in the Original and Revised Versions of Brahms's Piano Trio in B Major, Op. 8, Mvt. I: A Comparison by Means of Grundgestalt Analysis' (masters thesis, University of Massachusetts Amherst, 2007).

Finson, Jon W., *Robert Schumann: The Book of Songs* (Cambridge, MA: Harvard University Press, 2007).

Forte, Allen, 'Liszt's Experimental Idiom and Music of the Early Twentieth Century', *19th Century Music*, 10:3 (Spring 1987), 209–28 [special issue: *Resolutions I*].

Friedheim, Philip, 'First Version, Second Version, Alternate Version: Some Remarks on the Music of Liszt', *The Music Review*, 44 (1983), 194–202.

—, review, 'Neue Ausgabe sämtlicher Werke / New Liszt Edition. Series I: Werke für Klavier zu zwei Händen. Vol. I: Etüden I: Études d'exécution transcendante by Franz Liszt; Neue Ausgabe sämtlicher Werke / New Liszt Edition. Series I: Werke für Klavier zu zwei Händen. Vol. II: Etüden II by István Szelényi, Franz Liszt', *Journal of the American Musicological Society*, 26:1 (Spring 1973), 171–4.

Genette, Gérard, *Palimpsests: Literature in the Second Degree*, trans. Channa Newman and Claude Doubinsky (Lincoln, NE, and London: University of Nebraska Press, 1997).

Giani, Maurizio, 'Once More "Music and the Social Conscience": Reconsidering Liszt's Lyon', in Michael Saffle and Rossana Dalmonte (eds), *Liszt and the Birth of Modern Europe: Music as a Mirror of Religious, Political, Cultural, and Aesthetic Transformations*, Proceedings of the International Conference Held at the Villa Serbelloni, Bellagio (Como), 14–18 December 1998, Franz Liszt Studies Series, 9 (Hillsdale, NY: Pendragon Press, 2003), pp. 105–14.

Gibbs, Christopher H., 'The Presence of *Erlkönig*: Reception and Reworkings of a Schubert Lied' (PhD diss., Columbia University, 1992).

—, 'Writing Under the Influence? Salieri and Schubert's Early Opinion of Beethoven', *Current Musicology*, 75 (Spring 2003), 117–44.

Gibbs, Christopher H. and Dana Gooley (eds), *Liszt and His World* (Princeton: Princeton University Press, 2006).

Gil-Marcheux, Henri, 'LISZT: À propos de la technique de piano de Liszt', *Revue musicale*, 9:7 (1928), 76–88.

Girard, Henri, *Emile Deschamps, dilettante: Relations d'un poète romantique* (Paris: Paris E. Champion, 1921).

Goehr, Lydia, *Imaginary Museum of Musical Works: An Essay in the Philosophy of Music* (Oxford: Oxford University Press, 1992).

Gooley, Dana, 'The Battle against Instrumental Virtuosity in the Early Nineteenth Century', in Christopher Gibbs and Dana Gooley (eds), *Franz Liszt and His World* (Princeton: Princeton University Press), pp. 75–112.

—, 'The Virtuoso as Strategist', in William Weber (ed.), *The Musician as Entrepreneur, 1700 – 1914: Managers, Charlatans, and Idealists* (Bloomington: Indiana University Press, 2004), pp. 145–161.

—, *The Virtuoso Liszt* (Cambridge: Cambridge University Press, 2004).

Granat, Zbigniew, 'Rediscovering "Sonoristics": A Groundbreaking Theory from the Margins of Musicology', in Zdravko Blažeković and Barbara Dobbs Mackenzie (eds), *Music's Intellectual History* (New York: Répertoire International de Littérature Musicale, 2009), pp. 821–33.

Grove, George, 'Randhartinger, Benedikt', *A Dictionary of Music and Musicians*, ed. George Grove, 4 vols (London: MacMillan & Co., 1879), vol. 3, pp. 73–4.

Hallmark, Rufus E. (ed.), *German Lieder in the Nineteenth Century* (New York: Routledge 2010).

Hamad, Michael Abu, 'True Interpreters of Words: Tonal Distances in Franz Liszt's Early Songs' (PhD diss., Brandeis University, 2005).

Hamburger, Klára, 'Liszt's Confidante', *The Hungarian Quarterly*, 189 (2008), 163–9.

Hamilton, Kenneth, *After the Golden Age* (Oxford: Oxford University Press, 2008).

—, '"Not with a Bang but a Whimper": The Death of Liszt's *Sardanapale*', *Cambridge Opera Journal*, 8:1 (1996), 45–58.

—, 'The Opera Fantasias and Transcriptions of Franz Liszt: A Critical Study' (PhD diss., University of Oxford, 1989).

Hantz, Edwin, 'Motivic and Structural Unity in Liszt's "Blume Und Duft"', *In Theory Only* 6:3 (April 1982), 3–11

Harper-Scott, J.P.E. *Edward Elgar: Modernist* (Cambridge: Cambridge University Press, 2006)

Headington, Christopher, 'The Songs', in Alan Walker (ed.), *Franz Liszt: The Man and his Music* (New York: Taplinger Publishing, 1970), pp. 221–47.

Hegel, Georg W.F., *The Phenomenology of Spirit*, ed. and trans. Terry Pinkard (Cambridge: Cambridge University Press, 2018).

Hennemann, Monika, 'Liszt's Lieder', in Kenneth Hamilton (ed.), *The Cambridge Companion to Liszt* (Cambridge: Cambridge University Press, 2005), pp. 192–205.

Hoffmann, E.T.A., *E.T.A. Hoffmann's Musical Writings: Kreisleriana; The Poet and the Composer, Music Criticism*, ed. David Charlton, trans. Martyn Clarke (Cambridge: Cambridge University Press, 1989).

Hueffer, Francis, 'Liszt, Franz', *Grove Dictionary of Music and Musicians*, ed. George Grove, 4 vols (London: MacMillan & Co., 1879), vol. 2.

Hughes, Edwin, 'Liszt as Lieder Composer', *The Musical Quarterly*, 3:3 (July 1917), 390–409.

Husche, Wolfram, *Franz Liszt, Wirken und Wirkungen in Weimar* (Weimar: Weimarer Verlagsgesellschaft, 2010).

Ingarden, Roman, *The Work of Music and the Problem of Its Identity*, ed. Jean Gabbert Harrell, trans. Adam Czerniawski (London: MacMillan Press, 1986).

Jauss, Hans Robert, *Towards an Aesthetic of Reception*, trans. Paul de Man (Minneapolis: University of Minnesota Press, 1982).

Kallberg, Jeffrey, *Chopin at the Boundaries: Sex, History, Musical Genre* (Cambridge, MA: Harvard University Press, 1996).

Kasunic, David, 'On Jewishness and Genre', in Nicole Grimes, Siobhán Donovan, and Wolfgang Marx (eds), *Rethinking Hanslick: Music, Formalism, and Expression* (Rochester, NY: University of Rochester Press, 2013).

Kawabata, Mai, *Paganini: The Demonic Virtuoso* (Rochester, NY: The Boydell Press, 2013).

Kendall-Davies, Barbara, *Life and Work of Pauline Viardot Garcia*, vol. 1: *The Years of Fame 1836–1863*, 2nd edn (Newcastle: Cambridge Scholars Publishing, 2013).

Kerr, Greg, 'Utopia and Iconicity: Reading Saint-Simonian Texts', *Word and Image*, 28.3 (2012), 317–30.

Kleinertz, Rainer, 'Heinrich Heine on Liszt', in Christopher Gibbs and Dana Gooley (eds), *Franz Liszt and His World* (Princeton: Princeton University Press, 2006), pp. 231–54.

Korzybski, Alfred, *Science and Sanity: An Introduction to Non-Aristotelian Systems and General Semantics*, 5th edn (Brooklyn: Institute of General Semantics, 1994).

Kramer, Richard, *Distant Cycles* (Chicago: University of Chicago Press, 1994).

—, *Unfinished Music* (Oxford: Oxford University Press, 2008).

Kregor, Jonathan, *Liszt as Transcriber* (Cambridge: Cambridge University Press, 2010).

Letellier, Robert Ignatius, *Meyerbeer's Les Huguenots: An Evangel of Religion and Love* (Newcastle: Cambridge Scholars Publishing, 2015)

Locke, Ralph P., 'Liszt's Saint-Simonian Adventure', *19th Century Music*, 4:3 (Spring 1981), 209–30.

—, *Music, Musicians, and the Saint-Simonians* (Chicago, London: University of Chicago Press, 1986).

Lord, Alfred B., *The Singer of Tales* (Cambridge, MA: Harvard University Press, 1960).

Merrick, Paul, *Revolution and Religion in the Music of Liszt* (Cambridge: Cambridge University Press, 1987).

Middelton, Louisa M., 'Schröder-Devrient, Wilhelmine', *A Dictionary of Music and Musicians*, ed. George Grove, 4 vols (London: MacMillan & Co., 1879), vol. 3, pp. 315–18.

Millington, Barry, *Wagner*, rev. edn (Princeton: Princeton University Press, 1992).

Mitchell, Donald, *Gustav Mahler: The Wunderhorn Years* (Boulder, CO: Westview Press, 1975).

Noske, Frits, *French Song from Berlioz to Duparc*, trans. Rita Benton (New York: Dover Publications, 1970).

Pace, Ian, 'Notation, Time and the Performer's Relationship to the Score in Contemporary Music', in Darla Crispin (ed.), *Collected Writings of the Orpheus Institute: Unfolding Time: Studies in Temporality in Twentieth-Century Music* (Leuven: Leuven University Press, 2009), pp. 124–92.

Perten, Elizabeth, 'Liszt as Critic: Virtuosity, Aesthetics, and the Artist in Liszt's Weimar Prose (1848–1861)' (PhD diss., Brandeis University, 2014).

Pohl, C.F., 'Ludwig Tietze', *A Dictionary of Music and Musicians (A.D. 1450–1879)*, ed. George Grove, 4 vols (London: MacMillan & Co., 1879), vol. 4, p. 129.

Rehding, Alexander, 'TrisZtan: Or, the case of Liszt's "Ich möchte hingehn"', in Jim Samson and Bennett Zon (eds), *Nineteenth-Century Music: Selected Proceedings of the Tenth International Conference* (Aldershot and Burlington, VT: Ashgate, 2002), pp. 75–97.

Roberts, Paul, *Reading Franz Liszt* (London: Rowman & Littlefield / Amadeus Press, 2022).

Roseman, Sharon R., *The Tourism Imaginary and Pilgrimages to the Edges of the World* (Bristol: Channel View Publications, 2015).

Rosen, Charles, *The Romantic Generation* (Cambridge, MA: Harvard University Press, 1998).

Roynak, Jennifer, 'Performing the Lied, Performing the Self: Singing Subjectivity in Germany, 1790–1832' (PhD diss., University of Rochester, 2010).

Rutherford, Susan, '"La cantante delle passioni": Giuditta Pasta and the Idea of Operatic Performance', *Cambridge Opera Journal*, 19:2 (2007), 107–38.

Saffle, Michael, *Franz Liszt: A Research and Information Guide*, rev. 3rd edn (New York: Routledge, 2009).

—, *Liszt in Germany 1840–1845: A Study in Sources, Documents, and the History of Reception*, Franz Liszt Studies Series, 2 (Stuyvesant, NY: Pendragon Press, 1994).

Sallès, Antoine, *Liszt à Lyon: 1826, 1836, 1837, 1844, 1845* (Paris: E Fromont, 1911).

Samson, Jim, 'The Practice of Early-Nineteenth-Century Pianism', in Michael Talbot (ed.), *The Musical Work: Reality or Invention* (Liverpool: Liverpool University Press, 2000), pp. 110–27.

—, *Virtuosity and the Musical Work* (Cambridge: Cambridge University Press, 2003).

Searle, Humphrey, *The Music of Liszt*, rev. edn (London: Dover, 2012; orig. published 1954, rev. 1966).

Sitwell, Sacheverell, *Liszt* (London: Cassell and Company Ltd, 1934; rev. 1955).

Smaczny, Jan, 'Goethe and the Czechs', in Lorraine Byrne (ed.), *Goethe: Musical Poet, Musical Catalyst* (Dublin: Carysfort Press, 2004), pp. 159–84.

Smart, Mary Ann, 'Roles, Reputations, Shadows: Singers at the Opéra, 1828–1849', in David Charlton and Jonathan Cross (eds), *The Cambridge Companion of Grand Opera* (Cambridge: Cambridge University Press, 2003), pp. 108–31.

Stein, Deborah and Robert Spillman, *Poetry into Song* (Oxford: Oxford University Press, 1996).

Steiner, George, *Real Presences* (Chicago: University of Chicago Press, 1989).

Stevens, Robyn, 'The Garcia Family, Romanticism's Premiere Musical Dynasty: Their Legacy as Performers, Composers and Pedagogues' (DMA diss., University of Maryland, 2005).

Strohm, Richard, 'Looking Back at Ourselves: The Problem with the Musical Work-Concept', in Michael Talbot (ed.), *The Musical Work: Reality or Invention* (Liverpool: Liverpool University Press, 2000), pp.128–52.

Sulzer, Johann Georg, *Allgemeine Theorie der schönen Künste*, 2 vols (Leipzig: Weidmann, Reich, 1771–74), vol. 2.

Szabó-Knotik, Cornelia, 'Franz Liszt and Historicism', in Michael Saffle and Rossana Dalmonte (eds), *Liszt and the Birth of Modern Europe: Music as a Mirror of Religious, Political, Cultural, and Aesthetic Transformations*, Proceedings of the International Conference Held at the Villa Serbelloni, Bellagio (Como), 14–18 December 1998, Franz Liszt Studies Series, 9 (Hillsdale, NY: Pendragon Press, 2003), pp. 143–56.

Vaillancourt, Michael, 'Brahms's "Sinfonie-Serenade" and the Politics of Genre', *The Journal of Musicology*, 26:3 (Summer 2009), 379–403.

van Tour, Peter, *Counterpoint and Partimento: Methods of Teaching Composition in Late Eighteenth-Century Naples*, Studia Musicologica Upsaliensia, 25 (Uppsala: Uppsala Universitet, 2015).

Walker, Alan, *Franz Liszt*, 3 vols, rev. edn (Ithaca, NY: Cornell University Press, 1987–1997): Vol. 1: *The Virtuoso Years, 1811–1847* (1987); Vol. 2: *The Weimar Years, 1848–1861* (1989); Vol. 3: *The Final Years, 1861–1886* (1997).

—— (ed.), *Franz Liszt: The Man and his Music* (New York: Taplinger Publishing, 1970).

——, 'Liszt and the Lied', in *Reflections on Liszt* (Ithaca and London: Cornell University Press, 2011), pp. 150–74.

Wallenstein, Barry, *Visions and Revision: An Approach to Poetry* (New York: Thomas Y. Crowell, 1971).

Wilson, Karen Sue, 'A Historical Study and Stylistic Analysis of Franz Liszt's *Années de pèlerinage*' (PhD diss., University of North Carolina, 1977).

Williams, Adrian, *Portrait of Liszt by Himself and His Contemporaries* (Oxford: Clarendon Press, 1990).

Youens, Susan, 'Heine, Liszt and the Song of the Future', in Christopher Gibbs and Dana Gooley (eds), *Franz Liszt and His World* (Princeton: Princeton University Press, 2006), pp. 39–74.

Online sources

Eckhardt, Maria, Rena Charnin Mueller, and Alan Walker, 'Liszt, Franz', Grove Music Online, 2001, <https://www.oxfordmusiconline.com/grovemusic/view/10.1093/gmo/97815615926 30.001.0001/omo-9781561592630-e-0000048265> [accessed 29 September 2018].

Jolly, James, interview 'Inside Schumann's Dichterliebe,' <https://www.gramophone.co.uk/feature/inside-schumann-dichterliebe> [accessed 21 December 2018].

Koptiz, Klaus Martin, 'Caroline Unger', in *Musik und Gender im Internet*, <https://http://mugi.hfmt-hamburg.de/de/artikel/Caroline_Unger?size=2355> [accessed 14 May 2018].

Liszt, Franz, 'Im Rhein, im schönen Strome', Ben Bliss (tenor), Lachlan Glen (piano), Bruno Walter Auditorium, 4, April 2014, https://www.youtube.com/watch?v=cGAZf5HRILg [accessed 28 December 2018]

Lydon, Christopher, 'Harold Bloom's Moby-Dick', <http://radioopensource.org/harold-bloomsmelville/> [accessed 14 June 2016].

Online Chopin Variorum Edition, <http://www.chopinonline.ac.uk/ocve/> [accessed Feb 2018]

Pace, Ian, 'Beyond Werktreue: Ideologies of New Music Performance and Performers'. Paper presented at the lecture on 14 January 2014, Royal College of Music, <http://openaccess.city.ac.uk/6558/> [accessed 9 July 2018].

Rink, John, 'The Virtual Chopin', published by Cambridge University, 21 March, 2013: <https://www.youtube.com/watch?v=GJDnc_nZT-A> [accessed May 2018].

Index of Musical Works

General Index

Printed in the United States
by Baker & Taylor Publisher Services